MARX ON ECONOMICS

MARX
ON ECONOMICS

*

EDITED BY ROBERT FREEDMAN

INTRODUCTION BY HARRY SCHWARTZ

*

A HARVEST BOOK

HARCOURT, BRACE & WORLD, INC.

NEW YORK

Library of Congress Catalog Card Number: 61-7691

Printed in the United States of America

ISBN 0-15-657479-9

N O P Q

TO WILFRID HARRIS CROOK

PREFACE

This is a book on Marxian economics. Its general purpose is to permit the reader to discover the subtlety, complexity, and imaginative genius of Marx for himself.

Most students of Marxian economics rarely read the master, but are content to let his critics speak for him. This happens because the twenty-five hundred pages of *Capital,* three hundred pages of *The Critique of Political Economy,* more than four hundred pages of *Theories of Surplus Value,* his *Critique of the Gotha Programme, German Ideology, Communist Manifesto,* and other writings are forbidding in volume and turgid in prose. Beyond this, economic doctrines are scattered repetitiously throughout his works, seemingly without system. Marx often overwhelms his reader not only by the bulk of his writing, but also by the power of his expression and the force of his logic.

This volume has as its function bringing together in one place, as systematically arranged and logically ordered as possible, all of Marx's major statements respecting ideology and methodology, Marxian economics, and the shape of socialism and communism. The main focus of the collection is, of course, Marx's analysis of the nature of capitalism. Difficult decisions had to be made about when to cut and how to arrange the mass of material. In general, I have tried to organize the work in such a way as to make it possible for the reader to follow the course of the argument. I have tried to tie the selections together with brief summaries of the excerpts, without judgment or criticism.

Marx on Economics grew out of my own need in a course in comparative economic systems to present Marx's theories in such a way as to challenge the student's critical judgment. It should be useful not only to economists, but to students of Marx in other fields of inquiry. The book's intent is to provide the core of Marx's system essential to an adequate understanding of Marx whatever the particular interest of the reader. It is all too easy for students, in our time, to pass judgment on the intellectual work of this politically unpopular figure without examination of his ideas. Under such conditions, education conceived partly as the development of critical intelligence is impossible.

I acknowledge with greatest gratitude the literally indispensable assistance of Mary Elizabeth Finger, a person with first-rate critical sense and editorial skill, without whose aid this book never could have been completed. I would also like to acknowledge my wife, Evelyn, for her patient criticism and continuous encouragement; and the amazing speed and accuracy of my typist, Patricia Ryan.

ROBERT FREEDMAN

Colgate University
Hamilton, New York

INTRODUCTION

KARL MARX AND MARXIST ECONOMICS
BY HARRY SCHWARTZ

A striking feature of the 1960 Presidential campaign was the emphasis put by both candidates upon the importance of the Communist challenge to this country. Implicit in this was the concept of the importance that both men attached to a correct understanding of the system of ideas that we call Communism. Vice-President Richard Nixon felt this understanding to be so important that one of his first major moves after being nominated was the issuance of a formal document assailing the prevalent general ignorance of Communism and seeking to give a brief exposition and critique of Communist ideas. At about the same time in the late summer of 1960, Central Intelligence Director Allen Dulles made a speech urging that education about Communism be included widely in the curricula of our schools.

Basic to any understanding of Communism is an acquaintance with Marxism, the basic ideology from which Communist theory as it exists today has developed. Anyone with even an elementary understanding of Marxism must wince at the misunderstanding and misrepresentation of that doctrine so prevalent in our national life, in the speeches and writings of elected officials, politicians, educators, journalists, and others who should know better, but all too often do not. Since two wrongs do not make a right, this phenomenon is hardly defensible on the ground that Communist spokesmen, from Premier Nikita Khrushchev down, so often misunderstand and misrepresent our ideas.

Against the background of the international tensions of the years since World War II, this ignorance is understandable and its origins are clear. Since 1945, the United States and the free world have been engaged in a bitter cold war—and, at times,

shooting war—with the Communist world led by the Soviet
Union. Marxism, as the doctrine espoused by our opponents,
has been looked upon with fear and loathing, though Karl Marx
and Friedrich Engels—the founders of the doctrine—died long
before the 1917 Bolshevik Revolution. At the height of the
McCarthy hysteria in this country in the early nineteen fifties,
many people no doubt feared to have Marxist writings in their
homes or to study Marxist ideas in classrooms. All too often it
was forgotten that there is a very important difference between
propagandizing Marxism, on the one hand, and, on the other,
familiarizing oneself with Marxist ideology in an objective atmosphere where its merits and defects can be discussed.

   Yet it is precisely because of the great world struggle that
Americans need to understand Marxism. To a large extent, this
struggle is a struggle of ideas. To the extent that Communist
propaganda is based upon Marxism, a knowledge of that doctrine is essential if effective refutation is to be possible. There
are ideas in Marxism that can effectively be employed as ideological weapons against our Soviet-bloc propaganda foes. Much
of the most effective opposition to Stalinism before the tyrant's
death came from Yugoslav Marxists under President Tito and
from democratic socialists in many countries whose own ideology can be traced back to Marx and Engels.

   There is a much more basic argument, however—one tran-
scending the needs of the cold war—for encouraging intelligent
and educated Americans to understand the essentials of Marxism. One third of all humanity lives in societies in the Soviet bloc
in which Marxism—as modified by Lenin, Stalin, Khrushchev,
and Mao—is regarded as the source of all truth. In Western
Europe and Japan, strong socialist and communist parties representing varying currents of Marxist opinion exert enormous influence. In the underdeveloped countries of Asia, Africa, and
Latin America, Marxist ideas have played and still play a major
role in shaping the views of the intellectual elites from which are

drawn the leaders and policy-makers of today and tomorrow. It is literally impossible to understand the forces shaping the world of the second half of the twentieth century without understanding Marxism and its influence upon nations as different and as distant from each other as Sweden, Britain, the Soviet Union, Communist China, India, Ghana, Guinea, Cuba, and Mexico.

Nor can the intellectual history of the Western world—including the history of the United States—be understood without taking into account the enormous seminal influence of Marxist ideas upon many minds, both Marxists and bitter anti-Marxists. Earlier in this century, the impact of Marxism was clearly apparent in the writings of American titans like Thorstein Veblen and Charles and Mary Beard. In the nineteen thirties, scholars pointed out the parallels between some of the doctrines of the late John Maynard Keynes and Karl Marx. The fact that he has read Marx—without by any means accepting Marxism whole hog and uncritically—is evident in the current writings of Professor J. K. Galbraith, as well as in the writings of many other influential contemporary thinkers. The vast volume of polemical anti-Marxist writing in the Western world is implicit evidence of the importance of Marxist ideas and of the urgency with which many seek to refute them.

The late Joseph Schumpeter pointed out that the measure of the greatness of Marx's message is its continuing vitality. Schumpeter wrote, "We need not believe that a great achievement must necessarily be a source of light or faultless in either fundamental design or details. On the contrary, we may believe it to be a power of darkness; we may think it fundamentally wrong or disagree with it on any number of particular points. In the case of the Marxian system, such adverse judgment or even exact disproof, by its very failure to injure fatally, only serves to bring out the power of the structure." *

* Joseph A. Schumpeter, *Ten Great Economists from Marx to Keynes,* New York: Oxford University Press, 1951, pp. 3-4.

Against this background, let us look more closely at the authors of Marxism and at their doctrine. Karl Marx (1818-1883) has long overshadowed his colleague and friend Friedrich Engels (1820-1895), but their doctrine is essentially a joint product and would more justly be termed Marxism-Engelism. Products of a German bourgeois environment—Marx's father was a lawyer and Engels' a cotton-textile manufacturer—they were both deeply influenced by the intellectual ferment which helped bring on the revolutions of 1848. By that year, their basic ideas had already been formed and vividly stated in the *Communist Manifesto*. Marx lived his life primarily as an intellectual, working as an editor, a political commentator, a researcher, a propagandist, and a political organizer. Much of his adult life was spent reading and studying at home and in the British Museum in London. Engels was more the man of affairs; he managed textile mills whose profits helped support Marx and his family over long years when he earned little from his writings.

Marxism is a philosophy; it is not merely a theory of economics or sociology or history—all fields in which its impact has been great. Marx and Engels believed they had discovered nothing less than the laws of motion and of development of the universe, laws of animate and inanimate nature. The key to their philosophy is the concept of dialectical materialism. The materialistic aspect of this concept holds essentially that the world of our senses has an objective reality and is the sole reality. This is supplemented by the notion that all real phenomena in the universe change according to the tripartite dialectical pattern of thesis-antithesis-synthesis. From this materialist view flows the Marxist rejection of all forms of religion. The dialectical pattern is perhaps best exemplified by Marx's view of the class struggle in capitalist society as the mechanism through which a thesis and antithesis (capitalists and workers) interact to form a synthesis in the form of eventual socialism. Historical materialism,

Marxist economic theory, and the like are essentially the applications of dialectical materialism to different areas of human experience and activity. And it is this philosophical claim to the discovery of the laws of history that caused Marx and Engels to label their economic doctrine "scientific socialism" as against the allegedly "utopian socialism" of rival radical thinkers of the nineteenth century.

If one looks for the roots of Marxism's vitality today, after a century and more of its promulgation, one must look beyond its logical and factual virtues and defects. If Marx and Engels had been merely conventional academic philosophers and theoreticians, their ideas might today be only of interest to the historian of ideas. Their achievement was, rather, to formulate a philosophical system that provided justification and ammunition for all who were dissatisfied with bourgeois society as it was in the nineteenth and early twentieth centuries. Their doctrines had the power to move men to action, to articulate and systematize the grievances of millions of the poor and dispossessed.

This volume, *Marx on Economics,* edited by Robert Freedman, is devoted to an exposition of Marxist economic theory. Even the briefest of summaries makes clear how ideally suited this economic theory is to serve a revolutionary movement. To Marx and Engels, capitalism was fundamentally an act of robbery. The capitalist paid his worker—whose labor Marx and Engels saw as the sole source of exchange value—just enough to stay alive and raise his successor. But he took from the worker a much greater amount of product, thus compensating himself for what he had paid the worker and growing richer by the amount the worker had produced over and above the value of what he had received. The difference between what the worker produced and what he was paid, Marx and Engels termed surplus value. In their eyes, the capitalists' lust for more and more surplus value was insatiable, constituting a drive for ceaseless accumulation of capital, which permitted no real stability. From this simple mechanism of "robbery" and increasing capital accumulation, Marx and Engels drew far-reaching conclusions. They saw in the sweep of history capitalists growing richer and fewer, while the misery of the working class increased. This increasing polarization of society into a small clique of capitalists and a great mass of miserable exploited workers would continue, Marx and Engels thought, until the limits of endurance had been reached and the terrible system of exploitation would be destroyed by its victims. Marx described how he believed the process must end in Volume I of *Capital*:

Along with the constantly diminishing number of the magnates of capital, who usurp and monopolize all advantages . . . grows the mass of misery, oppression, slavery, degradation, exploitation; but with this too grows the revolt of the working class, a class always increasing in numbers, and disciplined, united, organized by the very mechanism of the process of capitalist production itself. The monopoly of capital becomes a fetter upon the mode of production, which has sprung up and flourished along with, and under it. Centralization of the means of production and socialization of labor at last reach a point where they become incompatible with their capitalist integument. This integument is burst asunder. The knell of capitalist private property sounds. The expropriators are expropriated.

Put so baldly, with no presentation of Marx's elaborate theoretical structure and his enormous volume of supporting factual material, it may seem that he and Engels were simply propagandists with no real claim to standing as social scientists. How incorrect such a judgment would be is apparent immediately in the eloquent tribute to capitalism the two men penned in their *Communist Manifesto* in 1848:

The bourgeoisie during its rule of scarce one hundred years has created more massive and more colossal productive forces than have all preceding generations together. Subjection of nature's forces to man, machinery, application of chemistry to industry and agriculture, steam navigation, railways, electric telegraphs, clearing of whole continents for cultivation, canalization of rivers, whole populations conjured out of the ground—what earlier century had even a presentiment that such productive forces slumbered in the lap of social labor?

Written more than a century ago, this is certainly one of the most eloquent testimonials ever written to capitalism's achievements. One looks in vain to modern Communist theoreticians for similar generous recognition of capitalism's contemporary achievements.

That Marx should have hated capitalism despite its achievements is more understandable to those who know how terrible was the poverty that afflicted most workers in the early and mid-nineteenth century in Western Europe. Where Marx went wrong was in failing to understand that there were less drastic solutions to the ills he denounced than the "expropriation of the expropriators" to which he looked forward so eagerly.

As the contents of *Marx on Economics* indicate, the great bulk of Marxist economic theory is a critique of capitalism and an attempt to forecast its "inevitable" development over time. Of what would follow capitalism if their forecast proved correct, Marx and Engels had very little to say, and of that little, part has long since been outrun by the march of events. In the *Communist Manifesto,* for example, they had listed ten measures which the victorious proletariat would take shortly after seizing power. At least half of those measures—among them free universal education for children, a heavy progressive income tax, and the gradual abolition of the distinction between town and country—are today regarded as commonplace in Western capitalist countries.

There has been much misunderstanding of Marxist predictions for the future postcapitalist world; for example, the misconception that Marxism is simply egalitarianism. In the *Critique of the Gotha Program,* Marx emphasized that egalitarian rewards could not be imposed immediately after the end of capitalism. He stressed that for some indefinite time afterward people would have to be given incentives in the form of unequal pay for different grades and amounts of work. Marx was fully aware of what stringent conditions would have to be met before his ultimate ideal of egalitarian Communism could be achieved. Writing in the *Critique of the Gotha Program* he said:

> In a higher phase of communist society, after the enslaving subordination of individuals under division of labor, and therewith also the antithesis between mental and physical labor, has vanished; after labor, from a mere means of life, has itself become the prime necessity of life; after the productive forces have also increased with the all-round development of the individual and all the springs of cooperative wealth flow more abundantly—only then can the narrow horizons of bourgeois rights be fully left behind and society inscribe on its banners: from each according to his ability, to each according to his needs!

This and other such visionary passages, however, are of little practical help in running a society and an economy. The rulers of Russia and of the countries which have fallen under Communist control after it have had to improvise and find their own solutions to problems which Marx and Engels refused to— and to a large extent could not—discuss in detail.

Whatever disadvantages Marxism's vagueness about the post-capitalist future may have had for Communist rulers facing concrete problems, they pale before its advantages. The ethereal character of the Marxist Utopia permits each man to read his own hopes and dreams into it, and then to compare this ideal future with the all too real and apparent defects, injustices, and evils of the existing society. Thus while Marx and Engels denounced "Utopian Socialists," the element of utopianism in their own doctrine served and serves as an element of political and propaganda strength. As a result, even before World War I, Marxist parties were strong in many parts of Western Europe, and the United States Socialist party, led by Eugene Debs, had significant strength. Since the Bolshevik Revolution, and even more since the creation of the Soviet bloc following World War II, Marxist utopianism has been an important Communist propaganda weapon throughout the world.

The history of the past century of controversy between Marxist economists and their opponents reveals elements of both strength and weakness in the economic theory of Marx and Engels. Let us look at each of these in turn.

Perhaps the main merit of Marxist economics from the present perspective is its preoccupation with economic change, with growth and development in economic life and institutions over time. This attention to economic life in the large—to macroeconomics, in current jargon—differs sharply from the main theme of orthodox economics over the past century. Most, though not all, of orthodox economics this past century has been concerned with what we now call microeconomics and with the concept of equilibrium. Orthodox economics—until it felt the impact of Keynes' *The General Theory of Employment, Interest and Money* in the nineteen thirties—had been largely concerned with the forces determining the prices of commodities in the market place, with the rational utilization of resources by an enterprise aiming at maximum profit, and the like. These are obviously important matters, but that they are too limited in scope to be the central theme of economics has been realized with particular force since World War II. Today the question of economic growth is at or near the center of attention of modern orthodox economics. It must be granted that Marx's and Engels' early realization of this problem's importance makes them in a certain sense more modern today, long after their death, than many of their opponents who lived, wrote, and thought after them.

A second merit of Marxist economics is its pioneering contribution to what is now called the theory of business cycles. Marx and Engels saw earlier than others that there were forces contained in the normal unregulated operation of capitalism which made for more or less periodic fluctuation upward and downward in production, investment, and employment. All this is commonplace today, but it was an achievement in its time. Marx himself never worked out a single comprehensive theory of business cycles, though much in his and Engels' writing stresses the view that depressions arise because the exploited masses are simply unable to buy all the output of rising production made possible by the constant accumulation of capital. But a careful survey of Marx's writings can find almost all the elements mentioned that later enter into different major business-cycle theories proposed by more orthodox theorists.

A third major achievement of Marxist economics was its correct prediction of the growth of what we would now call big business. While the main stream of orthodox economics focused primarily on models of markets in which perfect competition—with large numbers of buyers and sellers, none of them large enough alone to influence the price—was supposed to rule, Marx centered attention on the growth of huge aggregates of capital having substantial control over markets and capable of destroying many of their smaller competitors.

From a technical point of view, these are not inconsiderable achievements. At least partially, they balance the errors and wrong forecasts which also are part of Marxism. Let us turn to these now.

The most obvious criticism to be made of Marxist economic theory is simply that many of its key forecasts about the development of capitalism have been wrong. Marx's doctrine of the increasing misery of the working class has simply proved to be a fantastic miscalculation. The capitalist nations of the West have not seen a polarization of the population into a small group of extraordinarily wealthy capitalists facing an enormous mass of enslaved helots. For all of Marx's and Engels' genius, the course of history has proved to be much more complex than they thought it would be, and forces to which they paid little or no attention have proved to be of major importance. As a result, capitalism and private property still thrive in Western Europe and the United States, the areas on whose experience and history Marx and Engels built their theories. The areas in which Communist parties rule today are primarily countries that were overwhelmingly agricultural—Russia in 1917 and China in the late nineteen forties—when the Communists took over. And, of course, communization by military conquest such as took place in Eastern Europe and North Korea has no relevance at all to the Marxist analysis.

In retrospect, it is easy to see what went wrong with the Marxist analysis. Put most simply, that analysis failed to take into account adequately what proved to be the fact: that forces would arise which would permit the increasing wealth produced by capitalist societies to be shared among all major elements of the population rather than being entirely appropriated and monopolized by the capitalists Marx denounced. The growth of political democracy in the West gave the working class political power which was augmented in the economic sphere by the rise of trade unionism. Marx and Engels had thought of the state as simply an instrument of the ruling class. They had not anticipated the rise of the modern welfare state and of the modern mixed economies with their varying degrees of national economic planning cum capitalism. Ironically, of course, many of these changes which have made capitalism more viable than

Marx and Engels had thought it would be have resulted from the pressures and agitation of socialist parties and other groups influenced by Marxism. But the net result has been that Western capitalism today is far different from the system analyzed in Marxist economics.

If the original Marxist economics failed to take account of capitalism's ability to change and to become a far more humane system than Marx and Engels conceived it to be, that has not been true of many modern Marxists. The entire "revisionist" current in modern Marxism, which can be traced over many decades now from Eduard Bernstein in the past to the current doctrines of the Gaitskell wing of the British Labour party, of the German and Austrian Social Democratic parties, and of the heretical Yugoslav Communists, represents basically an attempt to modify Marxism to take account of the changing reality of capitalism. Even in the Soviet variant of Marxism—Marxism-Leninism—there is at least one major effort to wrestle with the disconcerting failure of the Marxist prediction about the increasing misery of the working class to come true. In his *Imperialism,* Lenin developed the ingenious theory that the huge profits extorted by capitalists from their colonial possessions gave them means by which to "bribe and corrupt" the upper strata of the working class at home. But even this, of course, is explicit recognition that events have not worked out as the Marxist classics thought they would.

The second major weakness of Marxist economics is its inapplicability to the concrete problems of operating an economy rationally and efficiently. In the last analysis, this weakness traces back to Marx's proposition that labor is the source of all value. The supposed proof of this proposition Marx offers is a logical *non sequitur,* since it ignores the key factor of relative scarcity, which is central among the price- and value-determining forces in any free market. Moreover, even if Marx's labor theory of value were true in any sense, it is a nonoperational concept, since not even Soviet economists have been able to create a calculus of labor values by reducing all types of skilled and trained labor to simple multiples of ordinary unskilled labor as Marx assumed could be done.

The weaknesses of the labor theory of value have become glaringly apparent in the operation of the Soviet and other Communist nations' economies where that theory has had great influence. Marx's refusal to consider interest on capital as a cost, for example, has led to great misallocation of resources because it has hindered Communist planners wrestling with the problem of time as a factor in making investment decisions. As Premier Khrushchev essentially acknowledged in August 1958 at the opening of the Kuibyshev hydroelectric station, Soviet planners misallocated resources by concentrating on hydroelectric stations, which seemed to give the cheapest electricity since they require no fuel cost. Hydroelectric power, however, is seen to be much more expensive than appears at first sight when the interest cost of the invested capital is taken into account. It was this essentially which Khrushchev was assessing when he called for a shift in emphasis from hydroelectric plants, requiring great capital investment tied up in construction for a long time, to thermal power plants, whose construction time is relatively short, so that a return on investment begins to be received much more quickly.

Nor has the labor theory of value provided any very useful guidance for the setting of prices by Soviet planners. The unsatisfactory nature of the Soviet price system is openly acknowledged in that country. Moreover, the penetration of mathematical economics into the Soviet Union in recent years has led to what is nothing less than an outright challenge to the labor theory of value. The recent work of Professor Leonid Kantorovich—the inventor of linear programming—amounts essentially to an attempt to introduce explicitly into Soviet economic calculation prices based on the relative scarcity of different goods as well as on their cost. The debate on this issue rages fiercely among Soviet economists, but the very fact that such debate is now permitted shows that fresh winds are blowing where an arid calm prevailed before.

A good many other detailed errors and failures of prophetic foresight in the main corpus of Marxist theory can be pointed out, but space permits only a brief mention of some of them here. The experience of the past two decades has made a mockery of the doctrine of the reserve army of the unemployed as the force permitting capitalists to grind down the conditions of the employed workers. In much of Western Europe and the United States there has been comparatively little unemployment, while such unemployment as has existed has not had the effects Marx expected. The unemployed have often been largely insulated from any impact on wages by the institution of unemployment insurance and by the ability of strong unions to defend their members' interests. Marx and Engels failed to see the displacement of the capitalist entrepreneur by the current crop of professional corporate managers, men who exercise—in Adolf Berle's felicitous phrase—power without property and who are themselves hired hands. Marx and Engels had great contempt for what they called the "idiocy of rural life" and failed to foresee the effective organization of commercial farmers into political blocs creating the present protectionist policies for agriculture in virtually every major Western country. Viewing economic motives as primary, they failed adequately to take account of nationalism, which, as much recent experience shows, is at least as dynamic and important a force in world political and economic affairs as the factors Marxism spotlights. It is all very well to urge the workers of the world to unite, but in actual practice Detroit automobile workers tend to feel as aggrieved as their employers do at the success with which European automobiles made by European workers are sold in the American market. Similar examples could obviously be multiplied many times.

History has already shown, however, that no amount of refutation on purely logical or factual bases is capable of destroying Marxism's influence. The reason is that Marxism has by now become a quasi-religious ideology for hundreds of millions of persons, an ideology thought to point the way to a better future. And by a simple feat of identification, the prestige of Marxism in the world grows more or less parallel with the increase of power and prestige of the Soviet bloc of nations. When the Soviet Union put Sputnik I into orbit, it ascribed that historic feat to the supposed advantages of its socialist system, thus implying ultimate credit for the inspiration given by Marx and Engels. And, similarly, the much more rapid rate of growth enjoyed by the Soviet economy over that of the United States acts as a potent argument for Marxism among the peoples of the world, particularly among the peoples of the underdeveloped nations. Thus in the battle for men's minds Marxism gains. At the same time, few realize that the Soviet-bloc nations have veered very sharply in many respects from the original doctrine, or that their economists today look ever more enviously at the calculus for rational allocation of resources developed by those whom Marx and Engels called contemptuously "vulgar economists." And ignored, too, by many is the reasonable suspicion that both Marx and Engels would have been repelled by the totalitarian darkness that covered Russia during the period of Stalinist "primitive accumulation" from the mid-twenties to the mid-fifties, and which envelopes China today in Mao Tse-tung's corresponding iron age.

As usual, the future is hidden from us by an impenetrable veil which, no doubt, hides many surprises for all. But already it is obvious that Marxist ideas have shaped the modern world powerfully and will continue helping to shape it for the indefinite future. As never before, therefore, the obligation is great for every intelligent citizen to familiarize himself with this doctrine that, for all its faults, has exerted so profound an influence on the minds and emotions of a large section of humanity.

Against this background, the usefulness of Professor Freedman's volume for the intelligent citizen should be apparent. It is a major contribution to solving the dilemma of the intelligent citizen who wants to acquaint himself with the basic ideas of Marxist economic theory but is understandably appalled by the task of wading through the three thick volumes of *Capital* as well as the rest of the great corpus of the writings of Marx and Engels. Professor Freedman has reduced this vast amount of writing to manageable form, integrating the key sections of different works in a logically coherent form and exposing the key ideas. And as against a mere summary or paraphrase of Marxist ideas, his reliance upon the actual writings of Marx and Engels permits the reader to taste the flavor of the original, to appreciate both the polemical skill and revolutionary fervor which are so characteristic of this body of doctrine. This volume should be a substantial contribution toward diminishing the ignorance of Marxism which, it is being increasingly realized, hampers many Americans in fully understanding and coping with the problems of the present most revolutionary age in human history.

CONTENTS

PART III: THE NATURE OF A COMMUNIST SOCIETY

A. *Value, Rent, and Money in a Communist Society 263*

B. *The Allocation of Output and Labor in a Socialist and Communist Society 267*

C. *The Relationship of Man to Work, Man to Man, and Man to the State 269*

Part **I** *The Ideological Underpinnings*

A.

ECONOMIC INTERPRETATION OF HISTORY

Summary: The first premise of human history is the existence of living people. Humans distinguish themselves from animals in that they *produce* the means of life. The manner in which they do this is determined by the means which they have found and have available to them. The act of production expresses the lives of individuals. They *are* what and how they produce. Thus the social and political organization of the state issues from the life process of individuals, not from their imagination, in forms which are a consequence of real life experience and are independent of the will of individuals. So it is also with the production of ideas and concepts and of the spiritual production of people, such as the language of politics, laws, morality, religion, metaphysics. What this means is that the remotest ideas and institutions of men are determined by the development of productive forces. "Consciousness can never be anything else than conscious existence, being, and the existence of men is their actual life process. . . ."

---

*

The first premise of all human history is, of course, the existence of living human individuals. Thus the first fact to be established is the physical organization of these individuals and their consequent relation to the rest of nature. Of course, we cannot here go either into the actual physical nature of man, or into the natural conditions in which man finds himself— geological, orohydrographical, climatic and so on. The writing of history must always set out from these natural bases and their modification in the course of history through the action of man.

Men can be distinguished from animals by consciousness, by religion or anything else you like. They themselves begin to distinguish themselves from animals as soon as they begin to *produce* their means of subsistence, a step which is conditioned by their physical organization. By producing their means of subsistence men are indirectly producing their actual material life.

The way in which men produce their means of subsistence depends first of all on the nature of the actual means they find in existence and have to reproduce. This mode of production must not be considered simply as being the reproduction of the physical existence of the individuals. Rather it is a definite form of activity of these individuals, a definite form of expressing their life, a definite *mode of life* on their part. As individuals express their life, so they are. What they are, therefore, coincides with their production, both with *what* they produce and with *how* they produce. The nature of individuals thus depends on the material conditions determining their production. . . .

The fact is, therefore, that definite individuals who are productively active in a definite way enter into these definite social and political relations. Empirical observation must in each separate instance bring out empirically, and without any mystification and speculation, the connection of the social and political structure with production. The social structure and the State are continually evolving out of the life-process of definite individuals, but of individuals, not as they may appear in their own or other people's imagination, but as they really are; i.e. as they are effective, produce materially, and are active under definite material limits, presuppositions and conditions independent of their will.

The production of ideas, of conceptions, of consciousness, is at first directly interwoven with the material activity and the material intercourse of men, the language of real life. Conceiving, thinking, the mental intercourse of men, appear at this stage as the direct efflux of their material behaviour. The same applies to mental production as expressed in the language of the politics, laws, morality, religion, metaphysics of a people. Men are the producers of their conceptions, ideas, etc.—real, active men, as they are conditioned by a definite development of their productive forces and of the intercourse corresponding to these, up to its furthest forms. Consciousness can never be anything else than conscious existence, and the existence of men is their actual life-process. . . .

. . . We set out from real, active men, and on the basis of their real life-process we demonstrate the development of the ideological reflexes and echoes of this life-process. The phantoms formed in the human brain are also, necessarily, sublimates of their material life-process, which is empirically verifiable and bound to material premises. Morality, religion, metaphysics, all the rest of ideology and their corresponding forms of consciousness, thus no longer retain the semblance of independence. They have no history, no development; but men, developing their material production and their material intercourse, alter, along with this their real existence, their thinking and the products of their thinking. Life is not determined by consciousness, but consciousness by life. . . .

The German Ideology, pp. 7, 13-15

Summary: Social change occurs according to the internal dynamics of a society, which, in turn, is a consequence of the "relations of production" of that society.

*

. . . In the social production which men carry on they enter into definite relations that are indispensable and independent of their will; these relations of production correspond to a definite stage of development of their material powers of production. The sum total of these relations of production constitutes the economic structure of society—the real foundation, on which rise legal and political superstructures and to which correspond definite forms of social consciousness. The mode of production in material life determines the general character of the social, political and spiritual processes of life. It is not the consciousness of men that determines their existence, but, on the contrary, their social existence determines their consciousness. At a certain stage of their development, the material forces of production in society come in conflict with the existing relations of production, or—what is but a legal expression for the same thing—with the property relations within which they had been at work before. From forms of development of the forces of production these relations turn into their fetters. Then comes the period of social revolution. With the change of the economic foundation the entire immense superstructure is more or less rapidly transformed. In considering such transformations the distinction should always be made between the material transformation of the economic conditions of production which can be determined with the precision of natural science, and the legal, political, religious, aesthetic or philosophic—in short ideological forms in which men become conscious of this conflict and fight it out. Just as our opinion of an individual is not based on what he thinks of himself, so can we not judge of such a period of transformation by its own consciousness; on the contrary, this consciousness must rather be explained from the contradictions of material life, from the existing conflict between the social forces of production and the relations of production. No social order ever disappears before all the productive forces, for which there is room in it, have been developed; and new higher relations of production never appear before the material conditions of their existence have matured in the womb of the old society. Therefore, mankind always takes up only such problems as it can solve; since, looking at the matter more closely, we will always find that the problem itself arises only when the material conditions necessary for its solution already exist or are at least in the process of formation. In broad outlines we can designate the Asiatic, the ancient, the feudal, and the modern bourgeois methods of production as so many epochs in the progress of the economic formation of society. The bourgeois relations of production are the last antagonistic form of the social process of production—antagonistic not in the sense of individual antagonism, but of one arising from conditions surrounding the life of individuals in society; at the same time the productive forces developing in the womb of bourgeois society create the material conditions for the solution of that antagonism. This social formation constitutes, therefore, the closing chapter of the prehistoric stage of human society.

*A Contribution to the Critique of
Political Economy,* pp. 11-13

Summary: But the scientist has a role to play despite the truth of the above.

*

. . . One nation can and should learn from others. And even when a society has got upon the right track for the discovery of the natural laws of its movement—and it is the ultimate aim of this work, to lay bare the economic law of motion of modern society—it can neither clear by bold leaps, nor remove by legal enactments, the obstacles offered by the successive phases of its normal development. But it can shorten and lessen the birth-pangs.

I, pp. 14-15*

* Symbols: *I, II,* and *III* refer to Karl Marx, *Capital,* Volumes I, II, and III, Charles Kerr edition, 1906, 1907, and 1909.—Ed.

Summary: Utopian socialists are no help in understanding social change because they believe that the course of history can be changed according to their personal preferences without regard to the scientific laws of social change.

*

We do not here refer to that literature which, in every great modern revolution, has always given voice to the demands of the proletariat, such as the writings of Babeuf and others.

The first direct attempts of the proletariat to attain its own ends—made in times of universal excitement, when feudal society was being overthrown—necessarily failed, owing to the then undeveloped state of the proletariat, as well as to the absence of the economic conditions for its emancipation, conditions that had yet to be produced, and could be produced by the impending bourgeois epoch alone. The revolutionary literature that accompanied these first movements of the proletariat had necessarily a reactionary character. It inculcated universal asceticism and social levelling in its crudest form.

The Socialist and Communist systems properly so called, those of St. Simon, Fourier, Owen and others, spring into existence in the early undeveloped period, described above, of the struggle between proletariat and bourgeoisie.

The founders of these systems see, indeed, the class antagonisms, as well as the action of the decomposing elements in the prevailing form of society. But the proletariat, as yet in its infancy, offers to them the spectacle of a class without any historical initiative or any independent political movement.

Since the development of class antagonism keeps even pace with the development of industry, the economic situation, as such Socialists find it, does not as yet offer to them the material conditions for the emancipation of the proletariat. They therefore search after a new social science, after new social laws, that are to create these conditions.

Historical action is to yield to their personal inventive action; historically created conditions of emancipation to phantastic ones; and the gradual, spontaneous class organisation of the proletariat to an organisation of society specially contrived by these inventors. Future history, resolves itself, in their eyes, into the propaganda and the practical carrying out of their social plans.

In the formation of their plans they are conscious of caring chiefly for the interests of the working class, as being the most suffering class. Only from the point of view of being the most suffering class does the proletariat exist for them.

The undeveloped state of the class struggle, as well as their own surroundings, causes Socialists of this kind to consider themselves far superior to all class antagonisms. They want to improve the condition of every member of society, even that of the most favoured. Hence, they habitually appeal to society at large, without distinction of class; nay, by preference, to the ruling class. For how can people, when once they understand their system, fail to see in it the best possible plan of the best possible state of society?

Hence, they reject all political, and especially all revolutionary action; they wish to attain their ends by peaceful means, and endeavour, by small experiments, necessarily doomed to failure, and by the force of example, to pave the way for the new social gospel.

Such phantastic pictures of future society, painted at a time when the proletariat is still in a very undeveloped state and has but a phantastic conception of its own position, correspond with the first instinctive yearnings of that class for a general reconstruction of society.

But these Socialist and Communist writings contain also a critical element. They attack every principle of existing society. Hence they are full of the most valuable materials for the enlightenment of the working class. The practical measures proposed in them—such as the abolition of the distinction between town and country; abolition of the family, of private gain and of the wage-system; the proclamation of social harmony; the conversion of the functions of the state into a mere superintendence of production—all these proposals point solely to the disappearance of class antagonisms which were, at that time, only just cropping up, and which, in these publications, are recognised in their earliest, indistinct and undefined forms only. These proposals, therefore, are of a purely utopian character.

The significance of Critical-Utopian Socialism and Communism bears an inverse relation to historical development. In proportion as the modern class struggle develops and takes definite shape, this phantastic standing apart from the contest, these phantastic attacks on it, lose all practical value and all theoretical justification. Therefore, although the originators of these systems were, in many respects, revolutionary, their disciples have, in every case, formed mere reactionary sects. They hold fast by the original views of their masters, in opposition to the progressive historical development of the proletariat. They, therefore, endeavour, and that consistently, to deaden the class struggle and to reconcile the class antagonisms. They still dream of experimental realisation of their social utopias, of founding isolated *phalanstères,* of establishing "Home Colonies," or setting up a "Little Icaria"—pocket editions of the New Jerusalem—and to realise all these castles in the air, they are compelled to appeal to the feelings and purses of the bourgeois. By degrees they sink into the category of the reactionary conservative Socialists depicted above, differing from these only by more systematic pedantry, and by their fanatical and superstitious belief in the miraculous effects of their social science.

They, therefore, violently oppose all political action on the part of the working class; such action, according to them, can only result from blind unbelief in the new gospel.

*Manifesto of the Communist
Party,* pp. 39-42

B.

THE CLASS STRUGGLE

Summary: The history of all societies has up to now been the history of class struggles. The bourgeoisie replaced the feudal nobility. The bourgeoisie "has created more massive and colossal productive forces than have all preceding generations together." The role of this class is to conquer nature by the continuous development of capital. In the process the bourgeoisie creates the weapon of its own destruction—the proletarians. As industrialism proceeds, the proletariat increases in size, unity, and power, while becoming more and more impoverished. Ultimately, the existence of the bourgeoisie is incompatible with society and that class will lose power to the revolutionary force of the industrial proletariat.

---

*

The history of all hitherto existing society is the history of class struggles.

Freeman and slave, patrician and plebeian, lord and serf, guild-master and journeyman, in a word, oppressor and oppressed, stood in constant opposition to one another, carried on an uninterrupted, now hidden, now open fight, a fight that each time ended, either in a revolutionary reconstitution of society at large, or in the common ruin of the contending classes.

In the earlier epochs of history, we find almost everywhere a complicated arrangement of society into various orders, a manifold gradation of social rank. In ancient Rome we have patricians, knights, plebeians, slaves; in the Middle Ages, feudal lords, vassals, guild-masters, journeymen, apprentices, serfs; in almost all of these classes, again, subordinate gradations.

The modern bourgeois society that has sprouted from the ruins of feudal society, has not done away with class antago-

12

nisms. It has but established new classes, new conditions of oppression, new forms of struggle in place of the old ones.

Our epoch, the epoch of the bourgeoisie, possesses, however, this distinctive feature: It has simplified the class antagonisms. Society as a whole is more and more splitting up into two great hostile camps, into two great classes directly facing each other—bourgeoisie and proletariat.

From the serfs of the Middle Ages sprang the chartered burghers of the earliest towns. From these burgesses the first elements of the bourgeoisie were developed.

The discovery of America, the rounding of the Cape, opened up fresh ground for the rising bourgeoisie. The East-Indian and Chinese markets, the colonisation of America, trade with the colonies, the increase in the means of exchange and in commodities generally, gave to commerce, to navigation, to industry, an impulse never before known, and thereby, to the revolutionary element in the tottering feudal society, a rapid development.

The feudal system of industry, in which industrial production was monopolised by closed guilds, now no longer sufficed for the growing wants of the new markets. The manufacturing system took its place. The guild-masters were pushed aside by the manufacturing middle class; division of labour between the different corporate guilds vanished in the face of division of labour in each single workshop.

Meantime the markets kept ever growing, the demand ever rising. Even manufacture no longer sufficed. Thereupon, steam and machinery revolutionised industrial production. The place of manufacture was taken by the giant, modern industry, the place of the industrial middle class, by industrial millionaires— the leaders of whole industrial armies, the modern bourgeois.

Modern industry has established the world market, for which the discovery of America paved the way. This market has given an immense development to commerce, to navigation, to communication by land. This development has, in its turn, reacted on the extension of industry; and in proportion as industry, commerce, navigation, railways extended, in the same proportion the bourgeoisie developed, increased its capital, and pushed into the background every class handed down from the Middle Ages.

We see, therefore, how the modern bourgeoisie is itself the product of a long course of development, of a series of revolutions in the modes of production and of exchange.

Each step in the development of the bourgeoisie was accompanied by a corresponding political advance of that class. An oppressed class under the sway of the feudal nobility, it became an armed and self-governing association in the mediaeval commune; here independent urban republic (as in Italy and Germany), there taxable "third estate" of the monarchy (as in France); afterwards, in the period of manufacture proper, serving either the semi-feudal or the absolute monarchy as a counterpoise against the nobility, and, in fact, corner-stone of the great monarchies in general—the bourgeoisie has at last, since the establishment of modern industry and of the world market, conquered for itself, in the modern representative state, exclusive political sway. The executive of the modern state is but a committee for managing the common affairs of the whole bourgeoisie.

The bourgeoisie has played a most revolutionary rôle in history.

The bourgeoisie, wherever it has got the upper hand, has put an end to all feudal, patriarchal, idyllic relations. It has pitilessly torn asunder the motley feudal ties that bound man to his "natural superiors," and has left no other bond between man and man than naked self-interest, than callous "cash payment." It has drowned the most heavenly ecstasies of religious fervour, of chivalrous enthusiasm, of philistine sentimentalism, in the icy water of egotistical calculation. It has resolved personal worth into exchange value, and in place of the numberless indefeasible chartered freedoms, has set up that single, unconscionable freedom—Free Trade. In one word, for exploitation, veiled by religious and political illusions, it has substituted naked, shameless, direct, brutal exploitation.

The bourgeoisie has stripped of its halo every occupation hitherto honoured and looked up to with reverent awe. It has converted the physician, the lawyer, the priest, the poet, the man of science, into its paid wage-labourers.

The bourgeoisie has torn away from the family its sentimental veil, and has reduced the family relation to a mere money relation.

The bourgeoisie has disclosed how it came to pass that the brutal display of vigour in the Middle Ages, which reactionaries so much admire, found its fitting complement in the most slothful indolence. It has been the first to show what man's activity can bring about. It has accomplished wonders far surpassing Egyptian pyramids, Roman aqueducts, and Gothic cathedrals; it has conducted expeditions that put in the shade all former migrations of nations and crusades.

The bourgeoisie cannot exist without constantly revolutionising the instruments of production, and thereby the relations of production, and with them the whole relations of society. Conservation of the old modes of production in unaltered form, was, on the contrary, the first condition of existence for all earlier industrial classes. Constant revolutionising of production, uninterrupted disturbance of all social conditions, everlasting uncertainty and agitation distinguish the bourgeois epoch from all earlier ones. All fixed, fast-frozen relations, with their train of ancient and venerable prejudices and opinions, are swept away, all new-formed ones become antiquated before they can ossify. All that is solid melts into air, all that is holy is profaned, and man is at last compelled to face with sober senses his real conditions of life and his relations with his kind.

The need of a constantly expanding market for its products chases the bourgeoisie over the whole surface of the globe. It must nestle everywhere, settle everywhere, establish connections everywhere.

The bourgeoisie has through its exploitation of the world market given a cosmopolitan character to production and consumption in every country. To the great chagrin of reactionaries, it has drawn from under the feet of industry the national ground on which it stood. All old-established national industries have been destroyed or are daily being destroyed. They are dislodged by new industries, whose introduction becomes a life and death question for all civilised nations, by industries that no longer work up indigenous raw material, but raw material drawn from the remotest zones; industries whose products are consumed, not only at home, but in every quarter of the globe. In place of the old wants, satisfied by the production of the country, we find new wants, requiring for their satisfaction the products of distant lands and climes. In place of the old local and national seclusion and self-sufficiency, we have intercourse in every direction, universal inter-dependence of nations. And as in material, so also in intellectual production. The intellectual creations of individual nations become common property. National one-sidedness and narrow-mindedness become more and more impossible, and from the numerous national and local literatures there arises a world literature.

The bourgeoisie, by the rapid improvement of all instruments of production, by the immensely facilitated means of communication, draws all nations, even the most barbarian, into civilisation. The cheap prices of its commodities are the heavy artillery with which it batters down all Chinese walls, with which it forces the barbarians' intensely obstinate hatred of foreigners to capitulate. It compels all nations, on pain of extinction, to adopt the bourgeois mode of production; it compels them to introduce what it calls civilisation into their midst, *i.e.,* to become bourgeois themselves. In a word, it creates a world after its own image.

The bourgeoisie has subjected the country to the rule of the towns. It has created enormous cities, has greatly increased the urban population as compared with the rural, and has thus rescued a considerable part of the population from the idiocy of rural life. Just as it has made the country dependent on the towns, so it has made barbarian and semi-barbarian countries dependent on the civilised ones, nations of peasants on nations of bourgeois, the East on the West.

More and more the bourgeoisie keeps doing away with the scattered state of the population, of the means of production, and of property. It has agglomerated population, centralised means of production, and has concentrated property in a few hands. The necessary consequence of this was political centralisation. Independent, or but loosely connected provinces, with separate interests, laws, governments and systems of taxation, became lumped together into one nation, with one government, one code of laws, one national class interest, one frontier and one customs tariff.

The bourgeoisie, during its rule of scarce one hundred years, has created more massive and more colossal productive forces than have all preceding generations together. Subjection of nature's forces to man, machinery, application of chemistry to industry and agriculture, steam-navigation, railways, electric telegraphs, clearing of whole continents for cultivation, canalisation of rivers, whole populations conjured out of the ground—what earlier century had even a presentiment that such productive forces slumbered in the lap of social labour?

We see then that the means of production and of exchange, which served as the foundation for the growth of the bourgeoisie, were generated in feudal society. At a certain stage in the development of these means of production and of exchange, the conditions under which feudal society produced and exchanged, the feudal organisation of agriculture and manufacturing industry, in a word, the feudal relations of property became no longer compatible with the already developed productive forces; they became so many fetters. They had to be burst asunder; they were burst asunder.

Into their place stepped free competition, accompanied by a social and political constitution adapted to it, and by the economic and political sway of the bourgeois class.

A similar movement is going on before our own eyes. Modern bourgeois society with its relations of production, of exchange and of property, a society that has conjured up such gigantic means of production and of exchange, is like the sorcerer who is no longer able to control the powers of the nether world whom he has called up by his spells. For many a decade past the history of industry and commerce is but the history of the revolt of modern productive forces against modern conditions of production, against the property relations that are the conditions for the existence of the bourgeoisie and of its rule. It is enough to mention the commercial crises that by their periodical return put the existence of the entire bourgeois society on trial, each time more threateningly. In these crises a great part not only of the existing products, but also of the previously created productive forces, are periodically destroyed. In these crises there breaks out an epidemic that, in all earlier epochs, would have seemed an absurdity—the epidemic of over-production. Society suddenly finds itself put back into a state of momentary barbarism; it appears as if a famine, a universal war of devastation had cut off the supply of every means of subsistence;

industry and commerce seem to be destroyed. And why? Because there is too much civilisation, too much means of subsistence, too much industry, too much commerce. The productive forces at the disposal of society no longer tend to further the development of the conditions of bourgeois property; on the contrary, they have become too powerful for these conditions, by which they are fettered, and no sooner do they overcome these fetters than they bring disorder into the whole of bourgeois society, endanger the existence of bourgeois property. The conditions of bourgeois society are too narrow to comprise the wealth created by them. And how does the bourgeoisie get over these crises? On the one hand by enforced destruction of a mass of productive forces; on the other, by the conquest of new markets, and by the more thorough exploitation of the old ones. That is to say, by paving the way for more extensive and more destructive crises, and by diminishing the means whereby crises are prevented.

The weapons with which the bourgeoisie felled feudalism to the ground are now turned against the bourgeoisie itself.

But not only has the bourgeoisie forged the weapons that bring death to itself; it has also called into existence the men who are to wield those weapons—the modern working class—the proletarians.

In proportion as the bourgeoisie, *i.e.,* capital, is developed, in the same proportion is the proletariat, the modern working class, developed—a class of labourers, who live only so long as they find work, and who find work only so long as their labour increases capital. These labourers, who must sell themselves piecemeal, are a commodity, like every other article of commerce, and are consequently exposed to all the vicissitudes of competition, to all the fluctuations of the market.

Owing to the extensive use of machinery and to division of labour, the work of the proletarians has lost all individual character, and, consequently, all charm for the workman. He becomes an appendage of the machine, and it is only the most simple, most monotonous, and most easily acquired knack, that is required of him. Hence, the cost of production of a workman is restricted, almost entirely, to the means of subsistence that he requires for his maintenance, and for the propagation of his race. But the price of a commodity, and therefore also of labour, is equal to its cost of production. In proportion, therefore, as the repulsiveness of the work increases, the wage decreases. Nay more, in proportion as the use of machinery and division of labour increases, in the same proportion the burden of toil also increases, whether by prolongation of the working hours, by increase of the work exacted in a given time, or by increased speed of the machinery, etc.

Modern industry has converted the little workshop of the patriarchal master into the great factory of the industrial capitalist. Masses of labourers, crowded into the factory, are organised like soldiers. As privates of the industrial army they are placed under the command of a perfect hierarchy of officers and sergeants. Not only are they slaves of the bourgeois class, and of the bourgeois state; they are daily and hourly enslaved by the machine, by the over-looker, and, above all, by the individual bourgeois manufacturer himself. The more openly this despotism proclaims gain to be its end and aim, the more petty, the more hateful and the more embittering it is.

The less the skill and exertion of strength implied in manual labour, in other words, the more modern industry develops, the more is the labour of men superseded by that of women. Differences of age and sex have no longer any distinctive social validity for the working class. All are instruments of labour, more or less expensive to use, according to their age and sex.

No sooner has the labourer received his wages in cash, for the moment escaping exploitation by the manufacturer, than he is set upon by the other portions of the bourgeoisie, the landlord, the shopkeeper, the pawnbroker, etc.

The lower strata of the middle class—the small tradespeople, shopkeepers, and retired tradesmen generally, the handicraftsmen and peasants—all these sink gradually into the proletariat, partly because their diminutive capital does not suffice for the scale on which modern industry is carried on, and is swamped in the competition with the large capitalists, partly because their specialised skill is rendered worthless by new methods of production. Thus the proletariat is recruited from all classes of the population.

The proletariat goes through various stages of development. With its birth begins its struggle with the bourgeoisie. At first the contest is carried on by individual labourers, then by the work people of a factory, then by the operatives of one trade, in one locality, against the individual bourgeois who directly exploits them. They direct their attacks not against the bourgeois conditions of production, but against the instruments of production themselves; they destroy imported wares that compete with their labour, they smash machinery to pieces, they set factories ablaze, they seek to restore by force the vanished status of the workman of the Middle Ages.

At this stage the labourers still form an incoherent mass scattered over the whole country, and broken up by their mutual competition. If anywhere they unite to form more compact bodies, this is not yet the consequence of their own active union, but of the union of the bourgeoisie, which class, in order to attain its own political ends, is compelled to set the whole proletariat in motion, and is moreover still able to do so for a time. At this stage, therefore, the proletarians do not fight their enemies, but the enemies of their enemies, the remnants of absolute monarchy, the landowners, the non-industrial bourgeois, the petty bourgeoisie. Thus the whole historical movement is concentrated in the hands of the bourgeoisie; every victory so obtained is a victory for the bourgeoisie.

But with the development of industry the proletariat not only increases in number; it becomes concentrated in greater masses, its strength grows, and it feels that strength more. The various interests and conditions of life within the ranks of the proletariat are more and more equalised, in proportion as machinery obliterates all distinctions of labour and nearly everywhere reduces wages to the same low level. The growing competition among the bourgeois, and the resulting commercial crises, make the wages of the workers ever more fluctuating. The unceasing improvement of machinery, ever more rapidly developing, makes their livelihood more and more precarious; the collisions between individual workmen and individual bourgeois take more and more the character of collisions between two classes. Thereupon the workers begin to form combinations (trade unions) against the bourgeoisie; they club together in order to keep up the rate of wages; they found permanent associations in order to make provision beforehand for these occasional revolts. Here and there the contest breaks out into riots.

Now and then the workers are victorious, but only for a time. The real fruit of their battles lies, not in the immediate result, but in the ever expanding union of the workers. This union is furthered by the improved means of communication which are created by modern industry, and which place the workers of different localities in contact with one another. It was just this contact that was needed to centralise the numerous local struggles, all of the same character, into one national struggle between classes. But every class struggle is a political struggle. And that union, to attain which the burghers of the Middle Ages, with their miserable highways, required centuries, the modern proletarians, thanks to railways, achieve in a few years.

This organisation of the proletarians into a class, and consequently into a political party, is continually being upset again by the competition between the workers themselves. But it ever rises up again, stronger, firmer, mightier. It compels legislative recognition of particular interests of the workers, by taking advantage of the divisions among the bourgeoisie itself. Thus the ten-hour bill in England was carried.

Altogether, collisions between the classes of the old society further the course of development of the proletariat in many ways. The bourgeoisie finds itself involved in a constant battle. At first with the aristocracy; later on, with those portions of the bourgeoisie itself whose interests have become antagonistic to the progress of industry; at all times with the bourgeoisie of foreign countries. In all these battles it sees itself compelled to appeal to the proletariat, to ask for its help, and thus, to drag it into the political arena. The bourgeoisie itself, therefore, supplies the proletariat with its own elements of political and general education, in other words, it furnishes the proletariat with weapons for fighting the bourgeoisie.

Further, as we have already seen, entire sections of the ruling classes are, by the advance of industry, precipitated into the proletariat, or are at least threatened in their conditions of existence. These also supply the proletariat with fresh elements of enlightenment and progress.

Finally, in times when the class struggle nears the decisive hour, the process of dissolution going on within the ruling class, in fact within the whole range of old society, assumes such a violent, glaring character, that a small section of the ruling class cuts itself adrift, and joins the revolutionary class, the class that holds the future in its hands. Just as, therefore, at an earlier period, a section of the nobility went over to the bourgeoisie, so now a portion of the bourgeoisie goes over to the proletariat, and in particular, a portion of the bourgeois ideologists, who have raised themselves to the level of comprehending theoretically the historical movement as a whole.

Of all the classes that stand face to face with the bourgeoisie today, the proletariat alone is a really revolutionary class. The other classes decay and finally disappear in the face of modern industry; the proletariat is its special and essential product.

The lower middle class, the small manfacturer, the shopkeeper, the artisan, the peasant, all these fight against the bourgeoisie, to save from extinction their existence as fractions of the middle class. They are therefore not revolutionary, but conservative. Nay more, they are reactionary, for they try to roll back the wheel of history. If by chance they are revolutionary, they are so only in view of their impending transfer into the proletariat; they thus defend not their present, but their future interests; they desert their own standpoint to adopt that of the proletariat.

The "dangerous class," the social scum (*Lumpenproletariat*), that passively rotting mass thrown off by the lowest layers of old society, may, here and there, be swept into the movement by a proletarian revolution; its conditions of life, however, prepare it far more for the part of a bribed tool of reactionary intrigue.

The social conditions of the old society no longer exist for the proletariat. The proletarian is without property; his relation to his wife and children has no longer anything in common with bourgeois family relations; modern industrial labour, modern subjection to capital, the same in England as in France, in America as in Germany, has stripped him of every trace of national character. Law, morality, religion, are to him so many bourgeois prejudices, behind which lurk in ambush just as many bourgeois interests.

All the preceding classes that got the upper hand, sought to fortify their already acquired status by subjecting society at large to their conditions of appropriation. The proletarians cannot become masters of the productive forces of society, except by abolishing their own previous mode of appropriation, and thereby also every other previous mode of appropriation. They have nothing of their own to secure and to fortify; their mission is to destroy all previous securities for, and insurances of, individual property.

All previous historical movements were movements of minorities, or in the interest of minorities. The proletarian movement is the self-conscious, independent movement of the immense majority, in the interest of the immense majority. The proletariat, the lowest stratum of our present society, cannot stir, cannot raise itself up, without the whole superincumbent strata of official society being sprung into the air.

Though not in substance, yet in form, the struggle of the proletariat with the bourgeoisie is at first a national struggle. The proletariat of each country must, of course, first of all settle matters with its own bourgeoisie.

In depicting the most general phases of the development of the proletariat, we traced the more or less veiled civil war, raging within existing society, up to the point where that war breaks out into open revolution, and where the violent overthrow of the bourgeoisie lays the foundation for the sway of the proletariat.

Hitherto, every form of society has been based, as we have already seen, on the antagonism of oppressing and oppressed classes. But in order to oppress a class, certain conditions must be assured to it under which it can, at least, continue its slavish existence. The serf, in the period of serfdom, raised himself to membership in the commune, just as the petty bourgeois, under the yoke of feudal absolutism, managed to develop into a bourgeois. The modern labourer, on the contrary, instead of rising with the progress of industry, sinks deeper and deeper below the conditions of existence of his own class. He becomes a pauper, and pauperism develops more rapidly than population and wealth. And here it becomes evident, that the bourgeoisie is unfit any longer to be the ruling class in society, and to impose its conditions of existence upon society as an overriding law. It is unfit to rule because it is incompetent to assure an existence to its slave within his slavery, because it cannot help letting him sink into such a state, that it has to feed him, instead of being fed by him. Society can no longer live under this bourgeoisie, in other words, its existence is no longer compatible with society.

The essential condition for the existence and sway of the bourgeois class, is the formation and augmentation of capital; the condition for capital is wage-labour. Wage-labour rests exclusively on competition between the labourers. The advance of industry, whose involuntary promoter is the bourgeoisie, replaces the isolation of the labourers, due to competition, by their revolutionary combination, due to association. The development of modern industry, therefore, cuts from under its feet the very foundation on which the bourgeoisie produces and appropriates products. What the bourgeoisie therefore produces, above all, are its own grave-diggers. Its fall and the victory of the proletariat are equally inevitable.

Manifesto of the Communist Party, pp. 9-21

Part **II** *Marxian Economic Analysis*

A.

LABOR THEORY OF VALUE

1. Value in Use and Value in Exchange

Summary: A commodity satisfies human wants. The utility of an object makes it a use value independent of the amount of labor required to create its useful qualities. Commodities constitute the substance of all wealth and are the material depositories of exchange value. At first sight, exchange value presents itself as a quantitative relation in which use values are exchanged and which constantly changes with time and place. This is not so. A good is exchanged for a wide variety of other goods equally. Exchange value expresses something equal in two commodities. If we leave out their use values, commodities have one common property, being products of human labor in the abstract. An article has value only because human labor in the abstract is embodied in it. However, there are some objects that are not commodities, yet command a price. Uncultivated land, for example, has a price, but does not contain value since it contains no human labor.

*

The wealth of those societies in which the capitalist mode of production prevails, presents itself as "an immense accumulation of commodities," its unit being a single commodity. Our investigation must therefore begin with the analysis of a commodity.

A commodity is, in the first place, an object outside us, a thing that by its properties satisfies human wants of some sort or another. The nature of such wants, whether, for instance, they spring from the stomach or from fancy, makes no difference. Neither are we here concerned to know how the object satisfies these wants, whether directly as means of subsistence, or indirectly as means of production.

Every useful thing, as iron, paper, &c., may be looked at from the two points of view of quality and quantity. It is an assemblage of many properties, and may therefore be of use in various ways. To discover the various use of things is the work of history. So also is the establishment of socially-recognised standards of measure for the quantities of these useful objects. The diversity of these measures has its origin partly in the diverse nature of the objects to be measured, partly in convention.

The utility of a thing makes it a use-value. But this utility is not a thing of air. Being limited by the physical properties of the commodity, it has no existence apart from that commodity. A commodity, such as iron, corn, or a diamond, is therefore, so far as it is a material thing, a use-value, something useful. This property of a commodity is independent of the amount of labour required to appropriate its useful qualities. When treating of use-value, we always assume to be dealing with definite quantities, such as dozens of watches, yards of linen, or tons of iron. The use-values of commodities furnish the material for a special study, that of the commercial knowledge of commodities. Use-values become a reality only by use or consumption: they also constitute the substance of all wealth, whatever may be the social form of that wealth. In the form of society we are about to consider, they are, in addition, the material depositories of exchange value.

Exchange value, at first sight, presents itself as a quantitative relation, as the proportion in which values in use of one sort are exchanged for those of another sort, a relation constantly changing with time and place. Hence exchange value appears to be something accidental and purely relative, and consequently an intrinsic value, *i.e.,* an exchange value that is inseparably connected with, inherent in commodities, seems a contradiction in terms. Let us consider the matter a little more closely.

A given commodity, *e.g.,* a quarter of wheat is exchanged for x blacking, y silk, or z gold, &c.—in short, for other commodities in the most different proportions. Instead of one exchange value, the wheat has, therefore, a great many. But since x blacking, y silk, or z gold, &c., each represent the exchange value of one quarter of wheat, x blacking, y silk, z gold, &c., must as exchange values be replaceable by each other, or equal to each other. Therefore, first: the valid exchange values of a given commodity express something equal; secondly, exchange value, generally, is only the mode of expression, the phenomenal form, of something contained in it, yet distinguishable from it.

Let us take two commodities, *e.g.,* corn and iron. The proportions in which they are exchangeable, whatever those proportions may be, can always be represented by an equation in which a given quantity of corn is equated to some quantity of iron: *e.g.,* 1 quarter corn = x cwt. iron. What does this equation tell us? It tells us that in two different things—in 1 quarter of corn and x cwt. of iron, there exists in equal quantities something common to both. The two things must therefore be equal to a third, which in itself is neither the one nor the other. Each of them, so far as it is exchange value, must therefore be reducible to this third. . . .

If then we leave out of consideration the use-value of commodities, they have only one common property left, that of being products of labour. But even the product of labour itself has undergone a change in our hands. If we make abstraction from its use-value, we make abstraction at the same time from the material elements and shapes that make the product a use-value; we see in it no longer a table, a house, yarn, or any other useful thing. Its existence as a material thing is put out of sight. Neither can it any longer be regarded as the product of the labour of the joiner, the mason, the spinner, or of any other definite kind of productive labour. Along with the useful qualities of the products themselves, we put out of sight both the useful character of the various kinds of labour embodied in them, and the concrete forms of that labour; there is nothing left but what is common to them all; all are reduced to one and the same sort of labour, human labour in the abstract.

Let us now consider the residue of each of these products; it consists of the same unsubstantial reality in each, a mere congelation of homogeneous human labour, of labour-power expended without regard to the mode of its expenditure. All that these things now tell us is, that human labour-power has been expended in their production, that human labor is embodied in them. When looked at as crystals of this social substance, common to them all, they are—Values. . . .

A use-value, or useful article, therefore, has value only because human labour in the abstract has been embodied or materialised in it. How, then, is the magnitude of this value to be measured? Plainly, by the quantity of the value-creating substance, the labour, contained in the article. The quantity of labour, however, is measured by its duration, and labour-time in its turn finds its standard in weeks, days, and hours.

I, pp. 41-45

Objects that in themselves are no commodities, such as conscience, honour, &c., are capable of being offered for sale by their holders, and of thus acquiring, through their price, the form of commodities. Hence an object may have a price without having value. The price in that case is imaginary, like certain quantities in mathematics. On the other hand, the imaginary price-form may sometimes conceal either a direct or indirect real value-relation; for instance, the price of uncultivated land, which is without value, because no human labour has been incorporated in it.

I, p. 115

2. *Socially Necessary Labor Time*

Summary: The value of a commodity is determined by the socially necessary labor time contained in it. Socially necessary labor time is the time required for production under normal conditions, with average degree of skill and intensity, using modern machinery. The greater the productivity of labor, the less is the labor time, and the less the value of a commodity. Some goods, like air, may be useful, but have no value since they embody no labor.

Use values are not simply the product of labor, but are a combination of matter (nature) and labor.

Different commodities require different degrees of skill. Skilled labor is simple labor intensified, a reduction that is always being made (presumably by the market) by a process that goes on behind the backs of the producers. Our task has been to get behind the phenomenon we see, that is, exchange value, to the value that lies behind it, socially necessary labor time.

*

Some people might think that if the value of a commodity is determined by the quantity of labour spent on it, the more idle and unskilful the labourer, the more valuable would his commodity be, because more time would be required in its production. The labour, however, that forms the substance of value, is homogeneous human labour, expenditure of one uniform

labour-power. The total labour-power of society, which is embodied in the sum total of the values of all commodities produced by that society, counts here as one homogeneous mass
of human labour-power, composed though it be of innumerable
individual units. Each of these units is the same as any other,
so far as it has the character of the average labour-power of
society, and takes effect as such; that is, so far as it requires
for producing a commodity, no more time than is needed on
an average, no more than is socially necessary. The labour-time
socially necessary is that required to produce an article under
the normal conditions of production, and with the average degree of skill and intensity prevalent at the time. The introduction
of power looms into England probably reduced by one half the
labour required to weave a given quantity of yarn into cloth.
The hand-loom weavers, as a matter of fact, continued to require the same time as before; but for all that, the product of
one hour of their labour represented after the change only half
an hour's social labour, and consequently fell to one half its
former value.

We see then that that which determines the magnitude of the
value of any article is the amount of labour socially necessary,
or the labour-time socially necessary for its production. Each
individual commodity, in this connexion, is to be considered
as an average sample of its class. Commodities, therefore, in
which equal quantities of labour are embodied, or which can
be produced in the same time, have the same value. The value
of one commodity is to the value of any other, as the labour-
time necessary for the production of the one is to that necessary
for the production of the other. "As values, all commodities
are only definite masses of congealed labour-time."

The value of a commodity would therefore remain constant,
if the labour-time required for its production also remained
constant. But the latter changes with every variation in the

productiveness of labour. This productiveness is determined by various circumstances, amongst others, by the average amount of skill of the workmen, the state of science, and the degree of its practical application, the social organisation of production, the extent and capabilities of the means of production, and by physical conditions. For example, the same amount of labour in favourable seasons is embodied in 8 bushels of corn, and in unfavourable, only in four. The same labour extracts from rich mines more metal than from poor mines. Diamonds are of very rare occurrence on the earth's surface, and hence their discovery costs, on an average, a great deal of labour-time. Consequently much labour is represented in a small compass. . . . In general, the greater the productiveness of labour, the less is the labour-time required for the production of an article, the less is the amount of labour crystallised in that article, and the less is its value; and *vice versâ,* the less the productiveness of labour, the greater is the labour-time required for the production of an article, and the greater is its value. The value of a commodity, therefore, varies directly as the quantity, and inversely as the productiveness, of the labour incorporated in it.

A thing can be a use-value, without having value. This is the case whenever its utility to man is not due to labour. Such are air, virgin soil, natural meadows, &c. A thing can be useful, and the product of human labour, without being a commodity. Whoever directly satisfies his wants with the produce of his own labour, creates, indeed, use-values, but not commodities. In order to produce the latter, he must not only produce use-values, but use-values for others, social use-values. Lastly, nothing can have value, without being an object of utility. If the thing is useless, so is the labour contained in it; the labour does not count as labour, and therefore creates no value. . . .

To all the different varieties of values in use there correspond as many different kinds of useful labour, classified according to the order, genus, species, and variety to which they belong in the social division of labour. This division of labour is a necessary condition for the production of commodities, but it does not follow conversely, that the production of commodities is a necessary condition for the division of labour. In the primitive Indian community there is social division of labour, without production of commodities. Or, to take an example nearer home, in every factory the labour is divided according to a system, but this division is not brought about by the operatives mutually exchanging their individual products. Only such products can become commodities with regard to each other, as result from different kinds of labour, each kind being carried on independently and for the account of private individuals.

To resume, then: In the use-value of each commodity there is contained useful labour, *i.e.,* productive activity of a definite kind and exercised with a definite aim. Use-values cannot confront each other as commodities, unless the useful labour embodied in them is qualitatively different in each of them. In a community, the produce of which in general takes the form of commodities, *i.e.,* in a community of commodity producers, this qualitative difference between the useful forms of labour that are carried on independently by individual producers, each on their own account, develops into a complex system, a social division of labour.

Anyhow, whether the coat be worn by the tailor or by his customer, in either case it operates as a use-value. Nor is the relation between the coat and the labour that produced it altered by the circumstance that tailoring may have become a special trade, an independent branch of the social division of labour. Wherever the want of clothing forced them to it, the human race made clothes for thousands of years, without a single man becoming a tailor. But coats and linen, like every other element of material wealth that is not the spontaneous produce of nature, must invariably owe their existence to a special productive activity, exercised with a definite aim, an activity that appropriates particular nature-given materials to particular human wants. So far therefore as labour is a creator of use-value, is useful labour, it is a necessary condition, independent of all forms of society, for the existence of the human race; it is an eternal nature-imposed necessity, without which there can be no material exchanges between man and Nature, and therefore no life.

The use-values, coat, linen, &c., *i.e.,* the bodies of commodities, are combinations of two elements—matter and labour. If we take away the useful labour expended upon them, a material substratum is always left, which is furnished by Nature without the help of man. The latter can work only as Nature does, that is by changing the form of matter. Nay more, in this work of changing the form he is constantly helped by natural forces. We see, then, that labour is not the only source of material wealth, of use-values produced by labour. As William Petty puts it, labour is its father and the earth its mother.

Let us now pass from the commodity considered as a use-value to the value of commodities.

By our assumption, the coat is worth twice as much as the linen. But this is a mere quantitative difference, which for the present does not concern us. We bear in mind, however, that if the value of the coat is double that of 10 yds. of linen, 20 yds. of linen must have the same value as one coat. So far as they are values, the coat and the linen are things of a like substance, objective expressions of essentially identical labour. But tailoring and weaving are, qualitatively, different kinds of labour. There are, however, states of society in which one and the same man does tailoring and weaving alternately, in which case these two forms of labour are mere modifications of the labour of the same individual, and not special and fixed functions of different persons; just as the coat which our tailor makes one day, and the trousers which he makes another day, imply only a variation in the labour of one and the same individual. Moreover, we see at a glance that, in our capitalist society, a given portion of human labour is, in accordance with the varying demand, at one time supplied in the form of tailoring, at another in the form of weaving. This change may possibly not take place without friction, but take place it must.

Productive activity, if we leave out of sight its special form, viz., the useful character of the labour, is nothing but the expenditure of human labour-power. Tailoring and weaving, though qualitatively different productive activities, are each a productive expenditure of human brains, nerves, and muscles, and in this sense are human labour. They are but two different modes of expending human labour-power. Of course, this labour-power, which remains the same under all its modifications, must have attained a certain pitch of development before it can be expended in a multiplicity of modes. But the value of a commodity represents human labour in the abstract, the expenditure of human labour in general. And just as in society, a general or a banker plays a great part, but mere man, on the other hand, a very shabby part, so here with mere human labour. It is the expenditure of simple labour-power, *i.e.,* of the labour-power which, on an average, apart from any special development, exists in the organism of every ordinary individual. Simple average labour, it is true, varies in character in different countries and at different times, but in a particular society it is given. Skilled labour counts only as simple labour intensified, or rather, as multiplied simple labour, a given quantity of skilled being considered equal to a greater quantity of simple labour. Experience shows that this reduction is constantly being made. A commodity may be the product of the most skilled labour, but its value, by equating it to the product of simple unskilled labour, represents a definite quantity of the latter labour alone. The different proportions in which different sorts of labour are reduced to unskilled labour as their standard, are established by a social process that goes on behind the backs of the producers, and, consequently, appear to be fixed by custom. For simplicity's sake we shall henceforth account every kind of labour to be unskilled, simple labour; by this we do no more than save ourselves the trouble of making the reduction.

Just as, therefore, in viewing the coat and linen as values, we abstract from their different use-values, so it is with the labour represented by those values: we disregard the difference between its useful forms, weaving and tailoring. As the use-values, coat and linen, are combinations of special productive activities with cloth and yarn, while the values, coat and linen, are, on the other hand, mere homogeneous congelations of in-differentiated labour, so the labour embodied in these latter values does not count by virtue of its productive relation to cloth and yarn, but only as being expenditure of human labour-power. Tailoring and weaving are necessary factors in the creation of the use-values, coat and linen, precisely because these two kinds of labour are of different qualities; but only in so far as abstraction is made from their special qualities, only in so far as both possess the same quality of being human labour, do tailoring and weaving form the substance of the values of the same articles.

Coats and linen, however, are not merely values, but values of definite magnitude, and according to our assumption, the coat is worth twice as much as the ten yards of linen. Whence this difference in their values? It is owing to the fact that the linen contains only half as much labour as the coat, and conse-quently, that in the production of the latter, labour-power must have been expended during twice the time necessary for the production of the former.

While, therefore, with reference to use-value, the labour contained in a commodity counts only qualitatively, with reference to value it counts only quantitatively, and must first be reduced to human labour pure and simple. In the former case, it is a question of How and What, in the latter of How much? How long a time? Since the magnitude of the value of a commodity represents only the quantity of labour embodied in it, it follows that all commodities, when taken in certain proportions, must be equal in value.

If the productive power of all the different sorts of useful labour required for the production of a coat remains unchanged, the sum of the values of the coat produced increases with their number. If one coat represents x days' labour, two coats represent 2x days' labour, and so on. But assume that the duration of the labour necessary for the production of a coat becomes doubled or halved. In the first case, one coat is worth as much as two coats were before; in the second case, two coats are only worth as much as one was before, although in both cases one coat renders the same service as before, and the useful labour embodied in it remains of the same quality. But the quantity of labour spent on its production has altered.

An increase in the quantity of use-values is an increase of material wealth. With two coats two men can be clothed, with one coat only one man. Nevertheless, an increased quantity of material wealth may correspond to a simultaneous fall in the magnitude of its value. This antagonistic movement has its origin in the two-fold character of labour. Productive power has reference, of course, only to labour of some useful concrete form; the efficacy of any special productive activity during a given time being dependent on its productiveness. Useful labour becomes, therefore, a more or less abundant source of products, in proportion to the rise or fall of its productiveness. On the other hand, no change in this productiveness affects the labour represented by value. Since productive power is an attribute of the concrete useful forms of labour, of course it can no longer have any bearing on that labour, so soon as we make abstraction from those concrete useful forms. However then productive power may vary, the same labour, exercised during equal periods of time, always yields equal amounts of value. But it will yield, during equal periods of time, different quantities of values in use; more, if the productive power rise, fewer, if it fall. The same change in productive power, which increases the fruitfulness of labour, and, in consequence, the quantity of use-values produced by that labour, will diminish the total value of this increased quantity of use-values, provided such change shorten the total labour-time necessary for their production; and *vice versâ*.

On the one hand all labour is, speaking physiologically, an expenditure of human labour-power, and in its character of identical abstract human labour, it creates and forms the value of commodities. On the other hand, all labour is the expenditure of human labour-power in a special form and with a definite aim, and in this, its character of concrete useful labour, it produces use-values. . . .

Commodities come into the world in the shape of use-values, articles, or goods, such as iron, linen, corn, &c. This is their plain, homely, bodily form. They are, however, commodities, only because they are something twofold, both objects of utility, and, at the same time, depositories of value. They manifest themselves therefore as commodities, or have the form of commodities, only in so far as they have two forms, a physical or natural form, and a value form.

The reality of the value of commodities differs in this respect from Dame Quickly, that we don't know "where to have it." The value of commodities is the very opposite of the coarse materiality of their substance, not an atom of matter enters into its composition. Turn and examine a single commodity, by itself, as we will. Yet in so far as it remains an object of value, it seems impossible to grasp it. If, however, we bear in mind that the value of commodities has a purely social reality, and that they acquire this reality only in so far as they are expressions or embodiments of one identical social substance, viz., human labour, it follows as a matter of course, that value can only manifest itself in the social relation of commodity to commodity. . . .

I, pp. 45-55

Hence, in determining the value of the yarn, or the labour-time required for its production, all the special processes carried on at various times and in different places, which were necessary, first to produce the cotton and the wasted portion of the spindle, and then with the cotton and spindle to spin the yarn, may together be looked on as different and successive phases of one and the same process. The whole of the labour in the yarn is past labour; and it is a matter of no importance that the operations necessary for the production of its constituent elements were carried on at times which, referred to the present, are more remote than the final operation of spinning. If a definite quantity of labour, say thirty days, is requisite to build a house, the total amount of labour incorporated in it is not altered by the fact that the work of the last day is done twenty-nine days later than that of the first. Therefore the labour contained in the raw material and the instruments of labour can be treated just as if it were labour expended in an earlier stage of the spinning process, before the labour of actual spinning commenced. . . .

Two conditions must nevertheless be fulfilled. First, the cotton and spindle must concur in the production of a use-value; they must in the present case become yarn. Value is independent of the particular use-value by which it is borne, but it must be embodied in a use-value of some kind. Secondly, the time occupied in the labor of production must not exceed the time really necessary under the given social conditions of the case. Therefore, if no more than 1 lb. of cotton be requisite to spin 1 lb. of yarn, care must be taken that no more than this weight of cotton is consumed in the production of 1 lb. of yarn; and similarly with regard to the spindle. Though the capitalist have a hobby, and use a gold instead of a steel spindle, yet the only labour that counts for anything in the value of the yarn is that which would be required to produce a steel spindle, because no more is necessary under the given social conditions.

I, pp. 209-210

Moreover, only so much of the time spent in the production of any article is counted, as, under the given social conditions, is necessary. The consequences of this are various. In the first place, it becomes necessary that the labour should be carried on under normal conditions. If a self-acting mule is the implement in general use for spinning, it would be absurd to supply the spinner with a distaff and spinning wheel. The cotton too must not be such rubbish as to cause extra waste in being worked, but must be of suitable quality. Otherwise the spinner would be found to spend more time in producing a pound of yarn than is socially necessary, in which case the excess of time would create neither value nor money. But whether the material factors of the process are of normal quality or not, depends not upon the labourer, but entirely upon the capitalist. Then again, the labour-power itself must be of average efficacy. In the trade in which it is being employed, it must possess the average skill, handiness and quickness prevalent in that trade, and our capi-

talist took good care to buy labour-power of such normal goodness. This power must be applied with the average amount of
exertion and with the usual degree of intensity; and the capitalist is as careful to see that this is done, as that his workmen
are not idle for a single moment. He has bought the use of the
labour-power for a definite period, and he insists upon his
rights. He has no intention of being robbed. Lastly, and for this
purpose our friend has a penal code of his own, all wasteful
consumption of raw material or instruments of labour is strictly
forbidden, because what is so wasted, represents labour super-
fluously expended, labour that does not count in the product
or enter into its value.

I, pp. 218-219

We stated, on a previous page, that in the creation of surplus-
value it does not in the least matter, whether the labour appropriated by the capitalist be simple unskilled labour of average
quality or more complicated skilled labour. All labour of a
higher or more complicated character than average labour is
expenditure of labour-power of a more costly kind, labour-
power whose production has cost more time and labour, and
which therefore has a higher value, than unskilled or simple
labour-power. This power being of higher value, its consumption is labour of a higher class, labour that creates in equal
times proportionally higher values than unskilled labour does.
Whatever difference in skill there may be between the labour
of a spinner and that of a jeweller, the portion of his labour by
which the jeweller merely replaces the value of his own labour-
power, does not in any way differ in quality from the additional
portion by which he creates surplus-value. In the making of
jewellery, just as in spinning, the surplus-value results only
from a quantitative excess of labour, from a lengthening-out of

one and the same labour-process, in the one case, of the process of making jewels, in the other of the process of making yarn.

But on the other hand, in every process of creating value, the reduction of skilled labour to average social labour, *e.g.,* one day of skilled to six days of unskilled labour, is unavoidable. We therefore save ourselves a superfluous operation, and simplify our analysis, by the assumption, that the labour of the workman employed by the capitalist is unskilled average labour.

I, pp. 220-221

3. Demand and Value

Summary: Although the value of a commodity is determined by the socially necessary labor time contained in it, if there is no demand for the commodity, it contains no value.

*

. . . If the community's want of linen, and such a want has a limit like every other want, should already be saturated by the products of rival weavers, our friend's product is superfluous, redundant, and consequently useless. Although people do not look a gift-horse in the mouth, our friend does not frequent the market for the purpose of making presents. But suppose his product turn out a real use-value, and thereby attracts money? The question arises, how much will it attract? No doubt the answer is already anticipated in the price of the article, in the exponent of the magnitude of its value. We leave out of consideration here any accidental miscalculation of value by our friend, a mistake that is soon rectified in the market. We suppose him to have spent on his product only that amount of labour-time that is on an average socially necessary. The

price then, is merely the money-name of the quantity of social
labour realised in his commodity. But without the leave, and
behind the back, of our weaver, the old fashioned mode of
weaving undergoes a change. The labour-time that yesterday
was without doubt socially necessary to the production of a
yard of linen, ceases to be so today, a fact which the owner
of the money is only too eager to prove from the prices quoted
by our friend's competitors. Unluckily for him, weavers are
not few and far between. Lastly, suppose that every piece of
linen in the market contains no more labour-time than is
socially necessary. In spite of this, all these pieces taken as a
whole, may have had superfluous labour-time spent upon them.
If the market cannot stomach the whole quantity at the normal
price of 2 shillings a yard, this proves that too great a portion of
the total labour of the community has been expended in the
form of weaving. The effect is the same as if each individual
weaver had expended more labour-time upon his particular
product than is socially necessary. Here we may say, with the
German proverb: caught together, hung together. All the linen
in the market counts but as one article of commerce, of which
each piece is only an aliquot part. And as a matter of fact, the
value also of each single yard is but the materialised form of
the same definite and socially fixed quantity of homogeneous
human labour.

I, pp. 120-121

. . . Every commodity must contain the necessary quantity
of labor, and at the same time only the proportional quantity of
the total social labor time must have been spent on the various
groups. For the use-value of things remains a prerequisite. The
use-value of the individual commodities depends on the par-

ticular need which each satisfies. But the use-value of the social mass of products depends on the extent to which it satisfies in quantity a definite social need for every particular kind of product in an adequate manner, so that the labor is proportionately distributed among the different spheres in keeping with these social needs, which are definite in quantity. (This point is to be noted in the distribution of capital to the various spheres of production.) The social need, that is the use-value on a social scale, appears here as a determining factor for the amount of social labor which is to be supplied by the various particular spheres. But it is only the same law, which showed itself in the individual commodity, namely that its use-value is the basis of its exchange-value and thus of its surplus-value. This point has any bearing upon the proportion between necessary and surplus-labor only in so far as a violation of this proportion makes it impossible to realise the value of the commodities and the surplus-value contained in it. For instance, take it that proportionally too much cotton goods have been produced, although only the labor-time necessary for this total product under the prevailing conditions is realised in it. But too much social labor has been expended in this particular line, in other words, a portion of this product is useless. The whole of it is therefore sold only as though it had been produced in the necessary proportion. This quantitative limit of the quota of social labor available for the various particular spheres is but a wider expression of the law of value, although the necessary labor time assumes a different meaning here. Only just so much of it is required for the satisfaction of the social needs. The limitation is here due to the use-value. Society can use only so much of its total labor for this particular kind of products under the prevailing conditions of production.

III, pp. 745-746

4. *The Value of Labor Power*

Summary: The laborer is obliged to sell his labor power to the capitalist because labor power is the only commodity which he has to sell. The capitalist (in the long run) is obliged to pay for labor power only the value which (like that of any commodity) is fundamentally determined by the labor time necessary for its production (and reproduction). Its value, therefore, is equal to its subsistence defined as a cultural minimum plus the expenses of education and training.

---

*

The . . . essential condition to the owner of money finding labour-power in the market as a commodity in this—that the labourer instead of being in the position to sell commodities in which his labour is incorporated, must be obliged to offer for sale as a commodity that very labour-power, which exists only in his living self.

In order that a man may be able to sell commodities other than labour-power, he must of course have the means of production, as raw material, implements, &c. No boots can be made without leather. He requires also the means of subsistence. Nobody—not even "a musician of the future" can live upon future products, or upon use-values in an unfinished state; and ever since the first moment of his appearance on the world's stage, man always has been, and must still be a consumer, both before and while he is producing. In a society where all products assume the form of commodities, these commodities must be sold after they have been produced; it is only after their sale

that they can serve in satisfying the requirements of their
producer. The time necessary for their sale is superadded to
that necessary for their production.

For the conversion of his money into capital, therefore, the
owner of money must meet in the market with the free labourer,
free in the double sense, that as a free man he can dispose of
his labour-power as his own commodity, and that on the other
hand he has no other commodity for sale, is short of everything
necessary for the realisation of his labour-power.

The question why this free labourer confronts him in the
market, has no interest for the owner of money, who regards
the labour market as a branch of the general market for commodities. And for the present it interests us just as little. We
cling to the fact theoretically, as he does practically. One thing,
however, is clear—nature does not produce on the one side
owners of money or commodities, and on the other men pos-
sessing nothing but their own labour-power. This relation has
no natural basis, neither is its social basis one that is common
to all historical periods. It is clearly the result of a past historical
development, the product of many economical revolutions, of
the extinction of a whole series of older forms of social production. . . .

We must now examine more closely this peculiar commodity,
labour-power. Like all others it has a value. How is that value
determined?

The value of labour-power is determined, as in the case
of every other commodity, by the labour-time necessary for
the production, and consequently also the reproduction, of this
special article. So far as it has value, it represents no more than
a definite quantity of the average labour of society incorporated
in it. Labour-power exists only as a capacity, or power of the
living individual. Its production consequently presupposes his
existence. Given the individual, the production of labour-power

consists in his reproduction of himself or his maintenance. For his maintenance he requires a given quantity of the means of subsistence. Therefore the labour-time requisite for the production of labour-power reduces itself to that necessary for the production of those means of subsistence; in other words, the value of labour-power is the value of the means of subsistence necessary for the maintenance of the labourer. Labour-power, however, becomes a reality only by its exercise; it sets itself in action only by working. But thereby a definite quantity of human muscle, nerve, brain, &c., is wasted, and these require to be restored. This increased expenditure demands a larger income. If the owner of labour-power works to-day, to-morrow he must again be able to repeat the same process in the same conditions as regards health and strength. His means of subsistence must therefore be sufficient to maintain him in his normal state as a labouring individual. His natural wants, such as food, clothing, fuel, and housing, vary according to the climatic and other physical conditions of his country. On the other hand, the number and extent of his so-called necessary wants, as also the modes of satisfying them, are themselves the product of historical development, and depend therefore to a great extent on the degree of civilisation of a country, more particularly on the conditions under which, and consequently on the habits and degree of comfort in which, the class of free labourers has been formed. In contradistinction therefore to the case of other commodities, there enters into the determination of the value of labour-power a historical and moral element. Nevertheless, in a given country, at a given period, the average quantity of the means of subsistence necessary for the labourer is practically known.

The owner of labour-power is mortal. If then his appearance in the market is to be continuous, and the continuous conversion of money into capital assumes this, the seller of labour-power must perpetuate himself, "in the way that every living individual perpetuates himself, by procreation." The labour-power withdrawn from the market by wear and tear and death, must be continually replaced by, at the very least, an equal amount of fresh labour-power. Hence the sum of the means of subsistence necessary for the production of labour-power must include the means necessary for the labourer's substitutes, *i.e.,* his children, in order that this race of peculiar commodity-owners may perpetuate its appearance in the market.

In order to modify the human organism, so that it may acquire skill and handiness in a given branch of industry, and become labour-power of a special kind, a special education or training is requisite, and this, on its part, costs an equivalent in commodities of a greater or less amount. This amount varies according to the more or less complicated character of the labour-power. The expenses of this education (excessively small in the case of ordinary labour-power), enter pro tanto into the total value spent in its production.

The value of labour-power resolves itself into the value of a definite quantity of the means of subsistence. It therefore varies with the value of these means or with the quantity of labour requisite for their production.

Some of the means of subsistence, such as food and fuel, are consumed daily, and a fresh supply must be provided daily. Others such as clothes and furniture last for longer periods and require to be replaced only at longer intervals. One article must be bought or paid for daily, another weekly, another quarterly, and so on. But in whatever way the sum total of these outlays may be spread over the year, they must be covered by the average income, taking one day with another. If the total of the commodities required daily for the production of labour-power = A, and those required weekly = B, and those required quarterly = C, and so on, the daily average of these commodities = $\dfrac{365A + 52B + 4C + \&c}{365}$. Suppose that in this mass of commodities requisite for the average day there are embodied 6 hours of social labour, then there is incorporated daily in labour-power half a day's average social labour, in other words, half a day's labour in requisite for the daily production of labour-power. This quantity of labour forms the value of a day's labour-power or the value of the labour-power daily reproduced. If half a day's average social labour is incorporated in three shillings, then three shillings is the price corresponding to the value of a day's labour-power. If its owner therefore offers it for sale at three shillings a day, its selling price is equal to its value, and according to our supposition, our friend Moneybags, who is intent upon converting his three shillings into capital, pays this value.

The minimum limit of the value of labour-power is determined by the value of the commodities, without the daily supply of which the labourer cannot renew his vital energy, consequently by the value of those means of subsistence that are physically indispensable. If the price of labour-power fall to this minimum, it falls below its value, since under such circumstances it can be maintained and developed only in a crippled state. But the value of every commodity is determined by the labour-time requisite to turn it out so as to be of normal quality.

It is a very cheap sort of sentimentality which declares this method of determining the value of labour-power, a method prescribed by the very nature of the case, to be a brutal method, and which wails with Rossi that, "To comprehend capacity for labour (puissance de travail) at the same time that we make abstraction from the means of subsistence of the labourers during the process of production, is to comprehend a phantom (être de raison). When we speak of labour, or capacity for labour, we speak at the same time of the labourer and his means of subsistence, of labourer and wages." When we speak of capacity for labour, we do not speak of labour, any more than when we speak of capacity for digestion, we speak of digestion. The latter process requires something more than a good stomach. When we speak of capacity for labour we do not abstract from the necessary means of subsistence. On the contrary, their value is expressed in its value. If his capacity for labour remains unsold, the labourer derives no benefit from it, but rather he will feel it to be a cruel nature-imposed necessity that this capacity has cost for its production a definite amount of the means of subsistence and that it will continue to do so for its reproduction. He will then agree with Sismondi: "that capacity for labour . . . is nothing unless it is sold."

One consequence of the peculiar nature of labour-power as a commodity is, that its use-value does not, on the conclusion of this contract between the buyer and seller, immediately pass into the hands of the former. Its value, like that of every other commodity, is already fixed before it goes into circulation, since a definite quantity of social labour has been spent upon it; but its use-value consists in the subsequent exercise of its force. The alienation of labour-power and its actual appropriation by the buyer, its employment as a use-value, are separated by an interval of time. But in those cases in which the formal alienation by sale of the use-value of a commodity, is not simultaneous with its actual delivery to the buyer, the money of the latter usually functions as means of payment. In every country in which the capitalist mode of production reigns, it is the custom not to pay for labour-power before it has been exercised for the period fixed by the contract, as for example, the end of each week. In all cases, therefore, the use-value of the labour-power is advanced to the capitalist: the labourer allows the buyer to consume it before he receives payment of the price; he everywhere gives credit to the capitalist. That this credit is no mere fiction, is shown not only by the occasional loss of wages on the bankruptcy of the capitalist, but also by a series of more enduring consequences. Nevertheless, whether money serves as a means of purchase or as a means of payment, this makes no alteration in the nature of the exchange of commodities. The price of the labour-power is fixed by the contract, although it is not realised till later, like the rent of a house. The labour-power is sold, although it is only paid for at a later period. It will, therefore, be useful, for a clear comprehension of the relation of the parties, to assume provisionally, that the possessor of labour-power, on the occasion of each sale, immediately receives the price stipulated to be paid for it.

We now know how the value paid by the purchaser to the possessor of this peculiar commodity, labour-power, is determined. The use-value which the former gets in exchange, manifests itself only in the actual usufruct, in the consumption of the labour-power. The money owner buys everything necessary for this purpose, such as raw material, in the market, and pays for it at its full value. The consumption of labour-power is at one and the same time the production of commodities and of surplus value. The consumption of labour-power is completed, as in the case of every other commodity, outside the limits of the market or of the sphere of circulation. Accompanied by Mr. Moneybags and by the possessor of labour-power, we therefore take leave for a time of this noisy sphere, where everything takes place on the surface and in view of all men, and follow them both into the hidden abode of production, on whose threshold there stares us in the face "No admittance except on business." Here we shall see, not only how capital produces, but how capital is produced. We shall at last force the secret of profit making.

This sphere that we are deserting, within whose boundaries the sale and purchase of labour-power goes, is in fact a very Eden of the innate rights of man. There alone rule Freedom, Equality, Property and Bentham. Freedom, because both buyer and seller of a commodity, say of labour-power, are constrained only by their own free will. They contract as free agents, and the agreement they come to, is but the form in which they give legal expression to their common will. Equality, because each enters into relation with the other, as with a simple owner of commodities, and they exchange equivalent for equivalent. Property, because each disposes only of what is his own. And Bentham, because each looks only to himself. The only force that brings them together and puts them in relation with each other, is the selfishness, the gain and the private interests of each. Each looks to himself only, and no one troubles himself about the rest, and just because they do so, do they all, in accordance with the pre-established harmony of things, or under the auspices of an all-shrewd providence, work together to their mutual advantage, for the common weal and in the interest of all.

On leaving this sphere of simple circulation or of exchange of commodities, which furnishes the "Free-trader Vulgaris" with his views and ideas, and with the standard by which he judges a society based on capital and wages, we think we can perceive a change in the physiognomy of our dramatis personae. He, who before was the money owner, now strides, in front as capitalist; the possessor of labour-power follows as his labourer. The one with an air of importance, smirking, intent on business; the other, timid and holding back, like one who is bringing his own hide to market and has nothing to expect but—a hiding.

I, pp. 187-196

Appendixes to the Labor Theory of Value

A. COMMODITY FETISHISM

Editor's note: Marx's theory of Commodity Fetishism adds nothing to his purely economic analysis, namely, the analysis of capitalist production, but is appended here to provide a perspective from which to better understand the thrust of Marx's critical view.

Summary: Bourgeois economists are prone to study the exchange relationship between commodities forgetting that what the relationship between material things really expresses is the social relationships between people. Thus, when Ricardo and others speak of value, rent, wages, profit, interest, et cetera as though they were the inevitable categories of economic life (without respect to time or culture), they obscure the class character of social relationships. These economic forms, really only characteristic of capitalism, appear to be eternal and therefore just. The superstructure which rests upon these forms—ethical, legal, and social—also appears eternal and just, instead of being the manifestation of a special form of social organization in a particular historical period.

---

*

A commodity is therefore a mysterious thing, simply because in it the social character of men's labour appears to them as an objective character stamped upon the product of that labour; because the relation of the producers to the sum total of their own labour is presented to them as a social relation, existing not between themselves, but between the products of their labour. This is the reason why the products of labour become commodities, social things whose qualities are at the same time perceptible and imperceptible by the senses. In the same way the light from an object is perceived by us not as the subjective excitation of our optic nerve, but as the objective form of something outside the eye itself. But, in the act of seeing, there is at all events, an actual passage of light from one thing to another, from the external object to the eye. There is a physical relation between physical things. But it is different with commodities. There, the existence of the things *quâ* commodities, and the value relation between the products of labour which stamps them as commodities, have absolutely no connection with their physical properties and with the material relations arising therefrom. There it is a definite social relation between men, that assumes, in their eyes, the fantastic form of a relation between things. In order, therefore, to find an analogy, we must have recourse to the mist-enveloped regions of the religious world. In that world the productions of the human brain appear as independent beings endowed with life, and entering into relation both with one another and the human race. So it is in the world of commodities with the products of men's hands. This I call the Fetishism which attaches itself to the products of labour, so soon as they are produced as commodities, and which is therefore inseparable from the production of commodities.

This Fetishism of commodities has its origin, as the foregoing analysis has already shown, in the peculiar social character of the labour that produces them.

As a general rule, articles of utility become commodities, only because they are products of the labour of private individuals or groups of individuals who carry on their work independently of each other. The sum total of the labour of all these private individuals forms the aggregate labour of society. Since the producers do not come into social contact

with each other until they exchange their products, the specific
social character of each producer's labour does not show itself
except in the act of exchange. In other words, the labour of
the individual asserts itself as a part of the labour of society,
only by means of the relations which the act of exchange estab-
lishes directly between the products, and indirectly, through
them, between the producers. To the latter, therefore, the
relations connecting the labour of one individual ‚with that
of the rest appear, not as direct social relations between individuals at work, but as what they really are, material relations
between persons and social relations between things. It is only
by being exchanged that the products of labour acquire, as
values, one uniform social status, distinct from their varied
forms of existence as objects of utility. This division of a
product into a useful thing and a value becomes practically
important, only when exchange has acquired such an extension
that useful articles are produced for the purpose of being exchanged, and their character as values has therefore to be taken
into account, beforehand, during production. From this moment
the labour of the individual producer acquires socially a two-
fold character. On the one hand, it must, as a definite useful
kind of labour, satisfy a definite social want, and thus hold its
place as part and parcel of the collective labour of all, as a
branch of a social division of labour that has sprung up spontaneously. On the other hand, it can satisfy the manifold wants
of the individual producer himself, only in so far as the mutual
exchangeability of all kinds of useful private labour is an established social fact, and therefore the private useful labour of
each producer ranks on an equality with that of all others. The
equalization of the most different kinds of labour can be the
result only of an abstraction from their inequalities, or of
reducing them to their common denominator, viz., expenditure
of human labour power or human labour in the abstract. The

two-fold social character of the labour of the individual appears to him, when reflected in his brain, only under those forms which are impressed upon that labour in everyday practice by the exchange of products. In this way, the character that his own labour possesses of being socially useful takes the form of the condition, that the product must be not only useful, but useful for others, and the social character that his particular labour has of being the equal of all other particular kinds of labour, takes the form that all the physically different articles that are the products of labour, have one common quality, viz, that of having value.

Hence, when we bring the products of our labour into relation with each other as values, it is not because we see in these articles the material receptacles of homogeneous human labour. Quite the contrary; whenever, by an exchange, we equate as values our different products, by that very act, we also equate, as human labour, the different kinds of labour expended upon them. We are not aware of this, nevertheless we do it. Value, therefore, does not stalk about with a label describing what it is. It is value, rather, that converts every product into a social hieroglyphic. Later on, we try to decipher the hieroglyphic, to get behind the secret of our own social products; for to stamp an object of utility as a value, is just as much a social product as language. The recent scientific discovery, that the products of labour, so far as they are values, are but material expressions of the human labour spent in their production, marks, indeed, an epoch in the history of the development of the human race, but, by no means, dissipates the mist through which the social character of labour appears to us to be an objective character of the products themselves. The fact, that in the particular form of production with which we are dealing, viz., the production of commodities, the specific social character of private labour carried on independently, consists in the equality of every kind of that labour, by virtue of its being human labour, which character, therefore, assumes in the product the form of value —this fact appears to the producers, notwithstanding the discovery above referred to, to be just as real and final, as the fact, that, after the discovery by science of the component gases of air, the atmosphere itself remained unaltered.

What, first of all, practically concerns producers when they make an exchange, is the question, how much of some other product they get for their own? In what proportions the products are exchangeable? When these proportions have, by custom, attained a certain stability, they appear to result from the nature of the products, so that, for instance, one ton of iron and two ounces of gold appear as naturally to be of equal value as a pound of gold and a pound of iron in spite of their different physical and chemical qualities appear to be of equal weight. The character of having value, when once impressed upon products, obtains fixity only by reason of their acting and re-acting upon each other as quantities of value. These quantities vary continually, independently of the will, foresight and action of the producers. To them, their own social action takes the form of the action of objects, which rule the producers instead of being ruled by them. It requires a fully developed production of commodities before, from accumulated experience alone, the scientific conviction springs up, that all the different kinds of private labour, which are carried on independently of each other, and yet as spontaneously developed branches of the social division of labour, are continually being reduced to the quantitive proportions in which society requires them. And why? Because, in the midst of all the accidental and ever fluctuating exchange-relations between the products, the labour-time socially necessary for their production forcibly asserts itself like an over-riding law of nature. The law of gravity thus asserts itself when a house falls about our ears. The determination of the magnitude of value by labour-time is therefore a secret, hidden under the apparent fluctuations in the relative values of commodities. Its discovery, while removing all appearance of mere accidentality from the determination of the magnitude of the values of products, yet in no way alters the mode in which that determination takes place.

I, pp. 83-87

Political economy has indeed analysed, however incompletely, value and its magnitude, and has discovered what lies beneath these forms. But it has never once asked the question why labour is represented by the value of its product and labour time by the magnitude of that value. These formulae, which bear stamped upon them in unmistakeable letters, that they belong to a state of society, in which the process of production has the mastery over man, instead of being controlled by him, such formulae appear to the bourgeois intellect to be as much a self-evident necessity imposed by nature as productive labour itself. Hence forms of social production that preceded the bourgeois form, are treated by the bourgeoisie in much the same way as the Fathers of the Church treated pre-Christian religions.

To what extent some economists are misled by the Fetishism inherent in commodities, or by the objective appearance of the social characteristics of labour, is shown, amongst other ways, by the dull and tedious quarrel over the part played by Nature in the formation of exchange value. Since exchange value is a definite social manner of expressing the amount of labour bestowed upon an object, Nature has no more to do with it, than it has in fixing the course of exchange.

The mode of production in which the product takes the form

of a commodity, or is produced directly for exchange, is the most general and most embryonic form of bourgeois production. It therefore makes its appearance at an early date in history, though not in the same predominating and characteristic manner as now-a-days. Hence its Fetish character is comparatively easy to be seen through. But when we come to more concrete forms, even this appearance of simplicity vanishes. Whence arose the illusions of the monetary system? To it gold and silver, when serving as money, did not represent a social relation between producers, but were natural objects with strange social properties. And modern economy, which looks down with such disdain on the monetary system, does not its superstition come out as clear as noon-day, whenever it treats of capital? How long is it since economy discarded the physiocratic illusion, that rents grow out of the soil and not out of society?

But not to anticipate, we will content ourselves with yet another example relating to the commodity form. Could commodities themselves speak, they would say: Our use-value may be a thing that interests men. It is no part of us as objects. What, however, does belong to us as objects, is our value. Our natural intercourse as commodities proves it. In the eyes of each other we are nothing but exchange values. Now listen how these commodities speak through the mouth of the economist. "Value"—(*i.e.*, exchange value) "is a property of things, riches"—(*i.e.*, use-value) "of man. Value, in this sense, necessarily implies exchanges, riches do not." "Riches" (use-value) "are the attribute of men, value is the attribute of commodities. A man or a community is rich, a pearl or a diamond is valuable. . . A pearl or a diamond is valuable" as a pearl or diamond. So far no chemist has ever discovered exchange value either in a pearl or a diamond. The economical discoverers of this chemical element, who by-the-bye lay special claim to critical acumen, find however, that the use-value of objects belongs to them independently of their material properties, while their value, on the other hand, forms a part of them as objects. What confirms them in this view, is the peculiar circumstances that the use-value of objects is realised without exchange, by means of a direct relation between the objects and man, while, on the other hand, their value is realised only by exchange, that is, by means of a social process. Who fails here to call to mind our good friend, Dogberry, who informs Neighbour Seacoal, that, "To be a well-favoured man is the gift of fortune; but reading and writing comes by nature."

I, pp. 92-96

Capital—Profit (Profit of Enterprise plus Interest), Land—Ground-Rent, Labor—Wages, this is the trinitarian formula which comprises all the secrets of the social process of production.

Furthermore, since interest, as previously demonstrated, appear as the characteristic product of capital, and profit of enterprise distinguishes itself from interest by appearing as wages independent of capital, the above trinitarian formula reduces itself more specifically to the following: Capital—Interest, Land—Ground-Rent, Labor—Wages. Here profit, the specific mark characterizing the form of surplus-value belonging to the capitalist mode of production, is happily eliminated.

Now, if we look more closely at this economic trinity, we observe:

1) The alleged sources of the annually available wealth belong to widely dissimilar spheres and have not the least analogy with one another. They have about the same relation to each other as lawyer's fees, carrots, and music.

Capital, Land, Labor! But capital is not a thing. It is a definite interrelation in social production belonging to a definite historical formation of society. This interrelation expresses itself through a certain thing and gives to this thing a specific social character. Capital is not the sum of the material and produced means of production. Capital means rather the means of production converted into capital, and means of production by themselves are no more capital than gold or silver are money in themselves. Capital signifies the means of production monopolized by a certain part of society, the products and material requirements of labor made independent of labor-power in living human beings and antagonistic to them, and personified in capital by this antagonism. Capital means not merely the products of the laborers made independent of them and turned into social powers, the products turned into rulers and buyers of their own producers, but also the social powers and the future . . . (illegible) form of labor, which antagonize the producers in the shape of qualities of their products. Here, then, we have a definite and, at first sight, very mystical, social form of one of the factors in a historically produced process of social production.

By the side of this factor we have the land, the unorganic nature as such, a crude and uncouth mass, in its whole primal wildness. Value is labor. Therefore surplus-value cannot be land. The absolute fertility of the soil accomplishes no more than that a certain quantity of labor produces a certain product conditioned upon the natural fertility of the soil. The difference in the fertility of the soil brings it about that the same quantities of labor and capital, hence the same value, express themselves in different quantities of agricultural products, so that these products have different individual values. The equalization of these individual values into market-values is responsible for the fact that the "advantages of fertile over inferior soil . . .

are transferred from the cultivator or consumer to the landlord."
(Ricardo, *Principles*, p. 6)

And finally, the third party in this conspiracy is a mere
ghost, "Labor," a mere abstraction, and which does not exist
when taken by itself, or, if we take . . . (illegible), the productive activity of human beings in general, by which they
promote the circulation of matter between themselves and
nature, divested not only of every definiteness of social form
and character, but even of its mere natural existence, independent of society, lifted above all societies, being the common
attribute of unsocial man as well as of man with any form of
society and a general expression and assertion of life.

III, pp. 947-949

In Capital—Profit, or better Capital—Interest, Land—Rent,
Labor—Wages of Labor, in this economic trinity expressing
professedly the connection of value and of wealth in general
with their sources, we have the complete mystification of the
capitalist mode of production, the transformation of social
conditions into things, the indiscriminate amalgamation of the
material conditions of production with their historical and social
forms. It is an enchanted, perverted, topsy-turvy world, in which
Mister Capital and Mistress Land carry on their goblin tricks
as social characters and at the same time as mere things. It is
the great merit of classic economy to have dissolved this false
appearance and illusion, this self-isolation and ossification of
the different social elements of wealth by themselves, this personification of things and conversion of conditions of production
into entities, this religion of everyday life. It did so by reducing
interest to a portion of profit, and rent to the surplus above the
average profit, so that both of them meet in surplus-value. It

represented the process of circulation as a mere metamorphosis of forms, and finally reduced value and surplus-value of commodities to labor in the actual process of production. Nevertheless even the best spokesmen of classic economy remained more or less the prisoners of the world of illusion which they had dissolved critically, and this could not well be otherwise from a bourgeois point of view. Consequently all of them fall more or less into inconsistencies, half-way statements, and unsolved contradictions. On the other hand, it is equally natural that the actual agents of production felt completely at home in these estranged and irrational forms of Capital—Interest, Land —Rent, Labor—Wages of Labor, for these are the forms of the illusion, in which they move about and in which they find their daily occupation. It is also quite natural that vulgar economy, which is nothing but a didactic, more or less dogmatic, translation of the ordinary conceptions of the agents of production and which arranges them in a certain intelligent order, should see in this trinity, which is devoid of all internal connection, the natural and indubitiable basis of its shallow assumption of importance. This formula corresponds at the same time to the interests of the ruling classes, by proclaiming the natural necessity and eternal justification of their sources of revenue and raising them to the position of a dogma.

III, pp. 966-967

Contrary to Adam Smith, David Ricardo elaborated with great clearness the determination of the value of a commodity by labor-time and showed that this law governs also such relations of capitalistic production which seem to contradict it most. Ricardo continues his investigations exclusively to the *quantitative determination of value* and as regards the latter he is at least conscious of the fact that the realization of the law depends upon certain historical conditions. He says, namely, that the determination of value by labor-time holds good for commodities "only as can be increased in quantity by the exertion of human industry, and on the production of which competition operates without restraint." What he really means is that the law of value presupposes for its full development an industrial society in which production is carried on a large scale and free competition prevails, *i.e.,* the modern capitalist society. In all other respects, Ricardo considers the capitalist form of labor as the eternal natural form of social labor. He makes the primitive fisherman and the primitive hunter straightway exchange their fish and game as owners of commodities, in proportion to the labor-time embodied in these exchange values. On this occasion he commits the anachronism of making the primitive fisherman and primitive hunter consult the annuity tables in current use on the London Exchange in the year 1817 in the calculation relating to their instruments. The "parallelograms of Mr. Owen" seem to be the only form of society outside of the bourgeois form with which he was acquainted. Although confined within this bourgeois horizon, Ricardo analyzes the bourgeois economy—which looks quite different to deeper insight than it does on the surface—with such keen power of theoretical penetration that Lord Brougham could say of him: "Mr. Ricardo seemed as if he had dropped from another planet."

*A Contribution to the Critique of
Political Economy,* pp. 68-70

B. THE DOCTRINE OF INCREASING MISERY*

Editor's note: That workers are progressively exploited as capital accumulation proceeds is basic to Marx's doctrine and lies at the heart of the theory of the ultimate destruction of the capitalist order due to internal contradictions. What Marx meant when referring to the "increasing misery" of the worker has been the subject of considerable comment. Did he mean that the *absolute* volume of goods and services available per worker would decline or did he mean that the laborer's *share* of a rising national income would be smaller?

Summary: The *value* of labor power is determined by the value of the necessities of life. However, it is possible, due to an increase in productivity, for labor and capital to share in increased output. Should wages rise due to increased output, they would be above their *value*. Although such an increase is quite likely, the fact that a disproportionate share of the increased output is appropriated by

---

* This section is drawn largely from the references contained in Thomas Sowell's "Marx's 'Increasing Misery' Doctrine," *American Economic Review,* March 1960, pp. 110-120. Sowell notes that the view that "Increasing Misery" means a decline in the absolute level of living is derived from the *Communist Manifesto* (*supra* p. 26), *Critique of the Gotha Programme,* p. 24 (". . . the system of wage labour is a system of slavery, and indeed a slavery which becomes more severe in proportion as the social productive forces of labour develop, whether the worker receives better or worse payment"), and *Capital,* Vol. I, pp. 708-709 (". . . in proportion as capital accumulates, the lot of the labourer, be his payment high or low, must grow worse. . . . Accumulation of wealth at one pole is, therefore, at the same time accumulation of misery, agony of toil, slavery, ignorance, brutality, mental degradation, at the opposite pole, *i.e.,* on the side of the class that produces its own product in the form of capital.") Sowell argues that it is the interpretation of these passages which is at issue.—Ed.

the capitalist widens the difference in the position of laborer and capitalist.

---

*

The value of labour-power is determined by the value of a given quantity of necessaries. It is the value and not the mass of these necessaries that varies with the productiveness of labour. It is, however, possible that, owing to an increase of productiveness, both the labourer, and the capitalist may simultaneously be able to appropriate a greater quantity of these necessaries, without any change in the price of labour-power or in surplus-value. If the value of labour-power be 3 shillings, and the necessary labour-time amount to 6 hours, if the surplus-value likewise be 3 shillings, and the surplus-labour 6 hours, then if the productiveness of labour were doubled without altering the ratio of necessary labour to surplus-labour, there would be no change of magnitude in surplus-value and price of labour-power. The only result would be that each of them would represent twice as many use-values as before; these use-values being twice as cheap as before. Although labour-power would be unchanged in price, it would be above its value. If, however, the prices of labour-power had fallen, not to 1s. 6d., the lowest possible point consistent with its new value, but to 2s. 10d. or 2s. 6d., still this lower price would represent an increased mass of necessaries. In this way it is possible with an increasing productiveness of labour, for the price of labour-power to keep on falling, and yet this fall to be accompanied by a constant growth in the mass of the labourer's means of subsistence. But even in such case, the fall in the value of labour-power would cause a corresponding rise of surplus-value, and thus the abyss between the labourer's position and that of the capitalist would keep widening.

I, p. 573

Summary: The value of wages is determined by the *quantity of labor necessaries cost,* not by the value of the *quantity of necessaries that labor receives.* It is the proportion of the working day which the laborer gets, his share of the national income, his relative wage, which determines his social position.

*

The value of wages has to be reckoned not on the basis of the quantity of necessaries which the worker receives, but on the basis of the quantity of labour which these necessaries cost—actually the proportion of the working day which he appropriates for himself; the proportionate share of the total product, or rather of the total value of this product, which the worker receives. It is possible that, reckoned in use values (quantity of commodities or money), his wages may rise as productivity increases, and yet reckoned in value they may fall, and *vice versa.* It is one of Ricardo's greatest merits that he made an examination of relative wages and established them as a definite category. Previously wages had always been looked upon as a simple element, and consequently the worker had been regarded as an animal. In Ricardo, however, he is considered in his social relationship. The position of the classes in relation to each other depends to a greater extent on the proportion which the wage forms than on the absolute amount of the wage.

Theories of Surplus Value, p. 320

A notable advance in the amount paid as wages presupposes a rapid increase of productive capital. The rapid increase of productive capital calls forth just as rapid an increase in wealth, luxury, social wants, and social comforts. Therefore, although the comforts of the laborer have risen, the social satisfaction which they give has fallen in comparison with these augmented comforts of the capitalist, which are unattainable for the laborer, and in comparison with the scale of general development society has reached. Our wants and their satisfaction have their origin in society; we therefore measure them in their relation to society, and not in relation to the objects which satisfy them. Since their nature is social, it is therefore relative.

"Wage-Labor and Capital" in *The Essentials of Marx*, p. 98

B.

THEORY OF EXPLOITATION

1. Constant and Variable Capital

Summary: Constant capital refers to that portion of the value of machinery and materials which is used up in production and added to the value of a product. Only the value of that portion of constant capital which is used up (depreciation and raw materials) is transferred to the value of the commodity. That part of capital represented by labor power, which in the process of production reproduces the equivalent of its own value plus a surplus value (which may vary according to circumstances), is called variable capital.

*

Value exists only in articles of utility, in objects: we leave out of consideration its purely symbolical representation by tokens. (Man himself, viewed as the impersonation of labour-power, is a natural object, a thing, although a living conscious thing; and labour is the manifestation of this power residing in him.) If therefore an article loses it utility, it also loses its value. The reason why means of production do not lose their value, at the same time that they lose their use-value, is this: they lose in the labour-process the original form of their use-value, only to assume in the product the form of a new use-value. But, however important it may be to value, that it should have some object of utility to embody itself in, yet it is a matter of complete indifference what particular object serves this purpose; this we saw when treating of the metamorphosis of commodities. Hence

72

it follows that in the labour-process the means of production transfer their value to the product only so far as along with their use-value they lose also their exchange value. They give up to the product that value alone which they themselves lose as means of production. But in this respect the material factors of the labour-process do not all behave alike.

The coal burnt under the boiler vanishes without leaving a trace; so, too, the tallow with which the axles of wheels are greased. Dye stuffs and other auxiliary substances also vanish but re-appear as properties of the product. Raw material forms the substance of the product, but only after it has changed its form. Hence raw material and auxiliary substances lost the characteristic form with which they are clothed on entering the labour-process. It is otherwise with the instruments of labour. Tools, machines, workshops, and vessels, are of use in the labour-process, only so long as they retain their original shape, and are ready each morning to renew the process with their shape unchanged. And just as during their lifetime, that is to say, during the continued labour-process in which they serve, they retain their shape independent of the product, so, too, they do after their death. The corpses of machines, tools, workshops, &c., are always separate and distinct from the product they helped to turn out. If we now consider the case of any instrument of labour during the whole period of its service, from the day of its entry into the workshop, till the day of its banishment into the lumber room, we find that during this period its use-value has been completely consumed, and therefore its exchange value completely transferred to the product. For instance, if a spinning machine lasts for 10 years, it is plain that during that working period its total value is gradually transferred to the product of the 10 years. The lifetime of an instrument of labour, therefore, is spent in the repetition of a greater or less number of similar operations. Its life may be compared with that of a human being. Every day brings a man 24 hours nearer to his grave: but how many days he has still to travel on that road, no man can tell accurately by merely looking at him. This difficulty, however, does not prevent life insurance offices from drawing, by means of the theory of averages, very accurate, and at the same time very profitable conclusions. So it is with the instruments of labour. It is known by experience how long on the average a machine of a particular kind will last. Suppose its use-value in the labour-process to last only six days. Then, on the average, it loses each day one-sixth of its use-value, and therefore parts with one-sixth of its value to the daily product. The wear and tear of all instruments, their daily loss of use-value, and the corresponding quantity of value they part with to the product, are accordingly calculated upon this basis.

It is thus strikingly clear, that means of production never transfer more value to the product than they themselves lose during the labour-process by the destruction of their own use-value. If such an instrument has no value to lose, if, in other words, it is not the product of human labour, it transfers no value to the product. It helps to create use-value without contributing to the formation of exchange value. In this class are included all means of production supplied by Nature without human assistance, such as land, wind, water, metals in situ, and timber in virgin forests.

Yet another interesting phenomenon here presents itself. Suppose a machine to be worth £1000, and to wear out in 1000 days. Then one thousandth part of the value of the machine is daily transferred to the day's product. At the same time, though with diminishing vitality, the machine as a whole continues to take part in the labour-process. Thus it appears that one factor of the labour-process, a means of production, continually enters as a whole into that process, while it enters into the process of the formation of value by fractions only. The difference between the two processes is here reflected in their material factors, by the same instrument of production taking part as a whole in the labour-process, while at the same time as an element in the formation of value, it enters only by fractions.

On the other hand, a means of production may take part as a whole in the formation of value, while into the labour-process it enters only bit by bit. Suppose that in spinning cotton, the waste for every 115 lbs. used amounts to 15 lbs., which is converted, not into yarn, but into "devil's dust." Now, although this 15 lbs. of cotton never becomes a constituent element of the yarn, yet assuming this amount of waste to be normal and inevitable under average conditions of spinning, its value is just as surely transferred to the value of the yarn, as is the value of the 100 lbs. that form the substance of the yarn. The use-value of 15 lbs. of cotton must vanish into dust, before 100 lbs. of yarn can be made. The destruction of this cotton is therefore a necessary condition in the production of the yarn. And because it is a necessary condition, and for no other reason, the value of that cotton is transferred to the product. The same holds good for every kind of refuse resulting from a labour-process, so far at least as such refuse cannot be further employed as a means in the production of new and independent use-values. Such an employment of refuse may be seen in the large machine works at Manchester, where mountains of iron turnings are carted away to the foundry in the evening, in order the next morning to re-appear in the workshops as solid masses of iron.

We have seen that the means of production transfer value to the new product, so far only as during the labour-process they lose value in the shape of their old use-value. The maximum loss of value that they can suffer in the process, is plainly limited by the amount of the original value with which they came into the process, or in other words, by the labour-time necessary for their production. Therefore the means of production can never add more value to the product than they themselves possess independently of the process in which they assist. However useful a given kind of raw material, or a machine, or other means of production may be, though it may cost £150, or, say, 500 days' labour, yet it cannot, under any circumstances, add to the value of the product more than £150. Its value is determined not by the labour-process into which it enters as a means of production, but by that out of which it has issued as a product. In the labour-process it only serves as a mere use-value, a thing with useful properties, and could not, therefore, transfer any value to the product, unless it possessed such value previously.

While productive labour is changing the means of production into constituent elements of a new product, their value undergoes a metempsychosis. It deserts the consumed body, to occupy the newly created one. But this transmigration takes place, as it were, behind the back of the labourer. He is unable to add new labour, to create new value, without at the same time preserving old values, and this, because the labour he adds must be of a specific useful kind; and he cannot do work of a useful kind, without employing products as the means of production of a new product, and thereby transferring their value to the new product. The property therefore which labour-power in action, living labour, possesses of preserving value, at the same time that it adds it, is a gift of Nature which costs the labourer nothing, but which is very advantageous to the capitalist inasmuch as it preserves the existing value of his capital. So long as trade is good, the capitalist is too much absorbed in money-grubbing to take notice of this gratuitous gift of labour. A violent interruption of the labour-process by a crisis, makes him sensitively aware of it.

As regards the means of production, what is really consumed is their use-value, and the consumption of this use-value by labour results in the product. There is no consumption of their value, and it would therefore be inaccurate to say that it is reproduced. It is rather preserved; not by reason of any operation it undergoes itself in the process; but because the article in which it originally exists, vanishes, it is true, but vanishes into some other article. Hence, in the value of the product, there is a re-appearance of the value of the means of production, but there is, strictly speaking, no reproduction of that value. That which is produced is a new use-value in which the old exchange-value re-appears.

It is otherwise with the subjective factor of the labour-process, with labour-power in action. While the labourer, by virtue of his labour being of a specialised kind that has a special object, preserves and transfers to the product the value of the means of production, he at the same time, by the mere act of working, creates each instant an additional or new value. Suppose the process of production to be stopped just when the workman has produced an equivalent for the value of his own labour-power, when, for example, by six hours' labour, he has added a value of three shillings. This value is the surplus, of the total value of the product, over the portion of its value that is due to the means of production. It is the only original bit of value formed during this process, the only portion of the value of the product created by this process. Of course, we do not forget that this new value only replaces the money advanced by the capitalist in the purchase of the labour-power, and spent by the labourer on the necessaries of life. With regard to the money spent, the new value is merely a reproduction; but, nevertheless, it is an actual, and not, as in the case of the value of the means of production, only an apparent, reproduction. The substitution of one value for another, is here effected by the creation of new value. . . .

By our explanation of the different parts played by the various factors of the labour-process in the formation of the product's value, we have, in fact, disclosed the characters of the different functions allotted to the different elements of capital in the process of expanding its own value. The surplus of the total value of the product, over the sum of the values of its constituent factors, is the surplus of the expanded capital over the capital originally advanced. The means of production on the one hand, labour-power on the other, are merely the different modes of existence which the value of the original capital assumed when from being money it was transformed into the various factors of the labour-process. That part of capital then, which is represented by the means of production, by the raw material, auxiliary material and the instruments of labour, does not, in the process of production, undergo any quantitative alteration of value. I therefore call it the constant part of capital, or, more shortly, *constant capital.*

On the other hand, that part of capital, represented by labour-power, does, in the process of production, undergo an alteration of value. It both reproduces the equivalent of its own value, and also produces an excess, a surplus-value, which may itself vary, may be more or less according to circumstances. This part of capital is continually being transformed from a constant into a variable magnitude. I therefore call it the variable part of capital, or, shortly, *variable capital.* The same elements of capital which, from the point of view of the labour-process, present themselves respectively as the objective and subjective factors, as means of production and labour-power, present themselves, from the point of view of the process of creating surplus-value, as constant and variable capital.

I, pp. 225-233

2. *Surplus Value*

Summary: Surplus value is the source of capitalist profit. It is obtained by the capitalist from the laborer in the following manner: The value of labor power (its market price) is only its subsistence (see Part II, A, 4). Since the laborer, working with modern machinery, is able to earn the value of subsistence (his wage) with only a few hours' work out of the working day, the value of his output for the remainder of the working day is appropriated by the capitalist as surplus value. Surplus value is the value created by the laborer but alienated by the capitalist.

---

*

The labour-process, turned into the process by which the capitalist consumes labour-power, exhibits two characteristic phenomena. First, the labourer works under the control of the capitalist to whom his labour belongs; the capitalist taking good care that the work is done in a proper manner, and that the means of production are used with intelligence, so that there is no unnecessary waste of raw material, and no wear and tear of the implements beyond what is necessarily caused by the work.

Secondly, the product is the property of the capitalist and not that of the labourer, its immediate producer. Suppose that a capitalist pays for a day's labour-power at its value; then the right to use that power for a day belongs to him, just as much as the right to use any other commodity, such as a horse that he has hired for the day. To the purchaser of a commodity belongs its use, and the seller of labour-power, by giving his labour, does no more, in reality, than part with the use-value that he has sold. From the instant he steps into the workshop, the use-value of his labour-power, and therefore also its use, which is labour, belongs to the capitalist. By the purchase of labour-power, the capitalist incorporates labour, as a living ferment, with the lifeless constituents of the product. From his point of view, the labour-process is nothing more than the consumption of the commodity purchased, *i.e.,* of labour-power; but this consumption cannot be effected except by supplying the labour-power with the means of production. The labour-process is a process between things that the capitalist has purchased, things that have become his property. The product of this process also belongs, therefore, to him, just as much as does the wine which is the product of a process of fermentation completed in his cellar.

I, p. 206

We assumed, on the occasion of its sale, that the value of a day's labour-power is three shillings, and that six hours' labour are incorporated in that sum; and consequently that this amount of labour is requisite to produce the necessaries of life daily required on an average by the labourer. If now our spinner by working for one hour, can convert $1\frac{2}{3}$ lbs. of cotton into $1\frac{2}{3}$ lbs. of yarn, it follows that in six hours he will convert 10 lbs. of cotton into 10 lbs. of yarn. Hence, during the spinning process, the cotton absorbs six hours' labour. The same quantity of labour is also embodied in a piece of gold of the value of three shillings. Consequently by the mere labour of spinning, a value of three shillings is added to the cotton.

Let us now consider the total value of the product, the 10 lbs.

of yarn. Two and a half days' labour have been embodied in it, of which two days were contained in the cotton and in the substance of the spindle worn away, and half a day was absorbed during the process of spinning. This two and a half days' labour is also represented by a piece of gold of the value of fifteen shillings. Hence, fifteen shillings is an adequate price for the 10 lbs. of yarn, or the price of one pound is eighteen-pence.

Our capitalist stares in astonishment. The value of the product is exactly equal to the value of the capital advanced. The value so advanced has not expanded, no surplus-value has been created, and consequently money has not been converted into capital. The price of the yarn is fifteen shillings, and fifteen shillings were spent in the open market upon the constituent elements of the product, or, what amounts to the same thing, upon the factors of the labour-process; ten shillings were paid for the cotton, two shillings for the substance of the spindle worn away, and three shillings for the labour-power. The swollen value of the yarn is of no avail, for it is merely the sum of the values formerly existing in the cotton, the spindle, and the labour-power; out of such a simple addition of existing values, no surplus-value can possibly arise. These separate values are now all concentrated in one thing; but so they were also in the sum of fifteen shillings, before it was split up into three parts, by the purchase of the commodities.

There is in reality nothing very strange in this result. The value of one pound of yarn being eighteenpence, if our capitalist buys 10 lbs. of yarn in the market, he must pay fifteen shillings for them. It is clear that, whether a man buys his house ready built, or gets it built for him, in neither case will the mode of acquisition increase the amount of money laid out on the house.

Our capitalist, who is at home in his vulgar economy, exclaims: "Oh! but I advanced my money for the express purpose of making more money." The way to Hell is paved with good intentions, and he might just as easily have intended to make money, without producing at all. He threatens all sorts of things. He won't be caught napping again. In future he will buy the commodities in the market, instead of manufacturing them himself. But if all his brother capitalists were to do the same, where would he find his commodities in the market? And his money he cannot eat. He tries persuasion. "Consider my abstinence; I might have played ducks and drakes with the 15 shillings; but instead of that I consumed it productively, and made yarn with it." Very well, and by way of reward he is now in possession of good yarn instead of a bad conscience; and as for playing the part of a miser, it would never do for him to relapse into such bad ways as that; we have seen before to what results such asceticism leads. Besides, where nothing is, the king has lost his rights: whatever may be the merit of his abstinence, there is nothing wherewith specially to remunerate it, because the value of the product is merely the sum of the values of the commodities that were thrown into the process of production. Let him therefore console himself with the reflection that virtue is its own reward. But no, he becomes importunate. He says: "The yarn is of no use to me: I produced it for sale." In that case let him sell it, or, still better, let him for the future produce only things for satisfying his personal wants, a remedy that his physician M'Culloch has already prescribed as infallible against an epidemic of over-production. He now gets obstinate. "Can the labourer," he asks, "merely with his arms and legs, produce commodities out of nothing? Did I not supply him with the materials, by means of which, and in which alone, his labour could be embodied? And as the greater part of society consists of such ne'er-do-weels, have I not rendered society incalculable service by my instruments of production, my cotton and my spindle, and not only society, but the labourer also, whom in addition I have provided with the necessaries of life? And am

I to be allowed nothing in return for all this service?" Well, but
has not the labourer rendered him the equivalent service of
changing his cotton and spindle into yarn? Moreover, there
is here no question of service. A service is nothing more than the
useful effect of a use-value, be it of a commodity, or be it of
labour. But here we are dealing with exchange-value. The capitalist paid to the labourer a value of 3 shillings, and the labourer
gave him back an exact equivalent in the value of 3 shillings,
added by him to the cotton: he gave him value for value. Our
friend, up to this time so purse-proud, suddenly assumes the
modest demeanour of his own workman, and exclaims: "Have
I myself not worked? Have I not performed the labour of superintendence and of overlooking the spinner? And does not this
labour, too, create value?" His overlooker and his manager try
to hide their smiles. Meanwhile, after a hearty laugh, he re-
assumes his usual mien. Though he chanted to us the whole
creed of the economists, in reality, he says, he would not give a
brass farthing for it. He leaves this and all such like subterfuges
and juggling tricks to the professors of political economy, who
are paid for it. He himself is a practical man; and though he
does not always consider what he says outside his business, yet
in his business he knows what he is about.

Let us examine the matter more closely. The value of a day's
labour-power amounts to 3 shillings, because on our assumption
half a day's labour is embodied in that quantity of labour-power,
i.e., because the means of subsistence that are daily required for
the production of labour-power, cost half a day's labour. But
the past labour that is embodied in the labour-power, and the
living labour that it can call into action; the daily cost of maintaining it, and its daily expenditure in work, are two totally
different things. The former determines the exchange-value of
the labour-power, the latter is its use-value. The fact that half
a day's labour is necessary to keep the labourer alive during 24

hours, does not in any way prevent him from working a whole day. Therefore, the value of labour-power, and the value which that labour-power creates in the labour process, are two entirely different magnitudes; and this difference of the two values was what the capitalist had in view, when he was purchasing the labour-power. The useful qualities that labour-power possesses, and by virtue of which it makes yarn or boots, were to him nothing more than a conditio sine qua non; for in order to create value, labour must be expended in a useful manner. What really influenced him was the specific use-value which this commodity possesses of being *a source not only of value, but of more value than it has itself*. This is the special service that the capitalist expects from labour-power, and in this transaction he acts in accordance with the "eternal laws" of the exchange of commodities. The seller of labour-power, like the seller of any other commodity, realises its exchange-value, and parts with its use-value. He cannot take the one without giving the other. The use-value of labour-power, or in other words, labour, belongs just as little to its seller, as the use-value of oil after it has been sold belongs to the dealer who has sold it. The owner of the money has paid the value of a day's labour-power; his, therefore, is the use of it for a day; a day's labour belongs to him. The circumstance, that on the one hand the daily sustenance of labour-power costs only half a day's labour, while on the other hand the very same labour-power can work during the whole day, that consequently the value which its use during one day creates, is double what he pays for that use, this circumstance is, without doubt, a piece of good luck for the buyer, but by no means an injury to the seller.

Our capitalist foresaw this state of things, and that was the cause of his laughter. The labourer therefore finds, in the workshop, the means of production necessary for working, not only during six, but during twelve hours. Just as during the six hours' process our 10 lbs. of cotton absorbed six hours' labour, and became 10 lbs. of yarn, so now, 20 lbs. of cotton will absorb 12 hours' labour and be changed into 20 lbs. of yarn. Let us now examine the product of this prolonged process. There is now materialised in this 20 lbs. of yarn the labour of five days, of which four days are due to the cotton and the lost steel of the spindle, the remaining day having been absorbed by the cotton during the spinning process. Expressed in gold, the labour of five days is thirty shillings. This is therefore the price of the 20 lbs. of yarn, giving, as before, eighteenpence as the price of a pound. But the sum of the values of the commodities that entered into the process amounts to 27 shillings. The value of the yarn is 30 shillings. Therefore the value of the product is $\frac{1}{9}$ greater than the value advanced for its production; 27 shillings have been transformed into 30 shillings; a surplus-value of 3 shillings has been created. The trick has at last succeeded; money has been converted into capital.

Every condition of the problem is satisfied, while the laws that regulate the exchange of commodities, have been in no way violated. Equivalent has been exchanged for equivalent. For the capitalist as buyer paid for each commodity, for the cotton, the spindle and the labour-power, its full value. He then did what is done by every purchaser of commodities; he consumed their use-value. The consumption of the labour-power, which was also the process of producing commodities, resulted in 20 lbs. of yarn, having a value of 30 shillings. The capitalist, formerly a buyer, now returns to market as a seller, of commodities. He sells his yarn at eighteenpence a pound, which is its exact value. Yet for all that he withdraws 3 shillings more from circulation than he originally threw into it. This metamorphosis, this conversion of money into capital, takes place both within the sphere of circulation and also outside it; within the circulation, because conditioned by the purchase of the labour-power in the market; outside the circulation, because what is done within it is only a stepping-stone to the production of surplus-

value, a process which is entirely confined to the sphere of production. Thus "tout est pour le mieux dans le meilleur des
mondes possibles."

By turning his money into commodities that serve as the
material elements of a new product, and as factors in the labour-
process, by incorporating living labour with their dead substance,
the capitalist at the same time converts value, *i.e.,* past, materialised, and dead labour into capital, into value big with value, a
live monster that is fruitful and multiplies.

If we now compare the two processes of producing value and
of creating surplus-value, we see that the latter is nothing but the
continuation of the former beyond a definite point. If on the
one hand the process be not carried beyond the point, where the
value paid by the capitalist for the labour-power is replaced by
an exact equivalent, it is simply a process of producing value; if,
on the other hand, it be continued beyond that point, it becomes
a process of creating surplus-value.

I, pp. 212-218

We know, however, from what has gone before, that the
labour-process may continue beyond the time necessary to reproduce and incorporate in the product a mere equivalent for
the value of the labour-power. Instead of the six hours that are
sufficient for the latter purpose, the process may continue for
twelve hours. The action of labour-power, therefore, not only
reproduces its own value, but produces value over and above
it. This surplus-value is the difference between the value of the
product and the value of the elements consumed in the formation
of that product, in other words, of the means of production and
the labour-power.

I, p. 232

3. The Rate of Surplus Value

Summary: The capital, C, necessary for the production of a commodity is made up of two parts: c—constant capital, and v—variable capital. $C = c + v$. Constant capital is defined as that portion of capital equipment (machinery, for example) worn away in the process of production plus raw and auxiliary materials. Although expensive machinery is used in the process of production, only that portion of machinery used up contributes to the value of a product and is counted as c. Variable capital, v, is the money spent for (the wage of) living labor and is equal to the laborer's subsistence.

However, variable capital is capable of creating surplus value, s. Thus the value of a commodity is $c + v + s$.

A laborer may work twelve hours per day and reproduce his own value, v, equal to his wage, in six hours. This is called "necessary labor time." The extra six hours which he works gratis for the capitalist is defined as the surplus value created by the laborer but appropriated by the capitalist. The *rate* of surplus value is the rate of exploitation of labor by capital. It may be defined as $\dfrac{s}{v} = \dfrac{\text{surplus labor}}{\text{necessary labor}}$.

---

*

The surplus-value generated in the process of production by C, the capital advanced, or in other words, the self-expansion of the value of the capital C, presents itself for our consideration, in the first place, as a surplus, as the amount by which the value of the product exceeds the value of its constituent element.

The capital C is made up of two components, one, the sum of money c laid out upon the means of production, and the other, the sum of money v expended upon the labour-power; c represents the portion that has become constant capital, and v the portion that has become variable capital. At first then, $C = c + v$: for example, if £500 is the capital advanced, its components may be such that the £500 = £410 const. + £90 var. When the process of production is finished, we get a commodity whose value = $(c + v) + s$, where s is the surplus-value; or taking our former figures, the value of this commodity may be (£410 const. + £90 var.) + £90 surpl. The original capital has now changed from C to C′, from £500 to £590. The difference is s or a surplus value of £90. Since the value of the constituent elements of the product is equal to the value of the advanced capital, it is mere tautology to say, that the excess of the value of the product over the value of its constituent elements, is equal to the expansion of the capital advanced or to the surplus-value produced.

Nevertheless, we must examine this tautology a little more closely. The two things compared are, the value of the product, and the value of its constituents consumed in the process of production. Now we have seen how that portion of the constant capital which consists of the instruments of labour, transfers to the product only a fraction of its value, while the remainder of that value continues to reside in those instruments. Since this remainder plays no part in the formation of value, we may at present leave it on one side. To introduce it into the calculation would make no difference. For instance, taking our former example, $c = £410$: suppose this sum to consist of £312 value of raw material, £44 value of auxiliary material, and £54 value of the machinery worn away in the process; and suppose that the total value of the machinery employed is £1,054. Out of this latter sum, then, we reckon as advanced for the purpose of turning out the product, the sum of £54 alone, which the machinery loses by wear and tear in the process; for this is all it parts with to the product. Now if we also reckon the remaining £1,000, which still continues in the machinery, as transferred to the product, we ought also to reckon it as part of the value advanced, and thus make it appear on both sides of our calculation. We should, in this way, get £1,500 on one side and £1,590 on the other. The difference of these two sums, or the surplus-value, would still be £90. Throughout this Book therefore, by constant capital advanced for the production of value, we always mean, unless the context is repugnant thereto, the value of the means of production actually consumed in the process, and that value alone.

This being so, let us return to the formula $C = c + v$, which we saw transformed into $C' = (c + v) + s$, C becoming C'. We know that the value of the constant capital is transferred to, and merely re-appears in the product. The new value actually created in the process, the value produced, or value-product, is therefore not the same as the value of the product; it is not, as it would at first sight appear $(c + v) + s$ or £410 const. + £90 var. + £90 surpl.; but $v + s$ or £90 var. + £90 surpl. not £590 but £180. If $c = o$, or in other words, if there were branches of industry in which the capitalist could dispense with all means of production made by previous labour, whether they be raw material, auxiliary material, or instruments of labour, employing only labour-power and materials supplied by Nature, in that case, there would be no constant capital to transfer to the product. This component of the value of the product, *i.e.,* the £410 in our example, would be eliminated, but the sum of £180, the amount of new value created, or the value produced, which contains £90 of surplus-value, would remain just as great as if c represented the highest value imaginable. We should have $C = (0 + v) = v$ or C' the expanded capital $= v + s$ and therefore $C' - C = s$ as before. On the other hand, if $s = 0$, or in other words, if the labour-power, whose value is advanced in the form of variable capital, were to produce only its equivalent, we should have $C = c + v$ or C' the value of the product $= (c + v) + 0$ or $C = C'$. The capital advanced would, in this case, not have expanded its value.

From what has gone before, we know that surplus-value is purely the result of a variation in the value of v, of that portion of the capital which is transformed into labour-power; consequently, $v + s = v + v'$ or v plus an increment of v. But the fact that it is v alone that varies, and the conditions of that variation, are obscured by the circumstance that in consequence of the increase in the variable component of the capital, there is also an increase in the sum total of the advanced capital. It was originally £500 and becomes £590. Therefore in order that our investigation may lead to accurate results, we must make abstraction from that portion of the value of the product, in which constant capital alone appears, and consequently must equate the constant capital to zero or make $c = 0$. This is merely an application of a mathematical rule, employed whenever we operate with constant and variable magnitudes, related to each other by the symbols of addition and subtraction only.

A further difficulty is caused by the original form of the variable capital. In our example, $C' =$ £410 const. + £90 var. + £90 surpl.; but £90 is a given and therefore a constant quantity; hence it appears absurd to treat it as variable. But in fact, the term £90 var. is here merely a symbol to show that this value undergoes a process. The portion of the capital invested in the purchase of labour-power is a definite quantity of materialised labour, a constant value like the value of the labour-power purchased. But in the process of production the place of the £90 is taken by the labour-power in action, dead labour is replaced by living labour, something stagnant by something flowing, a constant by a variable. The result is the reproduction of v plus an increment of v. From the point of view, then, of capitalist production, the whole process appears as the spontaneous variation of the originally constant value, which is transformed into labour-power. Both the process and its result, appear to be owing to this value. If, therefore, such expressions as " £90 variable capital," or "so much self-expanding value," appear contradictory, this is only because they bring to the surface a contradiction immanent in capitalist production.

At first sight it appears a strange proceeding, to equate the constant capital to zero. Yet it is what we do every day. If, for example, we wish to calculate the amount of England's profits from cotton industry, we first of all deduct the sums paid for cotton to the United States, India, Egypt and other countries; in other words, the value of the capital that merely re-appears in the value of the product, is put $= 0$.

Of course the ratio of surplus-value not only to that portion of the capital from which it immediately springs, and whose change of value it represents, but also to the sum total of the capital advanced is economically of very great importance. We shall, therefore, in the third book, treat of this ratio exhaustively. In order to enable one portion of a capital to expand its value by being converted into labour-power, it is necessary that another portion be converted into means of production. In order that variable capital may perform its function, constant capital must be advanced in proper proportion, a proportion given by the special technical conditions of each labour-process. The circumstance, however, that retorts and other vessels, are necessary to a chemical process, does not compel the chemist to notice them in the result of his analysis. If we look at the means of production, in their relation to the creation of value, and to the variation in the quantity of value, apart from anything else, they appear simply as the material in which labour-power, the value-creator, incorporates itself. Neither the nature, nor the value of this material is of any importance. The only requisite is

that there be a sufficient supply to absorb the labour expended
in the process of production. That supply once given, the material
may rise or fall in value, or even be, as land and the sea, without
any value in itself; but this will have no influence on the creation of value or on the variation in the quantity of value.

In the first place then we equate the constant capital to zero.
The capital advanced is consequently reduced from c + v to v,
and instead of the value of the product (c + v) + s we have
now the value produced (v + s). Given the new value produced = £180, which sum consequently represents the whole
labour expended during the process, then subtracting from it
£90 the value of the variable capital, we have remaining £90,
the amount of the surplus-value. This sum of £90 or s expresses
the absolute quantity of surplus-value produced. The relative
quantity produced, or the increase per cent of the variable
capital, is determined, it is plain, by the ratio of the surplus-value
to the variable capital, or is expressed by s/v. In our example
this ratio is 90/90, which gives an increase of 100%. This
relative increase in the value of the variable capital, or the
relative magnitude of the surplus-value, I call, "The rate of
surplus-value."

We have seen that the labourer, during one portion of the
labour-process, produces only the value of his labour-power,
that is, the value of his means of subsistence. Now since his
work forms part of a system, based on the social division of
labour, he does not directly produce the actual necessaries which
he himself consumes; he produces instead a particular commodity, yarn for example, whose value is equal to the value of
those necessaries or of the money with which they can be bought.
The portion of his day's labour devoted to this purpose, will be
greater or less, in proportion to the value of the necessaries that
he daily requires on an average, or, what amounts to the same
thing, in proportion to the labour-time required on an average
to produce them. If the value of those necessaries represents on

an average the expenditure of six hours' labour, the workman must on an average work for six hours to produce that value. If instead of working for the capitalist, he worked independently on his own account, he would, other things being equal, still be obliged to labour for the same number of hours, in order to produce the value of his labour-power, and thereby to gain the means of subsistence necessary for his conservation or continued reproduction. But as we have seen, during that portion of his day's labour in which he produces the value of his labour-power, say three shillings, he produces only an equivalent for the value of his labour-power already advanced by the capitalist; the new value created only replaces the variable capital advanced. It is owing to this fact, that the production of the new value of three shillings takes the semblance of a mere reproduction. That portion of the working day, then, during which this reproduction takes place, I call *"necessary"* labour-time, and the labour expended during that time I call *"necessary"* labour. Necessary, as regards the labourer, because independent of the particular social form of his labour; necessary, as regards capital, and the world of capitalists, because on the continued existence of the labourer depends their existence also.

During the second period of the labour-process, that in which his labour is no longer necessary labour, the workman, it is true, labours, expends labour-power; but his labour, being no longer necessary labour, he creates no value for himself. He creates surplus-value which, for the capitalist, has all the charms of a creation out of nothing. This portion of the working day, I name surplus labour-time, and to the labour expended during that time, I give the name of surplus-labour. It is every bit as important, for a correct understanding of surplus-value, to conceive it as a mere congelation of surplus-labour-time, as nothing but materialised surplus-labour, as it is, for a proper comprehension of value, to conceive it as a mere congelation of so many hours of labour, as nothing but materialised labour. The essential difference between the various economic forms of society, between, for instance, a society based on slave labour, and one based on wage labour, lies only in the mode in which this surplus-labour is in each case extracted from the actual producer, the labourer.

Since, on the one hand, the values of the variable capital and of the labour-power purchased by that capital are equal, and the value of this labour-power determines the necessary portion of the working day; and since, on the other hand, the surplus-value is determined by the surplus portion of the working day, it follows that surplus-value bears the same ratio to variable capital, that surplus-labour does to necessary labour, or in other words, the rate of surplus-value $\dfrac{s}{v} = \dfrac{\text{surplus labor}}{\text{necessary labor}}$.

Both ratios, $\dfrac{s}{v}$ and $\dfrac{\text{surplus labor}}{\text{necessary labor}}$ express the same thing in different ways; in the one case by reference to materialised, incorporated labour, in the other by reference to living, fluent labour.

The rate of surplus-value is therefore an exact expression for the degree of exploitation of labour-power by capital, or of the labourer by the capitalist.

I, pp. 235-241

Summary: Surplus value can be increased by the use of machinery. (1) Machinery increases the productivity of labor and therefore reduces the labor time necessary for the laborer to produce his subsistence. (2) It increases surplus value by making it possible to employ persons of slight muscular power—women and children. Since a subsistence wage must be great enough to support a *family,* employing the whole family makes possible the appropriation of a great deal more labor time for the same price. (3) Machinery prolongs the working day by providing the motive to the capitalist for doing so. Machinery does not tire by use and to leave it idle is costly. Thus there is the incentive to increase its use. Although labor depreciates according to use, machinery also depreciates due to the elements (rust, etc.). This latter is a motive for its full utilization. Also, there is "moral" depreciation (obsolescence due to improvements) which militate on behalf of fuller utilization— an increase in the working day. There is a contradiction which drives the capitalist to increase the working day. The more machinery employed relative to living labor, the less living labor is available for exploitation. To compensate for this decline in the source of surplus value, the capitalist must utilize the remaining labor more fully. (4) This latter leads to an *intensification* of the work of the laborer. He is compelled to work harder during the time that he works (machinery may be speeded up or discipline may be tightened).

---

*

John Stuart Mill says in his Principles of Political Economy: "It is questionable if all the mechanical inventions yet made have lighted the day's toil of any human being." That is, however, by no means the aim of the capitalistic application of machinery. Like every other increase in the productiveness of labour, machinery is intended to cheapen commodities, and, by shortening that portion of the working-day, in which the labourer works for himself, to lengthen the other portion that he gives, without an equivalent, to the capitalist. In short, it is a means for producing surplus-value.

I, p. 405

The startling point of Modern Industry is, as we have shown, the revolution in the instruments of labour, and this revolution attains its most highly developed form in the organised system of machinery in a factory. Before we inquire how human material is incorporated with this objective organism, let us consider some general effects of this revolution on the labourer himself.

Appropriation of supplementary Labour-power by Capital. The Employment of Women and Children.

In so far as machinery dispenses with muscular power, it becomes a means of employing labourers of slight muscular strength, and those whose bodily development is incomplete, but whose limbs are all the more supple. The labour of women and children was, therefore, the first thing sought for by capitalists who used machinery. That mighty substitute for labour and labourers was forthwith changed into a means for increasing the number of wage-labourers by enrolling, under the direct sway of capital, every member of the workman's family, without distinction of age or sex. Compulsory work for the capitalist usurped the place, not only of the children's play, but also of free labour at home within moderate limits for the support of the family.

The value of labour-power was determined, not only by the labour-time necessary to maintain the individual adult laborer, but also by that necessary to maintain his family. Machinery, by throwing every member of that family on to the labour market, spreads the value of the man's labour-power over his whole family. It thus depreciates his labour-power. To purchase the labour-power of a family of four workers may, perhaps, cost more than it formerly did to purchase the labour-power of the head of the family, but, in return, four days' labour takes the place of one, and their price falls in proportion to the excess of the surplus-labour of four over the surplus-labour of one. In order that the family may live, four people must now, not only labour, but expend surplus-labor for the capitalist. Thus we see, that machinery, while augmenting the human material that forms the principal object of capital's exploiting power, at the same time raises the degree of exploitation.

I, pp. 430-432

Prolongation of the working-day.

If machinery be the most powerful means for increasing the productiveness of labour—*i.e.*, for shortening the working time required in the production of a commodity, it becomes in the hands of capital the most powerful means, in those industries first invaded by it, for lengthening the working day beyond all bounds set by human nature. It creates, on the one hand, new conditions by which capital is enabled to give free scope to this its constant tendency, and on the other hand, new motives with which to whet capital's appetite for the labour of others.

In the first place, in form of machinery, the implements of labour become automatic, things moving and working independent of the workman. They are thenceforth an industrial *perpetuum mobile,* that would go on producing forever, did it not meet with certain natural obstructions in the weak bodies and the strong wills of its human attendants. The automaton, as capital, and because it is capital, is endowed, in the person of the capitalist, with intelligence and will; it is therefore animated by the longing to reduce to a minimum the resistance offered by that repellant yet elastic natural barrier, man. This resistance is moreover lessened by the apparent lightness of machine work, and by the more pliant and docile character of the women and children employed on it.

The productiveness of machinery is, as we saw, inversely proportional to the value transferred by it to the product. The longer the life of the machine, the greater is the mass of the products over which the value transmitted by the machine is spread, and the less is the portion of that value added to each single commodity. The active lifetime of a machine is, however, clearly dependent on the length of the working day, or on the duration of the daily labour-process multiplied by the number of days for which the process is carried on.

The wear and tear of a machine is not exactly proportional to its working time. And even if it were so, a machine working 16 hours daily for 7½ years, covers as long a working period as, and transmits to the total product no more value than, the same machine would if it worked only 8 hours daily for 15 years. But in the first case the value of the machine would be reproduced twice as quickly as in the latter, and the capitalist would, by this use of the machine, absorb in 7½ years as much surplus-value as in the second case he would in 15.

The material wear and tear of a machine is of two kinds. The one arises from use, as coins wear away by circulating, the other from non-use, as a sword rusts when left in its scabbard. The latter kind is due to the elements. The former is more or less directly proportional, the latter to a certain extent inversely proportional, to the use of the machine.

But in addition to the material wear and tear, a machine also undergoes, what we may call a moral depreciation. It loses exchange-value, either by machines of the same sort being produced cheaper than it, or by better machines entering into competition with it. In both cases, be the machine ever so young and full of life, its value is no longer determined by the labour actually materialised in it, but by the labour-time requisite to reproduce either it or the better machine. It has, therefore, lost value more or less. The shorter the period taken to reproduce its total value, the less is the danger of moral depreciation; and the longer the working day, the shorter is that period. When machinery is first introduced into an industry, new methods of reproducing it more cheaply follow blow upon blow, and so do improvements, that not only affect individual parts and details of the machine, but its entire build. It is, therefore, in the early days of the life of machinery that this special incentive to the prolongation of the working day makes itself felt most acutely.

Given the length of the working day, all other circumstances remaining the same, the exploitation of double the number of workmen demands, not only a doubling of that part of constant capital which is invested in machinery and buildings, but also of that part which is laid out in raw material and auxiliary substances. The lengthening of the working day, on the other hand, allows of production on an extended scale without any alteration in the amount of capital laid out on machinery and buildings. Not only is there, therefore, an increase of surplus-value, but the outlay necessary to obtain it diminishes. It is true that this takes place, more or less, with every lengthening of the working day; but in the case under consideration, the change is more marked, because the capital converted into the instruments of labour preponderates to a greater degree. The development of the factory system fixes a constantly increasing portion of the capital in a form, in which, on the one hand, its value is capable of continual self-expansion, and in which, on the other hand, it loses both use-value and exchange-value whenever it loses contact with living labour. "When a labourer," said Mr. Ashworth, a cotton magnate, to Professor Nassau W. Senior, "lays down his spade, he renders useless, for that period, a capital worth eighteen-pence. When one of our people leaves the mill, he renders useless a capital that has cost £100,000." Only fancy! making "useless" for a single moment, a capital that has cost £100,-000! It is, in truth, monstrous, that a single one of our people should ever leave the factory! The increased use of our machinery, as Senior after the instruction he received from

Ashworth clearly perceives, makes a constantly increasing lengthening of the working day "desirable."

Machinery produces relative surplus-value; not only by directly depreciating the value of labour-power, and by indirectly cheapening the same through cheapening the commodities that enter into its reproduction, but also, when it is first introduced sporadically into an industry, by converting the labour employed by the owner of that machinery, into labour of a higher degree and greater efficacy, by raising the social value of the article produced above its individual value, and thus enabling the capitalist to replace the value of a day's labour-power by a smaller portion of the value of the day's product. During this transition period, when the use of machinery is a sort of monopoly, the profits are therefore exceptional, and the capitalist endeavours to exploit thoroughly "the sunny time of this his first love," by prolonging the working day as much as possible. The magnitude of the profit whets his appetite for more profit.

As the use of machinery becomes more general in a particular industry, the social value of the product sinks down to its individual value, and the law that surplus-value does not arise from the labour-power that has been replaced by the machinery, but from the labour-power actually employed in working with the machinery, asserts itself. Surplus-value arises from the variable capital alone, and we saw that the amount of surplus-value depends on two factors, *viz.,* the rate of surplus-value and the number of the workmen simultaneously employed. Given the length of the working day, the rate of surplus-value is determined by the relative duration of the necessary labour and of the surplus-labour in a day. The number of the labourers simultaneously employed depends, on its side, on the ratio of the variable to the constant capital. Now, however much the use of machinery may increase the surplus

labour at the expense of the necessary labour by heightening
the productiveness of labour, it is clear that it attains this result,
only by diminishing the number of workmen employed by a
given amount of capital. It converts what was formerly variable
capital, invested in labour-power, into machinery, which, being
constant capital, does not produce surplus-value. It is impossible, for instance, to squeeze as much surplus-value out of 2
as out of 24 labourers. If each of these 24 men gives only one
hour of surplus-labour in 12, the 24 men give together 24
hours of surplus-labour, while 24 hours is the total labour of
the two men. Hence, the application of machinery to the production of surplus-value implies a contradiction which is immanent in it, since, of the two factors of the surplus-value
created by a given amount of capital, one, the rate of surplus-
value cannot be increased, except by diminishing the other, the
number of workmen. This contradiction comes to light, as soon
as by the general employment of machinery in a given industry,
the value of the machine-produced commodity regulates the
value of all commodities of the same sort; and it is this contradiction, that in its turn, drives the capitalist, without his
being conscious of the fact, to excessive lengthening of the
working day, in order that he may compensate the decrease in
the relative number of labourers exploited, by an increase not
only of the relative, but of the absolute surplus-labour.

If, then, the capitalistic employment of machinery, on the
one hand, supplies new and powerful motives to an excessive
lengthening of the working day, and radically changes, as well
the methods of labour, as also the character of the social working organism, in such a manner as to break down all opposition
to this tendency, on the other hand it produces, partly by opening out to the capitalist new strata of the working class, previously inaccessible to him, partly by setting free the labourers
it supplants, a surplus working population, which is compelled

to submit to the dictation of capital. Hence that remarkable
phenomenon in the history of Modern Industry, that machinery
sweeps away every moral and natural restriction on the length
of the working day. Hence, too, the economical paradox, that
the most powerful instrument for shortening labour-time, becomes the most unfailing means for placing every moment of
the labourer's time and that of his family, at the disposal of
the capitalist for the purpose of expanding the value of his
capital. "If," dreamed Aristotle, the greatest thinker of an-
tiquity, "if every tool, when summoned, or even of its own
accord, could do the work that befits it, just as the creations
of Daedalus moved of themselves, or the tripods of Hephaestos
went of their own accord to their sacred work, if the weavers'
shuttles were to weave of themselves, then there would be no
need either of apprentices for the master workers, or of slaves
for the lords." And Antiparos, a Greek poet of the time of
Cicero, hailed the invention of the water-wheel for grinding
corn, an invention that is the elementary form of all machinery,
as the giver of freedom to female slaves, and the bringer back
of the golden age. Oh! those heathens! They understood, as
the learned Bastiat, and before him the still wiser MacCulloch
have discovered, nothing of political economy and Christianity.
They did not, for example, comprehend that machinery is the
surest means of lengthening the working day. They perhaps
excused the slavery of one on the ground that it was a means
to the full development of another. But to preach slavery of
the masses, in order that a few crude and half-educated par-
venus, might become "eminent spinners," "extensive sausage
makers," and "influential shoe-black dealers," to do this, they
lacked the bump of Christianity.

I, pp. 440-446

Intensification of Labour.

The immoderate lengthening of the working day, produced by machinery in the hands of capital, leads to a reaction on the part of society, the very sources of whose life are menaced; and, thence, to a normal working day whose length is fixed by law. Thenceforth a phenomenon that we have already met with, namely, the intensification of labour, develops into great importance. Our analysis of absolute surplus-value had reference primarily to the extension or duration of the labour, its intensity being assumed as given. We now proceed to consider the substitution of a more intensified labour for labour of more extensive duration, and the degree of the former.

It is self-evident, that in proportion as the use of machinery spreads, and the experience of a special class of workmen habituated to machinery accumulates, the rapidity and intensity of labour increase as a natural consequence. Thus in England, during half a century, lengthening of the working day went hand in hand with increasing intensity of factory labour. Nevertheless the reader will clearly see, that where we have labour, not carried on by fits and starts, but repeated day after day with unvarying uniformity, a point must inevitably be reached, where extension of the working day and intensity of the labour mutually exclude one another, in such a way that lengthening of the working day becomes compatible only with a lower degree of intensity, and, a higher degree of intensity, only with a shortening of the working day. So soon as the gradually surging revolt of the working class compelled Parliament to shorten compulsorily the hours of labour, and to begin by imposing a normal working day on factories proper, so soon consequently as an increased production of surplus value by the prolongation of the working day was once for all put a stop to, from that moment capital threw itself with all its might into the production of relative surplus-value, by hastening on the further improvement of machinery. At the same time a change took place in the nature of relative surplus-value. Generally speaking, the mode of producing relative surplus-value consists in raising the productive power of the workman, so as to enable him to produce more in a given time with the same expenditure of labour. Labour-time continues to transmit as before the same value to the total product, but this unchanged amount of exchange value is spread over more use-values; hence the value of each single commodity sinks. Otherwise, however, so soon as the compulsory shortening of the hours of labour takes place. The immense impetus it gives to the development of productive power, and to economy in the means of production, imposes on the workman increased expenditure of labour in a given time, heightened tension of labour-power, and closer filling up of the pores of the working day, or condensation of labour to a degree that is attainable only within the limits of the shortened working day. This condensation of a greater mass of labour into a given period thenceforward counts for what it really is, a greater quantity of labour. In addition to a measure of its extension, *i.e.,* duration, labour now acquires a measure of its intensity or of the degree of its condensation or density. The denser hour of the ten hours' working-day contains more labour, *i.e.,* expended labour-power, than the more porous hour of the twelve hours' working-day. The product therefore of one of the former hours has as much or more value than has the product of $1\frac{1}{5}$ of the latter hours. Apart from the increased yield of relative surplus-value through the heightened productiveness of labour, the same mass of value is now produced for the capitalist, say, by $3\frac{1}{3}$ hours of surplus labour, and $6\frac{2}{3}$ hours of necessary labour, as was previously produced by four hours of surplus labour and eight hours of necessary labour.

We now come to the question: How is the labour intensified? The first effect of shortening the working day results from the self-evident law, that the efficiency of labour-power is in an inverse ratio to the duration of its expenditure. Hence, within certain limits what is lost by shortening the duration is gained by the increasing tension of labour-power. That the workman moreover really does expend more labour-power is ensured by the mode in which the capitalist pays him. In those industries, such as potteries, where machinery plays little or no part, the introduction of the Factory Acts has strikingly shown that the mere shortening of the working-day increases to a wonderful degree the regularity, uniformity, order, continuity, and energy of the labour. It seemed, however, doubtful whether this effect was produced in the factory proper, where the dependence of the workman on the continuous and uniform motion of the machinery had already created the strictest discipline. Hence, when in 1844 the reduction of the working-day to less than twelve hours was being debated, the masters almost unanimously declared "that their overlookers in the different rooms took good care that the hands lost no time," that the "extent of vigilance and attention on the part of the workmen was hardly capable of being increased," and therefore, that the speed of the machinery and other conditions remaining unaltered, "to expect in a well-managed factory any important result from increased attention of the workmen was an absurdity." This assertion was contradicted by experiments. Mr. Robert Gardner reduced the hours of labour in his two large factories at Preston, on and after the 20th April, 1844, from twelve to eleven hours a day. The result of about a year's working was that "the same amount of product for the same cost was received, and the workpeople as a whole earned in eleven hours as much wages as they did before in twelve."

I, pp. 447-449

C.

ACCUMULATION AND THE FALLING RATE OF PROFIT

1. Organic Composition of Capital

Summary: Thus far we have seen that constant capital (machinery) has the function of increasing the productivity of variable capital (labor) and becomes a powerful lever of accumulation. As capital accumulates, the proportion of constant to variable capital increases. This change in the technical composition of capital is a relative, rather than an absolute, matter. The absolute amount of variable capital may increase, but the proportion of it relative to constant capital will decline.

---

*

According to the economists themselves, it is neither the actual extent of social wealth, nor the magnitude of the capital already functioning, that lead to a rise of wages, but only the constant growth of accumulation and the degree of rapidity of that growth. (Adam Smith, Book I., chapter 8.) So far, we have only considered one special phase of this process, that in which the increase of capital occurs along with a constant technical composition of capital. But the process goes beyond this phase.

Once given the general basis of the capitalistic system, then, in the course of accumulation, a point is reached at which the development of the productivity of social labour becomes the most powerful lever of accumulation. "The same cause," says Adam Smith, "which raises the wages of labour, the increase of stock, tends to increase its productive powers, and to make a smaller quantity of labour produce a greater quantity of work."

Apart from natural conditions, such as fertility of the soil, &c., and from the skill of independent and isolated producers (shown rather qualitatively in the goodness than quantitatively in the mass of their products), the degree of productivity of labour, in a given society, is expressed in the relative extent of the means of production that one labourer, during a given time, with the same tension of labour-power, turns into products. The mass of the means of production which he thus transforms, increases with the productiveness of his labour. But those means of production play a double part. The increase of some is a consequence, that of the others a condition of the increasing productivity of labour. *E.g.,* with the division of labour in manufacture, and with the use of machinery, more raw material is worked up in the same time, and, therefore, a greater mass of raw material and auxiliary substances enter into the labour-process. That is the consequence of the increasing productivity of labour. On the other hand, the mass of machinery, beasts of burden, mineral manures, drainpipes, &c., is a condition of the increasing productivity of labour. So also is it with the means of production concentrated in buildings, furnaces, means of transport, &c. But whether condition or consequence, the growing extent of the means of production, as compared with the labour-power incorporated with them, is an expression of the growing productiveness of labour. The increase of the latter appears, therefore, in the diminution of the mass of labour in proportion to the mass of means of production moved by it, or in the diminution of the subjective factor of the labour process as compared with the objective factor.

This change in the technical composition of capital, this growth in the mass of means of production, as compared with the mass of the labour-power that vivifies them, is reflected again in its value-composition, by the increase of the constant constituent of capital at the expense of its variable constituent. There may be, *e.g.,* originally 50 per cent. of a capital laid out in means of production, and 50 per cent. in the labour-power; later on, with the development of the productivity of labour, 80 per cent. in means of production, 20 per cent. in labour-power, and so on. This law of the progressive increase in constant capital, in proportion to the variable, is confirmed at every step (as already shown) by the comparative analysis of the prices of commodities, whether we compare different economic epochs or different nations in the same epoch. The relative magnitude of the element of price, which represents the value of the means of production only, or the constant part of capital consumed, is in direct, the relative magnitude of the other element of price that pays labour (the variable part of capital) is in inverse proportion to the advance of accumulation.

This diminution in the variable part of capital as compared with the constant, or the altered value-composition of the capital, however, only shows approximately the change in the composition of its material constituents. If, *e.g.,* the capital-value employed to-day in spinning is $\frac{7}{8}$ constant and $\frac{1}{8}$ variable, whilst at the beginning of the 18th century it was $\frac{1}{2}$ constant and $\frac{1}{2}$ variable, on the other hand, the mass of raw material, instruments of labour, &c., that a certain quantity of spinning labour consumes productively to-day, is many hundred times greater than at the beginning of the 18th century. The reason is simply that, with the increasing productivity of labour, not only does the mass of the means of production consumed by it increase, but their value compared with their mass diminishes. Their value therefore rises absolutely, but not in proportion to their mass. The increase of the difference between constant and variable capital is, therefore, much less than that of the difference between the mass of the means of production into which the constant, and the mass of the labour-power into which the variable, capital is converted. The former difference increases with the latter, but in a smaller degree.

But, if the progress of accumulation lessens the relative magnitude of the variable part of capital, it by no means, in doing this, excludes the possibility of a rise in its absolute magnitude. Suppose that a capital-value at first is divided into 50 per cent. of constant and 50 per cent. of variable capital; later into 80 per cent. of constant and 20 per cent. of variable. If in the meantime the original capital, say £6,000 has increased to £18,000, its variable constituent has also increased. It was £3,000, it is now £3,600. But whereas formerly an increase of capital by 20 per cent. would have sufficed to raise the demand for labour 20 per cent., now this latter rise requires a tripling of the original capital.

I, pp. 681-683

The accumulation of capital, though originally appearing as its quantitative extension only, is effected, as we have seen, under a progressive qualitative change in its composition, under a constant increase of its constant, at the expense of its variable constituent.

The specifically capitalist mode of production, the development of the productive power of labour corresponding to it, and the change thence resulting in the organic composition of capital, do not merely keep pace with the advance of accumulation, or with the growth of social wealth. They develop at a much quicker rate, because mere accumulation, the absolute increase of the total social capital, is accompanied by the centralisation of the individual capitals of which that total is made up; and because the change in the technological composition of the additional capital goes hand in hand with a similar change in the technological composition of the original capital. With the advance of accumulation, therefore, the proportion of constant to variable capital changes. [If] it was originally say 1:1, it now becomes successively 2:1, 3:1, 4:1, 5:1, 7:1, &c., so that, as the capital increases, instead of $\frac{1}{2}$ of its total value, only $\frac{1}{3}$, $\frac{1}{4}$, $\frac{1}{5}$, $\frac{1}{6}$, $\frac{1}{8}$, &c., is transformed into labour-power, and, on the other hand, $\frac{2}{3}$, $\frac{3}{4}$, $\frac{4}{5}$, $\frac{5}{6}$, $\frac{7}{8}$ into means of production.

I, pp. 689-690

2. *The Falling Rate of Profit*

Summary: As accumulation proceeds, the proportion of constant capital to variable capital increases. This means that the rate of profit, S/C (= S/c + v), must decline. This is because surplus value (V) can be derived only from (V) variable capital. The proportion of c to v increases even though the absolute amount of v may increase (or remain the same, as in our example). What is true of different stages for the same country is also true of contemporaneous stages of development of different countries. The differences between two national rates of profit may be eliminated or reversed if labor is less productive in one country than the other. In countries at different stages of development with different organic compositions of capital, the country with a short normal working day may have a higher rate of surplus value than a country with a longer normal working day.

There is nothing in the law of the tendency for the rate of profit to decline to prevent the absolute amount of appropriated surplus labor or, for that matter, the total volume of employment from growing. The increase in the *relative* mass of materialized labor (constant capital) causes the rate of profit to have a tendency to fall.

If the laboring population increases, so long as constant capital increases in greater proportion, the rate of profit may decline while the mass of profit as well as employment increases. Not only may there be an absolute increase in profit as accumulation proceeds, there must be such an increase for these reasons: The process of accumulation which momentarily brings about a relative increase in demand for variable capital (labor) relative to constant capital on the one hand raises wages, increasing the population by encouraging marriage. But, on the other hand, high wages accelerate the introduction of machinery, creating unemployment which would result in an increase in the total population, since "poverty propagates its kind." For these reasons, accumulation must be accompanied by a growth in surplus labor and therefore by the growth of the absolute amount of profit. Yet constant capital must increase even more swiftly than variable so that the net result is still a falling rate of profit.

Accumulation increases the total volume of capital and the number of capitalists, reducing the number of independent producers, thus increasing the labor force. This increases the basis of the mass of profit. Yet accumulation of constant capital increases even faster, reducing the *rate* of profit while its *mass* increases.

Capitalists with large accumulations of capital may have larger masses of profit than smaller capitalists earning high rates of profit. When capitalists lower prices to drive out competitors, it is believed (by vulgar economists) that the purpose is to make a larger *mass* of profit at the expense of a lower *rate* of profit. Also it is argued that the degree of competition or monopoly accounts for the differing rate of profit in different businesses. This shows a misunderstanding of what the rate of profit really means and represents the crude idea that profits are an *arbitrary* addition to cost (which can be manipulated at will).

It is true that as capital accumulates prices decline and the mass of profit increases with sales. The price falls because as more constant capital is used in production, the proportion of living labor, and materialized labor, such as raw materials and wear and tear, declines. Because of the cheapening of production the mass of profits will grow if the rate of relative or absolute surplus value increases. But since the amount of living labor in a commodity decreases, the mass of profits will decline. Thus the cheapening of constant capital can only delay the decline in profit due to the rapid decrease in variable (living) capital.

To say that the price of a commodity has fallen is to say that a certain quantity of labor is realized in more commodities. For the most part, the rate of profit will fall despite the increase in the rate of surplus value, because (1) a larger realized surplus value of a smaller amount of added labor is smaller than the smaller proportion of surplus value realized on the much larger former total labor, and (2) because the organic composition of capital has increased.

Despite the fact that capitalist production results in a decrease in the price of commodities and an increase in the mass of profits, in the long run these phenomena must be accompanied by a decline in the rate of profit due to the increased organic composition of capital.

---

*

THE THEORY OF THE LAW.

With a given wage and working day, a certain variable capital, for instance of 100, represents a certain number of employed laborers. It is the index of this number. For instance, let 100 p.st. be the wages of 100 laborers for one week. If these laborers perform the same amount of necessary as of surplus-labor, in other words, if they work daily as much time for themselves as they do for the capitalist, or, in still other words, if they require as much time for the reproduction of their wages as they do for the production of surplus-value for the capitalist, then they would produce a total value of 200 p.st., and the surplus-value would amount to 100 p.st. The rate of surplus-value, $\frac{s}{V}$, would be 100%. But we have seen that this rate of surplus-value would express itself in considerably different rates of profit, according to the different volumes of constant capitals c and consequently of total capitals C. For the rate of profit is calculated by the formula $\frac{s}{C}$.

Take it that the rate of surplus-value is 100%. Now, if

$c = 50$, and $v = 100$, then $p' = \frac{100}{150}$, or $66\frac{2}{3}\%$.

$c = 100$, and $v = 100$, then $p' = \frac{100}{200}$, or 50%.

$c = 200$, and $v = 100$, then $p' = \frac{100}{300}$, or $33\frac{1}{3}\%$.

$c = 300$, and $v = 100$, then $p' = \frac{100}{400}$, or 25%.

$c = 400$, and $v = 100$, then $p' = \frac{100}{500}$, or 20%.

In this way, the same rate of surplus-value, with the same degree of labor exploitation, would express itself in a falling rate of profit, because the material growth of the constant capital, and consequently of the total capital, implies their growth in value, although not in the same proportion.

If it is furthermore assumed that this gradual change in the composition of capital is not confined to some individual spheres of production, but occurs more or less in all, or at least in the most important ones, so that they imply changes in the organic average composition of the total capital of a certain society, then the gradual and relative growth of the constant over the variable capital must necessarily lead to *a gradual fall of the average rate of profit,* so long as the rate of surplus-value, or the intensity of exploitation of labor by capital, remain the same. Now we have seen that it is one of the laws of capitalist production that its development carries with it a relative decrease of variable as compared with constant capital, and consequently as compared to the total capital, which it sets in motion. This is only another way of saying that the same number of laborers, the same quantity of labor-power set in motion by a variable capital of a given value, consume in production an ever increasing quantity of means of production, such as machinery and all sorts of fixed capital, raw and auxiliary materials, and consequently a constant capital of ever increasing value and volume, during the same period of time, owing to the peculiar methods of production developing within the capitalist system. This progressive relative decrease of the variable capital as compared to the constant, and consequently to the total, capital is identical with the progressive higher organic composition of the average social capital. It is, in another way, but an expression of the progressive development of the productive powers of society, which is manifested by the fact that the same number of laborers, in the same time, convert an ever growing quantity of raw and auxiliary materials into products, thanks to the growing application of machinery and fixed capital in general, so that less labor is needed for the production of the same, or of more, commodities. This growing value and volume of constant capital corresponds to a progressive cheapening of products, although the increase in the value of the constant capital indicates but imperfectly the growth in the actual mass of use-values represented by the material of the constant capital. Every individual product, taken by itself, contains a smaller quantity of labor than the same product did on a lower scale of production, in which the capital invested in wages occupies a far greater space compared to the capital invested in means of production. The hypothetical series placed at the beginning of this chapter expresses, therefore, the actual tendency of capitalist production. This mode of production produces a progressive decrease of the variable capital as compared to the constant capital, and consequently a continuously rising organic composition of the total capital. The immediate result of this is that the rate of surplus-value, at the same degree of labor-exploitation, expresses itself in a continually falling average rate of profit. (We shall see later why this fall does not manifest itself in an absolute form, but rather as a tendency toward a progressive fall.) This progressive tendency of the average rate of profit to fall is, therefore, but a peculiar expression of capitalist production for the fact that the social productivity of labor is progressively increasing. This is not saying that the rate of profit may not fall temporarily for other reasons. But it demonstrates at least that it is the nature of the capitalist mode of production, and a logical necessity of its development, to give expression to the average rate of surplus-value by a falling rate of average profit. Since the mass of the employed living labor is continually on the decline compared to the mass of materialised labor incorporated in productively consumed means of production, it follows that that portion of living labor, which is unpaid and represents surplus-value, must also be continually on the decrease compared to the volume and value of the invested total capital. Seeing that the proportion of the mass of surplus-value to the value of the invested total capital forms the rate of profit, this rate must fall continuously.

Simple as this law appears from the foregoing statements, all of political economy has so far tried in vain to discover it, as we shall see later on. The economists saw the problem and cudgeled their brains in tortuous attempts to interpret it. Since this law is of great importance for capitalist production, it may be said to be that mystery whose solution has been the goal of the entire political economy since Adam Smith. The difference between the various schools since Adam Smith consists in their different attempts to solve this riddle. If we consider, on the other hand, that political economy up to the present has been tinkering with the distinction between constant and variable capital without ever defining it accurately; that it never separated surplus-value from profit, and never even considered profit in its purely theoretical form, that is, separated from its different subdivisions, such as industrial profit, commercial profit, interest, ground rent; that it never thoroughly analyzed the differences in the organic composition of capital, and for this reason never thought of analyzing the formation of an average rate of profit; if we consider all this, we no longer wonder at its failure to solve the riddle.

We intentionally analyze first this law, before we pass on to a consideration of the different independent categories into which profit is subdivided. The fact that this analysis is made independently of the subdivisions of profit, which fall to the share of different categories of persons, shows in itself that this law, in its general workings, is independent of those subdivisions and of the mutual relations of the resulting categories of profit. The profit to which we are here referring is but another name for surplus-value itself, which is merely observed in its relation to the total capital, instead of its relation to the variable capital from which it arises. The fall in the rate of profit therefore expresses the falling relation of surplus-value itself to the total capital, and is for this reason independent of any division of this profit among various participants.

We have seen that a certain stage of capitalist development, in which the organic composition of capital, c:v shows the proportion of 50:100, expresses a rate of surplus-value of 100% by a rate of profit of $66\frac{2}{3}\%$, and that a higher stage, in which c:v shows the proportion 400:100, expresses the same rate of surplus-value by a rate of profit of only 20%. What is true of different successive stages in the same country, is also true of different contemporaneous stages of development in different countries. In an undeveloped country, in which the first-named composition of capital is the rule, the average rate of profit would be $66\frac{2}{3}\%$, while in a country with the other, higher, stage of development, the average rate of profit would be 20%.

The difference between two national rates of profit might be eliminated, or even reversed, if labor were less productive in the less developed country, so that a larger quantity of labor would be incorporated in a smaller quantity of the same commodities, a larger exchange-value represented by a smaller use-value, so that the laborer would consume a larger portion of his time in the reproduction of his own means of subsistence, or of their value, and have less time to spare for the production of surplus-value, and consequently would perform less surplus-labor, so that the rate of surplus-value would be lower. For instance, if the laborer of the less developed country were to work two-thirds of the working day for himself, and one-third for the capitalist, then, referring to the above illustration, the same labor-power would be paid with $133\frac{1}{3}$ and would furnish a surplus of only $66\frac{2}{3}$. A constant capital of 50 would correspond to a variable capital of $133\frac{1}{3}$. The rate of surplus-value would then amount to $133\frac{1}{3}:66\frac{2}{3} = 50\%$, and the rate of profit to $183\frac{1}{3}:66\frac{2}{3} =$ about $36\frac{1}{2}\%$. . . .

In countries with capitalist production in different stages of development, and consequently with capitals of different organic composition, a country with a short normal working day may have a higher rate of surplus-value (the one factor which determines the rate of profit) than a country with a long normal working day. In the first place, if the English working day of 10 hours, on account of its higher intensity, is equal to an Austrian working day of 14 hours, then dividing the working day equally in both instances, 5 hours of English surplus-labor may represent a greater value on the world-market than 7 hours of Austrian surplus-labor. In the second place, a larger portion of the English working day may represent surplus-labor than of the Austrian working day.

The law of the falling tendency of the rate of profit, which is the expression of the same, or even of a higher, rate of surplus-value, says in so many words: If you take any quantity of the average social capital, say a capital of 100, you will find that an ever larger portion of it is invested in means of production, and an ever smaller portion in living labor. Since, then, the aggregate mass of the living labor operating the means of production decreases in comparison to the value of these means of production, it follows that the unpaid labor, and that portion of value in which it is expressed, must decline as compared to the value of the advanced total capital. Or, an ever smaller aliquot part of the invested total capital is converted into living labor, and this capital absorbs in proportion to its magnitude less and less surplus-labor, although the proportion of the unpaid part of the employed labor may simultaneously grow as compared with the paid part. The relative decrease of the variable, and the relative increase of the constant, capital, while both parts may grow absolutely in magnitude, is but another expression for the increased productivity of labor.

Let a capital of 100 consist of 80c + 20v, and let the 20v stand for 20 laborers. Let the rate of surplus-value be 100%, that is to say, the laborers work one-half of the day for themselves and the other half for the capitalist. Now take a less developed country, in which a capital of 100 is composed of 20c + 80v, and let these 80v stand for 80 laborers. But let these laborers work two-thirds of the day for themselves, and only one-third for the capitalists. Assuming all other things to be equal, the laborers in the first case will produce a value of 40, while those in the second case will produce a value of 120. The first capital produces 80c + 20v + 20s = 120; rate of profit 20%. The second capital produces 20c + 80v + 40s = 140; rate of profit 40%. In other words, the rate of profit in the second case is double that of the first case, and yet the rate of surplus-value in the first case is 100%, while it is only 50% in the second case. But a capital of the same magnitude appropriates in the first case the surplus-labor of only 20 laborers, while it appropriates that of 80 laborers in the second case.

The law of the falling tendency of the rate of profit, or of the relative decline of the appropriated surplus-labor compared to the mass of materialised labor set in motion by living labor does not argue in any way against the fact that the absolute mass of the employed and exploited labor set in motion by the social capital, and consequently the absolute mass of the surplus-labor appropriated by it, may grow. Nor does it argue against the fact that the capitals controlled by individual capitalists may dispose of a growing mass of labor and surplus-labor, even though the number of the laborers employed by them may not grow.

Take for illustration's sake a certain population of working people, for instance, two millions. Assume, furthermore, that the length and intensity of the average working day, and the level of wages, and thereby the proportion between necessary and surplus-labor, are given. In that case the aggregate labor of these two millions, and their surplus-labor expressed in surplus-value, represent always the same magnitude of values. But with the growth of the mass of the constant (fixed and circulating) capital, which this labor manipulates, the proportion of this produced quantity of values declines as compared to the value of this total capital. And the value of this capital grows with its mass, although not in the same proportion. This proportion, and consequently the rate of profit, falls in spite of the fact that the same mass of living labor is controlled as before, and the same amount of surplus-labor absorbed by the capital. This proportion changes, not because the mass of living labor decreases, but because the mass of the materialised labor set in motion by living labor increases. It is a relative decrease, not an absolute one, and has really nothing to do with the absolute magnitude of the labor and surplus-labor set in motion. The fall of the rate of profit is not due to an absolute, but only to a relative decrease of the variable part of the total capital, that is, its decrease as compared with the constant part.

The same thing which applies to any given mass of labor and surplus-labor, applies also to a growing number of laborers, and thus under the above assumptions, to any growing mass of the controlled labor in general and to its unpaid part, the surplus-labor, in particular. If the laboring population increases from two million to three million, if, furthermore, the variable capital invested in wages also rises to three million from its former amount of two million, while the constant capital rises from four million to fifteen million, then the mass of surplus-labor, and of surplus-value, under the above assumption of a constant working day and a constant rate of surplus-value, rises by 50%, that is, from two million to three million. Nevertheless, in spite of this growth in the absolute mass of surplus-labor and surplus-value by 50%, the proportion of the variable to the constant capital would fall from 2:4 to 3:15, and the proportion of the surplus-value to the total capital, expressed in millions, would be

$$\text{I. } 4c + 2v + 2s; \ C = 6, \ p' = 33\tfrac{1}{3}\%.$$
$$\text{II. } 15c + 3v + 3s; \ C = 18, \ p' = 16\tfrac{2}{3}\%.$$

While the mass of surplus-value has increased by one-half, the rate of profit has fallen by one-half. However, the profit is only the surplus-value calculated on the total social capital, so that its absolute magnitude, socially considered, is the same as the absolute magnitude of the surplus-value. In this case, the absolute magnitude of the profit would have grown by 50%, in spite of its enormous relative decrease compared to the advanced total capital, or in spite of the enormous fall of the average rate of profit. We see, then, that in spite of the progressive fall of the rate of profit, there may be an absolute increase of the number of laborers employed by capital, an absolute increase of the labor set in motion by it, an absolute increase of the mass of surplus-labor absorbed, a resulting absolute increase of the produced surplus-value, and consequently an absolute increase in the mass of the produced profit. And this increase may be progressive. And it *may* not only be so. On the basis of capitalist production, it *must* be so, aside from temporary fluctuations.

The capitalist process of production is essentially a process of accumulation. We have shown that the mass of values, which must be simply reproduced and maintained, increases progressively with the development of capitalist production to the extent that the productivity of labor grows, even if the employed labor-power should remain constant. But the development of social productivity carries with it a still greater increase of the produced use-values, of which the means of production form a part. And the additional labor, whose appropriation reconverts this additional value into capital, does not depend on the value, but on the mass of these means of production (including the means of subsistence), because the laborer in the productive process is not operating with the exchange-value, but with the use-value of the means of production. Accumulation itself, however, and the concentration of capital that goes with it, is a material means of increasing the productive power. Now, this growth of the means of production includes the increase of the laboring population, the creation of a laboring population which corresponds to the surplus-capital or even exceeds its general requirements, leading to an overpopulation of working people. A momentary excess of the surplus-capital over the laboring population controlled by it would have a two-fold effect. It would, on the one hand, mitigate the conditions, which decimate the offspring of the laboring class and would facilitate marriages among them, by raising wages. This would tend to increase the laboring population. On the other hand, it would employ the methods by which relative surplus-value is created (introduction and improvement of machinery) and thereby create still more rapidly an artificial relative overpopulation, which in its turn would be a hothouse for the actual propagation of its numbers, since under capitalist production poverty propagates its kind. The nature of the capitalist process of accumulation, which process is but an element in the capitalist process of production, implies as a matter of course that the increased mass of means of production, which is to be converted into capital, must always find on hand a corresponding increase, or even an excess, of laboring people for exploitation. The progress of the process of production and accumulation *must,* therefore, be accompanied by a growth of the mass of available and appropriated surplus-labor, and consequently by a growth of the absolute mass of profit appropriated by the social capital. But the same laws of production and accumulation increase the volume and value of the constant capital in a more rapid progression than those of the variable capital invested in living labor. The same laws, then, produce for the social capital an increase in the absolute mass of profit and a falling rate of profit.

We leave out of consideration the fact that the same amount of values represents a progressively increasing mass of use-values and enjoyments to the extent that the capitalist process of production carries with it a development of the productive power of social labor, a multiplication of the lines of production, and an increase of products.

The development of capitalist production and accumulation lifts the processes of labor to a higher scale and gives them greater dimensions, which imply larger investments of capital for each individual establishment. A growing concentration of capitals (accompanied by a growing number of capitalists, though not to the same extent) is therefore one of the material requirements of capitalist production as well as one of the results produced by it. Hand in hand with it, and mutually interacting, goes a progressive expropriation of the more or less direct producers. It is, then, a matter of course for the capitalists that they should control increasing armies of laborers (no matter how much the variable capital may relatively decrease in comparison to the constant capital), and that the mass of surplus-value, and of profit, appropriated by them, should grow simultaneously with the fall of the rate of profit, and in spite of it. The same causes which concentrate masses of laborers under the control of capitalists, are precisely those which also swell the mass of fixed capital, auxiliary and raw materials in a growing proportion as compared to the mass of the employed living labor.

It requires but a passing notice at this point, that, given a certain laboring population, the mass of surplus-value, and therefore the absolute mass of profit, must grow if the rate of surplus-value increases by a prolongation or intensification of the working day, or by a lowering of the value of wages through a development of the productive power of labor, and must do so in spite of the relative decrease of the variable capital compared to the constant.

The same development of the productive power of social labor, the same laws, which express themselves in a relative fall of the variable as compared to the total capital and in a correspondingly hastened accumulation, while this accumulation in its turn becomes the starting point of a further development of the productive power and of a further relative fall of the variable capital, this same development manifests itself, aside from temporary fluctuations, by a growing increase of the employed total labor-power, a growing increase of the absolute mass of surplus-value, and consequently of profits.

Now, in what form must this two-faced law with the same

causes for a decrease of the *rate* of profits and a simultaneous increase of the absolute mass of profits show itself? A law based on the fact that under certain conditions the appropriated mass of surplus-labor, and consequently of surplus-value, increases, and that, so far as the total capital is concerned, or the individual capital as an aliquot part of the total capital, profit and surplus-value are identical magnitudes?

Take that aliquot part of capital which is the basis of our calculation of the rate of profit, for instance 100. These 100 illustrate the average composition of the total capital, say 80c + 20v. We have seen in the second part of this volume, that the average rate of profit is determined, not by the particular composition of individual capital, but by the average composition of social capital. If the variable capital decreases as compared to the constant, or to the total capital, then the rate of profit, or the relative magnitude of surplus-value calculated on the total capital, falls even though the intensity of exploitation were to remain the same, or even to increase. But it is not this relative magnitude alone which falls. The magnitude of the surplus-value or profit absorbed by the total capital of 100 also falls absolutely. At a rate of surplus-value of 100%, a capital of 60 + 40 produces a mass of surplus-value and profit amounting to 40; a capital of 70c + 30v a mass of profit of 30; a capital of 80c + 20v produces only 20 of profit. This fall refers to the mass of surplus-value, and thus of profit, and is due to the fact that the total capital of 100, with the same intensity of labor exploitation, employs less living labor, sets in motion less labor-power, and therefore produces less surplus-value. Taking any aliquot part of the social capital, that is, of capital of average composition, as a standard by which to measure surplus-value—and this is done in all calculations of profit—a relative fall of surplus-value is identical with its absolute fall. The rate of profit sinks in the above cases from 40% to 30% and 20%, because the mass of surplus-value, and of profit, produced by the same capital falls absolutely from 40 to 30 and 20. Since the magnitude of the value of capital, by which the surplus-value is measured, is given as 100, a fall in the proportion of surplus-value to this given magnitude can be only another expression for the fact that surplus-value and profit decrease absolutely. This is, of course, a tautology. But we have demonstrated that the nature of the capitalist process of production brings about this decrease.

On the other hand, the same causes which bring about an absolute decrease of surplus-value and profit on a given capital, and consequently in the percentage of the rate of profit, produce an increase of the absolute mass of surplus-value and profit appropriated by the total capital (that is, by the capitalists as a whole). How can this be explained, and what is the only way in which this can be explained, or what are the conditions on which this apparent contradiction is based?

While any aliquot part, any 100 of the social capital, any 100 of average social composition, is a given magnitude, for which a fall in the rate of profit implies a fall in the absolute magnitude of profit, just because the capital which serves as a standard of measurement is a constant magnitude, the magnitude of the social capital, on the other hand, as well as that of the capital in the hands of individual capitalists, is variable, and in keeping with our assumptions it must vary inversely to the decrease of its variable portion.

In our former illustration, when the percentage of composition was 60c + 40v, the corresponding surplus-value and profit was 40, and the rate of profit 40%. Take it that the total capital in this stage of composition was one million. In that case the total surplus-value, and total profit, amounted to 400,000. Now, if the composition changes later to 80c + 20v, while the degree of labor exploitation remains the same, then the surplus-value

and profit for each 100 is 20. But as we have demonstrated that
the absolute mass of surplus-value and profit increases in spite
of the fall of the rate of profit, in spite of the decrease in the
production of surplus-value by a capital of 100, that it grows,
say, from 400,000 to 440,000, there is no other way in which
this could be brought about than by a growth of the total capital
to 2,200,000 to the extent that this new composition developed.
The mass of the total capital set in motion has risen by 220%,
while the rate of profit has fallen by 50%. If the total capital
had only been doubled, it could have produced no more surplus-
value and profit with a rate of profit of 20% than the old capital
of 1,000,000 at a rate of 40%. If it had grown to less than
twice its old size, it would have produced less surplus-value or
profit than the old capital of 1,000,000, which, with its former
composition, would have had to grow from 1,000,000 to no
more than 1,100,000, in order to raise its surplus-value from
400,000 to 440,000.

III, pp. 247-260

A fall in the rate of profit by 50% means its fall by one-half.
If the mass of profit is to remain the same, the capital must be
doubled. In order that the mass of profit made at a declining
rate of profit may remain the same as before, the multiplier
indicating the growth of the total capital must be equal to the
divisor indicating the fall of the rate of profit. If the rate of
profit falls from 40 to 20, the total capital must rise at the rate
of 20 to 40, in order that the result may remain the same. If
the rate of profit had fallen from 40 to 8, the capital would
have to increase at the rate of 8 to 40, or five times its value.
A capital of 1,000,000 at a rate of 40% produces 400,000, and
a capital of 5,000,000 at a rate of 8% likewise produces 400,-

000. This applies, so long as the result is to remain the same. But if the result is to be higher, then the capital must grow at a faster rate than the rate of profit falls. In other words, in order that the variable portion of the total capital may not only remain the same, but may also increase absolutely, although its percentage in the total capital falls, the total capital must grow at a higher rate than the percentage of the variable capital falls. It must grow at such a rate that it requires in its new composition not merely the same old variable capital, but more than it for the purchase of labor-power. If the variable portion of a capital of 100 falls from 40 to 20, the total capital must rise higher than 200, in order to be able to employ a larger variable capital than 40.

Even if the mass of the exploited laboring population were to remain constant, and only the length and intensity of the working day to increase, the mass of the invested capital would have to increase, since it must rise for the mere purpose of employing the same mass of labor under the old conditions of exploitation as soon as the composition of capital varies.

In short, the same development of the social productivity of labor expresses itself in the course of capitalist production on the one hand in a tendency to a progressive fall of the rate of profit, and on the other hand in a progressive increase of the absolute mass of the appropriated surplus-value, or profit; so that on the whole a relative decrease of variable capital and profit is accompanied by an absolute increase of both. This twofold effect, as we have seen, can express itself only in a growth of the total capital at a ratio more rapid than that expressed by the fall in the rate of profit. In order that an absolutely increased variable capital may be employed in a capital of higher composition, that is, a capital in which the constant capital has relatively increased still more than the variable, the total capital must not only grow in proportion to its higher composition, but even still more rapidly. If follows, then, that an ever larger quantity of capital is required in order to employ the same, and still more an increased amount of labor-power, to the extent that the capitalist mode of production develops. The increasing productivity of labor thus creates necessarily and permanently an apparent overpopulation of laboring people. If the variable capital forms only one-sixth of the total capital instead of one-half, as before, then the total capital must be trebled in order to employ the same amount of labor-power. And if the labor-power to be employed is doubled, then the total capital must be multiplied by six.

Political economy has so far been unable to explain the law of the falling tendency of the rate of profit. So it pointed as a consolation to the increasing mass of profit, the increase in the absolute magnitude of profit for the individual capitalist as well as for the social capital, but even this consolation was based on mere commonplaces and probabilities.

It is simply a tautology to say that the mass of profit is determined by two factors, namely first the rate of profit, and secondly by the mass of capital invested at this rate. It is therefore but a corollary of this tautology to say that there is a possibility for the increase of the mass of profit even though the rate of profit may fall at the same time. This does not help us to get one step farther, since there is also a possibility that the capital may increase without resulting in an increase of the mass of profit, and that it may even increase while the mass of profit is already falling. For 100 at 25% make 25, while 400 at 5% make only 20. But if the same causes, which bring about a fall in the rate of profit, promote the accumulation, that is, the formation of additional capital, and if each additional capital employs additional labor and produces additional surplus-value; when, on the other hand, the mere fall in the rate of profit implies the fact that the constant capital, and with it the total old capital, have increased, then this process ceases to be mysterious. We shall see later, to what falsifications of calculations some people have recourse in order to deny the possibility of an increase in the mass of profits while the rate of profits is simultaneously decreasing.

We have shown that the same causes, which bring about a tendency of the average rate of profits to fall, necessitate also an accelerated accumulation of capital and consequently an increase in the absolute magnitude, or total mass, of the surplus-labor (surplus-value, profit) appropriated by it. Just as everything is reversed in competition, and thus in the consciousness of its agents, so is also this law, this internal and necessary connection between two apparent contradictions. It is evident, within the proportions indicated above, that a capitalist disposing of a large capital will receive a larger mass of profits than a small capitalist making apparently high profits. A superficial observation of competition shows furthermore that under certain circumstances, when the greater capitalist wishes to make room for himself on the market by pushing aside the smaller ones, as happens in times of commercial crises, he makes a practical use of this, that is, he lowers his rate of profit intentionally in order to crowd the smaller ones off the field. Particularly merchant's capital, as we shall show at length later on, shows symptoms, which seem to attribute the fall in profits to an expansion of the business, and thus of capital. We shall later on give a scientific expression for this false conception. Similar superficial observations result from the comparison of rates of profit made in some particular lines of business, according to whether they are subject to free competition or to monopoly. The utterly shallow conception existing in the heads of the agents of competition is found in our Roscher, namely the idea that a reduction of the rate of profits is "more prudent and humane." The fall in the rate of profit is in this case attributed to an increase of capital, it appears as a *consequence* of this increase, and of the resultant calculation of the capitalist that the mass of profits to be pocketed by him will be greater at a smaller rate of profits. This entire conception (with the exception of that of Adam Smith, which we shall mention later) rests on the utter misapprehension of what the average rate of profit represents and on the crude idea that prices are indeed determined by adding a more or less arbitrary amount of profit to the actual value of the commodities. Crude as these ideas are, they arise necessarily out of the inverted aspect which the immanent laws of capitalist production represent under competition.

The law that the fall in the rate of profit due to the development of the productive powers is accompanied by an increase in the mass of profit expresses itself furthermore in the fact that a fall in the price of commodities produced by capital is accompanied by a relative increase of the masses of profit contained in them and realised by their sale.

Since the development of the productive powers and the higher composition of capital corresponding to it set in motion an ever increasing quantity of means of production with an ever decreasing quantity of labor, every aliquot part of the total product, every single commodity, or every particular quantity of commodities in the total mass of products absorbs less living labor, and also contains less materialised labor, both as to the wear and tear of fixed capital and to the raw and auxiliary materials consumed. Every single commodity, then, contains a smaller amount of labor materialised in means of production and of labor newly added during production. Hence the price of the individual commodity falls. The mass of profits contained in the individual commodities may nevertheless increase, if the rate of the absolute or relative surplus-value grows. The commodity then contains less newly added labor, but its unpaid portion grows over its paid portion. However, this is the case only within certain limits. In the course of the development of production, with the enormously growing absolute decrease of the amount of living labor newly embodied in the individual commodities, the mass of unpaid labor contained in them will likewise decrease absolutely, however much it may have grown as compared to their paid portion. The mass of profit on each individual commodity will decrease considerably with the development of the productive power of labor, in spite of the increase of the rate of surplus-value. And this reduction, the same as the fall in the rate of profits, is only delayed by the cheapening of the elements of constant capital and the other circumstances mentioned in the first part of this volume, which increase the rate of profit at a stable, or even falling, rate of surplus-value.

To say that the price of the individual commodities falls, which together make up the total product of the capital, is simply to say that a certain quantity of labor is realised in a larger quantity of commodities, so that each individual commodity contains less labor than before. This is the case even if the price of one of the parts of constant capital, such as raw material, etc., should rise. With the exception of a few cases (for instance, if the productive power of labor cheapens all the elements of constant and variable capital uniformly) the rate of profit will fall in spite of the increased rate of surplus-value, 1), because even a larger unpaid portion of the smaller total amount of newly added labor is smaller than a smaller aliquot portion of unpaid labor was in the former large amount of total labor, and 2), because the higher composition of the capital is expressed through the individual commodity by the fact that that portion of its value, in which newly added labor is materialised, decreases as compared to that portion of its value, which represents raw material, auxiliary material, and wear and tear of fixed capital. This change in the proportions of the various component parts of the price of the individual commodities, the decrease of that portion of their price, in which newly added labor is materialised, and the increase of that portion, in which formerly materialised labor is represented, is that form which expresses through the price of the individual commodities the decrease of the variable capital as compared to the constant capital. To the extent that this decrease is absolute for a certain amount of capital, for instance 100, it is also absolute for every individual commodity as an aliquot part of the reproduced capital. However, the rate of profit, if calculated merely on the elements of the price of the individual commodity, would be different from what it actually is. . . .

Although the *rate* of profit must be calculated by measuring the mass of the produced and realised surplus-value by the consumed portion of capital reappearing in the commodities as well as by the sum of this portion plus that portion of capital which, though not consumed, is employed and continues to serve in production, the *mass* of profit cannot be equal to anything but the mass of profit, or surplus-value, contained in the commodities themselves and to be realised by their sale.

If the productivity of industry increases, the prices of the individual commodities fall. There is less paid and unpaid labor contained in them. Let the same labor produce, say, thrice its former product. Then the individual product requires two-thirds less labor. And since the profit can constitute but a portion of the amount of labor congealed in the individual commodities, the mass of profit in the individual commodities must decrease. And this must hold good, within certain limits, even if the rate of surplus-value should rise. In any case, the mass of profits on the total product does not fall below the original mass of profits so long as the capital employs the same number of laborers at the same degree of exploitation. (This may also take place, if fewer laborers are employed at a higher rate of exploitation.) For to the same extent that the mass of profit on the individual product decreases does the number of products increase. The mass of profits remains the same, only it is distributed differently over the total amount of commodities. Nor does this alter the division of the amount of value created by newly added labor between the laborers and capitalists. The mass of profit cannot increase, so long as the same amount of labor is employed, unless the unpaid surplus-labor increases, or, supposing the intensity of exploitation to remain the same, unless the number of laborers grows. Or, both of these causes may, of course, combine to produce this result. In all these cases, which, however, according to our assumption, presuppose an increase of the constant capital as compared to the variable and an increase in the magnitude of the total capital, the individual commodity contains a smaller mass of profit and the rate of profit falls even if it is calculated on the individual commodity. A given quantity of additional labor is materialised in a larger quantity of commodities. The price of the individual commodities falls. Abstractly speaking, the rate of profit may remain the same, even though the price of the individual commodity may fall as a result of an increase in the productivity of labor and a simultaneous increase in the number of these cheaper commodities, for instance, if the increase in the productivity of labor extended its effects uniformly and simultaneously to all the elements of the commodities, so that the total price of the commodities would fall in the same proportion in which the productivity of labor would increase, while on the other hand the mutual relations of the different elements of the price of commodities would remain the same. The rate of profit might even rise, if a rise in the rate of surplus-value were accompanied by a considerable reduction in the value of the elements of constant, and particularly of fixed, capital. But in reality, as we have seen, the rate of profit will fall in the long run. In any case, a fall in the price of any individual commodity does not by itself give a clue to the rate of profit. Everything depends on the magnitude of the total capital invested in its production. For instance, if the price of one yard of fabric falls from 3 sh. to $1\frac{2}{3}$ sh.; if we know that it contained before this reduction in price $1\frac{2}{3}$ sh. worth of constant capital, yarn, etc., $\frac{2}{3}$ sh. wages, and $\frac{1}{3}$ sh. profit, while it contains after this reduction 1 sh. of constant capital, $\frac{1}{3}$ sh. of wages, and $\frac{1}{3}$ sh. of profit, we cannot tell whether the rate of profit has remained the same or not. This depends on the question, whether the advanced total capital has increased, and how much, and how many yards of fabric more it produces in a given time.

This phenomenon arising from the nature of the capitalist mode of production, namely, that an increase in the productivity of labor implies a fall in the price of the individual commodity, or of a certain mass of commodities, an increase in the number of commodities, a reduction of the mass of profit in the individual commodity and of the rate of profit on the aggregate of commodities, an increase of the mass of profit in the total quantity of commodities, this phenomenon shows itself on the surface only in a reduction of the mass of profit in the individual commodities, in a fall of their prices, in an increase of the mass of profits in the augmented number of commodities as a whole, which have been produced by the total capital of society or by that of the individual capitalist. It is then imagined that the capitalist adds less profits to the price of the individual commodities on his own free volition and makes up for it by the returns on a greater number of commodities produced by him. This conception rests upon the idea of profit upon alienation, which in its turn is deduced from the ideas of merchant's capital.

We have seen previously, in parts four and seven of Book I, that the growth in the mass of commodities resulting from the productivity of labor and the consequent cheapening of the commodities as such (unless these commodities become determining elements in the price of labor-power) do not affect the proportion between paid and unpaid labor in the individual commodities, in spite of the fall in price.

Since everything appears inverted under competition, the individual capitalist may imagine: 1) That he is reducing his profit on the individual commodity by cutting its price, but still making a greater profit on account of the larger quantity of commodities which he is selling; 2) that he is fixing the price of the individual commodities and determining the price of the total product by multiplication, while the original process is really one of division (see Book I, chapter XII) and the multiplication is correct only in a secondary way, being based on that division. The vulgar economist does practically no more than to translate the queer concepts of the capitalists, who are in the thralls of competition, into a more theoretical and generalising language and to attempt a vindication of the correctness of those conceptions.

Practically, a fall in the prices of commodities and a rise in the mass of profits contained in the augmented mass of these cheapened commodities is but another expression for the law of the falling rate of profit with a simultaneous increase in the mass of profits.

III, pp. 260-271

Summary: The fall in the average rate of profit is a long-run tendency which in the short run may be counteracted by (1) an increase in the intensity of exploitation, (2) depression of wages below their value, (3) reduction in the cost of elements of constant capital, (4) relative overpopulation, and (5) foreign trade.

The raising of the intensity of exploitation was partially discussed above (under B, Section 3). Depressing the wage rate below its value (presumably by the market) is a very important short-run check on the decline in the rate of profit. Constant capital may be cheapened if, for example, its cost of production is reduced.

Relative overpopulation makes cheap labor available to new lines of production, thus making them profitable. This raises the average rate of profit (of all industries). But these new industries will be subject to the same laws of accumulation and their rates of profit will eventually decline.

Foreign trade cheapens the element of constant capital by (1) cheapening the necessaries of life, (2) permitting an expansion of the scale of production. Foreign trade further aids capitalist development by providing an ever-expanding market.

Capital invested in foreign trade yields a higher rate of profit than a like domestic investment because it competes with less highly developed productive facilities, so that commodities can be sold above their values even when sold at lower prices than competing countries sell the same commodities for. Labor in advanced countries may produce articles of higher quality than competing labor in backward countries, yet be paid as if they were of the same quality. Also, capital invested in colonies may be highly profitable because coolies and slaves are easy to exploit.

---

*

Counteracting Causes.

If we consider the enormous development of the productive powers of labor, even comparing but the last 30 years with all former periods; if we consider in particular the enormous mass of fixed capital, aside from machinery in the strict meaning of the term, passing into the process of social production as a whole, then the difficulty, which has hitherto troubled the vulgar economists, namely that of finding an explanation for the falling rate of profit, gives way to its opposite, namely to the question; How is it that this fall is not greater and more rapid? There must be some counteracting influences at work, which thwart and annul the effects of this general law, leaving to it merely the character of a tendency. For this reason we have referred to the fall of the average rate of profit as a tendency to fall.

The following are the general counterbalancing causes:

I. *Raising the Intensity of Exploitation.*

The rate at which labor is exploited, the appropriation of surplus-labor and surplus-value, is raised by a prolongation of the working day and an intensification of labor. These two points have been fully discussed in volume I as incidents to the production of absolute and relative surplus-value. There are many ways of intensifying labor, which imply an increase of the constant capital as compared to the variable, and consequently a fall in the rate of profit, for instance setting a laborer to watch a larger number of machines. In such cases—and in the majority of manipulations serving to produce relative surplus-value— the same causes, which bring about an increase in the rate of surplus-value, may also imply a fall in the mass of surplus-value, looking upon the matter from the point of view of the total quantities of invested capital. But there are other means of intensification, such as increasing the speed of machinery, which, although consuming more raw material, and, so far as the fixed capital is concerned, wearing out the machinery so much faster, nevertheless do not affect the relation of its value to the price of labor set in motion by it. It is particularly the prolongation of the working day, this invention of modern industry, which increases the mass of appropriated surplus-labor without essentially altering the proportion of the employed labor-power to the constant capital set in motion by it, and which tends to reduce this capital relatively, if anything. For the rest, we have already demonstrated—what constitutes the real secret of the tendency of the rate of profit to fall—that the manipulations made for the purpose of producing relative surplus-value amount on the whole to this: That on one side as much as possible of a certain quantity of labor is transformed into surplus-value, and that on the other hand as little labor as possible is employed in proportion to the invested capital, so that the same causes, which permit the raising of the intensity of exploitation, forbid the exploitation of the same quantity of labor by the same capital as before. These are the warring tendencies, which, while aiming at a raise in the rate of surplus-value, have at the same time a tendency to bring about a fall in the mass of surplus-value, and therefore of the rate of surplus-value produced by a certain capital. It is furthermore appropriate to mention at this point the extensive introduction of female and child labor. . . .

Whatever tends to promote the production of relative surplus-value by mere improvements in methods, for instance in agriculture, without altering the magnitude of the invested capital, has the same effect. While the constant capital does not increase relatively to the variable in such cases, taking the variable capital as an index of the amount of labor-power employed, the mass of the product *does* increase in proportion to the labor-power employed. The same takes place, when the productive power of labor (whether its product passes into the consumption of the laborer or into the elements of constant capital) is freed from obstacles of circulation, of arbitrary or other restrictions which become obstacles in course of time, in short, of fetters of all kinds, without touching directly the proportion between the variable and the constant capital.

It might be asked, whether the causes checking the fall of the rate of profit, but always hastening it in the last analysis, include the temporary raise in surplus-value above the average level, which recur now in this, now in that line of production for the benefit of those individual capitalists, who make use of inventions, etc., before they are generally introduced. This question must be answered in the affirmative.

The mass of surplus-value produced by a capital of a certain magnitude is the product of two factors, namely of the rate of surplus-value multiplied by the number of laborers employed at this rate. Hence it depends on the number of laborers, when the rate of surplus-value is given, and on the rate of surplus-value, when the number of laborers is given. In short, it depends on the composite proportion of the absolute magnitudes of the variable capital and the rate of surplus-value. Now we have seen, that on an average the same causes, which raise the rate of relative surplus-value, lower the mass of the employed labor-power. It is evident, however, that there will be a more or less in this according to the definite proportion, in which the opposite movements exert themselves, and that the tendency to reduce the rate of profit will be particularly checked by a raise in the rate of absolute surplus-value due to a prolongation of the working day.

We saw in the case of the rate of profit, that a fall in the rate was generally accompanied by an increase in the mass of profit, on account of the increasing mass of the total capital employed. From the point of view of the total variable capital of society, the surplus-value produced by it is equal to the profit produced by it. Both the absolute mass and the absolute rate of surplus-value have thus increased. The one has increased, because the quantity of labor-power employed by society has grown, the other, because the intensity of exploitation of this labor-power has increased. But in the case of a capital of a given magnitude, for instance 100, the rate of surplus-value may increase, while the mass may decrease on an average; for the rate is determined by the proportion, in which the variable capital produces value, while its mass is determined by the proportional part which the variable capital constitutes in the total capital.

The rise in the rate of surplus-value is a factor, which determines also the mass of surplus-value and thereby the rate of profit, for it takes place especially under conditions, in which, as we have seen, the constant capital is either not increased at all relatively to the variable capital, or not increased in proportion. This factor does not suspend the general law. But it causes that law to become more of a tendency, that is, a law whose absolute enforcement is checked, retarded, weakened, by counteracting influences. Since the same causes, which raise the rate of surplus-value (even a prolongation of the working time is a result of large scale industry), also tend to decrease the labor-power employed by a certain capital, it follows that these same causes also tend to reduce the rate of profit and to check the speed of this fall. If one laborer is compelled to perform as much labor as would be rationally performed by two, and if this is done under circumstances, in which this one laborer can replace three, then this one will produce as much surplus-labor as was formerly produced by two, and to that extent the rate of surplus-value will have risen. But this one will not produce as much as formerly three, and to that extent the mass of surplus-value will have decreased. But this reduction in mass will be compensated, or limited, by the rise in the rate of surplus-value. If the entire population is employed at a higher rate of surplus-value, the mass of surplus-value will increase, although the population may remain the same. It will increase still more, if the population increases at the same time. And although this goes hand in hand with a relative reduction of the number of laborers employed in proportion to the magnitude of the total capital, yet this reduction is checked or moderated by the rise in the rate of surplus-value.

Before leaving this point, we wish to emphasize once more that, with a capital of a certain magnitude, the *rate* of surplus-value may rise, while its *mass* is decreasing, and vice versa. The mass of surplus-value is equal to the rate multiplied by the number of laborers; however, this rate is never calculated on the total, but only on the variable capital, actually only for a day at a time. On the other hand, with a given magnitude of a certain capital, the *rate of profit* can never fall or rise, without a simultaneous fall or rise in the *mass of surplus-value*.

II. *Depression of Wages Below their Value.*

This is mentioned only empirically at this place, since it, like many other things, which might be enumerated here, has nothing to do with the general analysis of capital, but belongs in a presentation of competition, which is not given in this work. However, it is one of the most important causes checking the tendency of the rate of profit to fall.

III. *Cheapening of the Elements of Constant Capital.*

Everything that has been said in the first part of this volume about the causes, which raise the rate of profit while the rate of surplus-value remains the same, or independently of the rate of surplus-value, belongs here. This applies particularly to the fact that, from the point of view of the total capital, the value of the constant capital does not increase in the same proportion as its material volume. For instance, the quantity of cotton, which a single European spinning operator works up in a modern factory, has grown in a colossal degree compared to the quantity formerly worked up by a European operator with a spinning wheel. But the value of the worked-up cotton has not grown in proportion to its mass. The same holds good of machinery and other fixed capital. In short, the same development, which increases the mass of the constant capital relatively over that of the variable, reduces the value of its elements as a result of the increased productivity of labor. In this way the value of the constant capital although continually increasing, is prevented from increasing at the same rate as its material volume, that is, the material volume of the means of production set in motion by the same amount of labor-power. In exceptional cases the mass of the elements of constant capital may even increase, while its value remains the same or even falls.

The foregoing bears upon the depreciation of existing capital (that is, of its material elements) which comes with the development of industry. This is another one of the causes which by their constant effects tend to check the fall of the rate of profit, although it may under certain circumstances reduce the mass of profit by reducing the mass of capital yielding a profit. This shows once more that the same causes, which bring about a tendency of the rate of profit to fall, also check the realisation of this tendency.

IV. *Relative Overpopulation.*

The production of a relative surplus-population is inseparable from the development of the productivity of labor expressed by a fall in the rate of profit, and the two go hand in hand. The relative overpopulation becomes so much more apparent in a certain country, the more the capitalist mode of production is developed in it. This, again, is on the one hand a reason, which explains why the imperfect subordination of labor to capital continues in many lines of production, and continues longer than seems at first glance compatible with the general stage of development. This is due to the cheapness and mass of the disposable or unemployed wage laborers, and to the greater resistance, which some lines of production, by their nature, oppose to a transformation of manufacture into machine production. On the other hand, new lines of production are opened up, especially for the production of luxuries, and these lines take for their basis this relative overpopulation set free in other lines of production by the increase of their constant capital. These new lines start out with living labor as their predominating element, and go by degrees through the same evolution as the other lines of production. In either case the variable capital constitutes a considerable proportion of the total capital and wages are below the average, so that both the rate and mass of surplus-value are exceptionally high. Since the average rate of profit is formed by leveling the rates of profit in the individual lines of production, the same cause, which brings about a falling tendency of the rate of profit, once more produces a counterbalance to this tendency and paralyses its effects more or less.

V. *Foreign Trade.*

To the extent that foreign trade cheapens partly the elements of constant capital, partly the necessities of life for which the variable capital is exchanged, it tends to raise the rate of profit by raising the rate of surplus-value and lowering the value of the constant capital. It exerts itself generally in this direction by permitting an expansion of the scale of production. But by this means it hastens on one hand the process of accumulation, on the other the reduction of the variable as compared to the constant capital, and thus a fall in the rate of profit. In the same way the expansion of foreign trade, which is the basis of the capitalist mode of production in its stages of infancy, has become its own product in the further progress of capitalist development through its innate necessities, through its need of an ever expanding market. Here we see once more the dual nature of these effects. (Ricardo entirely overlooked this side of foreign trade.)

Another question, which by its special nature is really beyond the scope of our analysis, is the following: Is the average rate of profit raised by the higher rate of profit, which capital invested in foreign, and particularly in colonial trade, realises?

Capitals invested in foreign trade are in a position to yield a higher rate of profit, because, in the first place, they come in competition with commodities produced in other countries with lesser facilities of production, so that an advanced country is enabled to sell its goods above their value even when it sells them cheaper than the competing countries. To the extent that the labor of the advanced countries is here exploited as a labor of a higher specific weight, the rate of profit rises, because labor which has not been paid as being of a higher quality is sold as such. The same condition may obtain in the relations with a certain country, into which commodities are exported and from which commodities are imported. This country may offer more materialised labor in goods than it receives, and yet it may receive in return commodities cheaper than it could produce them. In the same way a manufacturer, who exploits a new invention before it has become general, undersells his competitors and yet sells his commodities above their individual values, that is to say, he exploits the specifically higher productive power of the labor employed by him as surplus-value. By this means he secures a surplus-profit. On the other hand, capitals invested in colonies, etc., may yield a higher rate of profit for the simple reason that the rate of profit is higher there on account of the backward development, and for the added reason, that slaves, coolies, etc., permit a better exploitation of labor. We see no reason, why these higher rates of profit realised by capitals invested in certain lines and sent home by them should not enter as elements into the average rate of profit and tend to keep it up to that extent. We see so much less reason for the contrary opinion, when it is assumed that such favored lines of investment are subject to the laws of free competition. What Ricardo has in mind as objections, is mainly this: With the higher prices realised in foreign trade, commodities are bought abroad and sent home. These commodities are sold on the home market, and this can constitute at best but a temporary advantage of the favored spheres of production over others. This aspect of the matter is changed, when we no longer look upon it from the point of view of money. The favored country recovers more labor in exchange for less labor, although this difference, this surplus, is pocketed by a certain class, as it is in any exchange between labor and capital. So far as the rate of profit is higher, because it is generally higher in the colonial country, it may go hand in hand with a low level of prices, if the natural conditions are favorable. It is true that a compensation takes place, but it is not a compensation on the old level, as Ricardo thinks.

However, this same foreign trade develops the capitalist mode of production in the home country. And this implies the relative decrease of the variable as compared to the constant capital, while it produces, on the other hand, an over-production for the foreign market, so that it has once more the opposite effect in its further course.

And so we have seen in a general way, that the same causes, which produce a falling tendency in the rate of profit, also call forth counter-effects, which check and partly paralyse this fall. This law is not suspended, but its effect is weakened. Otherwise it would not be the fall of the average rate of profit, which would be unintelligible, but rather the relative slowness of this fall. The law therefore shows itself only as a tendency, whose effects become clearly marked only under certain conditions and in the course of long periods.

Before passing on to something new, we will, for the sake of preventing misunderstanding, repeat two statements, which we have substantiated at different times.

1) The same process, which brings about a cheapening of commodities in the course of development of the capitalist mode of production, also causes a change in the organic composition of the social capital invested in the production of commodities, and thereby lowers the rate of profit. We must be careful, then, not to confound the reduction in the relative cost of an individual commodity, including that portion of its cost which repre

sents wear and tear of machinery, with the relative rise in the value of the constant as compared to the variable capital, although vice versa every reduction in the relative cost of the constant capital, whose material elements retain the same volume or increase in volume, tends to raise the rate of profit, in other words, tends to reduce the value of the constant capital to that extent as compared with the shrinking proportions of the employed variable capital.

2) The fact that the additional living labor contained in the individual commodities, which together make up the product of the capital, stands in a decreasing proportion to the materials and instruments of labor consumed by them; the fact, that an ever decreasing quantity of additional living labor is materialised in them, because their production requires less labor to the extent that the productive power of society is developed—this fact does not touch the proportion, according to which the living labor contained in the commodities is divided into paid and unpaid labor. On the other hand, although the total quantity of additional living labor contained in them decreases, the unpaid portion increases over the paid portion, either by an absolute, or by a proportional reduction of the paid portion; for the same mode of production, which reduces the total quantity of the additional living labor in the commodities, is accompanied by a rise of the absolute and relative surplus-value. The falling tendency of the rate of profit is accompanied by a rising tendency of the rate of surplus-value, that is, in the rate of exploitation. Nothing is more absurd, for this reason, than to explain a fall in the rate of profit by a rise in the rate of wages, although there may be exceptional cases where this may apply. Statistics do not become available for actual analyses of the rates of wages in different epochs and countries, until the conditions, which shape the rate of profit, are thoroughly understood. The rate of profit does not fall, because labor becomes less productive, but

because it becomes more productive. Both phenomena, the rise in the rate of surplus-value and the fall in the rate of profit, are but specific forms through which the productivity of labor seeks a capitalistic expression.

III, pp. 272-281

3. Equalization of the Rate of Profit

Summary: Different industries have different organic compositions of capital. Profits will be equal only in those industries with the same organic composition of capital, the same rate of surplus value, and the same time of turnover. Yet, unless the rate of profit in various lines of industry is the same, the theory of value (here expounded) would be irreconcilable with the real phenomena of production, and we would have to give up our attempt to understand these phenomena.

An example will show how the average rate of profit is formed from different organic compositions of capital and how the *values* of commodities are transformed into their *prices.* If the rate of surplus value (exploitation) is the same in all industries (for example, 100%), then the rate of profit for each industry will differ depending upon its organic composition of capital. For example, if $S/c + v = 20/80 + 20 = 20\%$ ($v = s$ at 100% S/v) in one industry, then $S/c + v = 40/60 + 40 = 40\%$ in another. The "value" of the product of each industry is then found. Assuming in the first case c (used up) to be 50, which makes $c + v + s = 90$ ($50c + 20v + 20s$), and in the second instance where $c = 51$, the value of the product is 131 ($51c + 40v + 40s$).

Competition brings about an equalization of the rates of profit in different industries, reducing them all to the average. It is done in this way. All the compositions of capital (all the c's and v's) are added up and divided by the number of cases. This turns out to be 78c and 22v. Since the rate of exploitation is 100%, average profit is 22%. The "prices" of commodities are then recalculated, using S = 22 (the new average S = 22 since S/v 100%). Then the "price" in the first example is 92 (whereas its former "value" was 90) and in the second instance the "price" is 113 (whereas its value was 131). The important conclusion is that price deviates from value + 2 in the first case and −18 in the second.

---

*

. . . different lines of industry may have different rates of profit, corresponding to differences in the organic composition of capitals, and, within the limits indicated, also corresponding to different times of turn-over; the law (as a general tendency) that profits are proportioned as the magnitudes of the capitals, or that capitals of equal magnitude yield equal profits in equal times, applies only to capitals of the same organic composition, with the same rate of surplus-value, and the same time of turnover. And these statements hold good on the assumption, which has been the basis of all our analyses so far, namely that the commodities are sold at their values. On the other hand there is no doubt that, aside from unessential, accidental, and mutually compensating distinctions, a difference in the average rate of profit of the various lines of industry does not exist in reality, and could not exist without abolishing the entire system of capitalist production. It would seem, then, as though the theory of value were irreconcilable at this point with the actual process, irreconcilable with the real phenomena of production, so that we should have to give up the attempt to understand these phenomena. . . .

The organic composition of capital depends at each stage on two circumstances: First, on the technical relation of the employed labor-power to the mass of the employed means of production; secondly, on the price of these means of production. We

have seen that this composition must be considered according to
its percentages. We express the organic composition of a certain
capital, consisting of four-fifths of constant, and one-fifth of variable capital, by the formula 80c + 20v. We furthermore assume
in this comparison that the rate of surplus-value is unchangeable.
Let it be, for instance, 100%. The capital of 80c + 20v then
produces a surplus-value of 20s, and this is equal to a rate of
profit of 20% on the total capital. The magnitude of the actual
value of the product of this capital depends on the magnitude
of the fixed part of the constant capital, and on the amount of it
passing by wear and tear over to the product. But as this circumstance is immaterial so far as the rate of profit and the present
analysis are concerned, we assume for the sake of simplicity that
the constant capital is transferred everywhere uniformly and entirely to the annual product of the capitals named. It is further
assumed that these capitals realise equal quantities of surplus-
value in the different spheres of production, proportional to the
magnitude of their variable parts. In other words, we disregard
for the present the difference which may be produced in this
respect by the different lengths of the periods of turn-over. This
point will be discussed later.

Let us compare five different spheres of production, and let
the capital in each one have a different organic composition, as
follows:

Capitals	Rate of Surplus Value	Surplus Value	Value of Product	Rate of Profit
I. 80c 20v	100%	20	120	20%
II. 70c 30v	100%	30	130	30%
III. 60c 40v	100%	40	140	40%
IV. 85c 15v	100%	15	115	15%
V. 95c 5v	100%	5	105	5%

Here we have considerably different rates of profit in different spheres of production with the same degree of exploitation, corresponding to the different organic composition of these capitals.

The grand total of the capitals invested in these five spheres of production is 500; the grand total of the surplus-value produced by them is 110; the total value of all commodities produced by them is 610. If we consider the amount of 500 as one single capital, and capitals I to V as its component parts (about analogous to the different departments of a cotton mill which has different proportions of constant and variable capital in its carding, preparatory spinning, spinning, and weaving rooms, on the basis of which the average proportion for the whole factory is calculated), then we should put down the average composition of this capital of 500 as $390c + 110v$, or, in percentages, as $78c + 22v$. In other words, if we regard each one of the capitals of 100 as one-fifth of the total capital, its average composition would be $78c + 22v$; and every 100 would make an average surplus-value of 22. The average rate of profit would, therefore, be 22%, and, finally, the price of every fifth of the total product produced by the capital of 500 would be 122. The product of each 100 of the advanced total capital would have to be sold, then, at 122.

But in order not to arrive at entirely wrong conclusions, it is necessary to assume that not all cost-prices are equal to 100.

With a composition of $80c + 20v$, and a rate of surplus-value of 100, the total value of the commodities produced by the first capital of 100 would be $80c + 20v + 20s$, or 120, provided that the whole constant capital is transferred to the product of the year. Now, this may happen under certain circumstances in some spheres of production. But it will hardly be the case where the proportion of c to v is that of four to one. We must, therefore, remember in comparing the values produced by each

100 of the different capitals, that they will differ according to the different composition of c as to fixed and circulating parts, and that the fixed portions of different capitals will wear out more or less rapidly, thus transferring unequal quantities of value to the product in equal periods of time. But this is immaterial so far as the rate of profit is concerned. Whether the 80c transfer the value of 80, or 50, or 5, to the annual product, whether the annual product is consequently $80c + 20v + 20s = 120$, or $50c + 20v + 20s = 90$, or $5c + 20v + 20s = 45$, in all of these cases the excess of the value of the product over its cost-price is 20, and in every case these 20 are calculated on a capital of 100 in ascertaining the rate of profit. The rate of profit of capital I is, therefore, in every case 20%. In order to make this still plainer, we transfer in the following table different portions of the constant capital of the same five capitals to the value of their product.

Capitals	Rate of Surplus Value	Surplus Value	Rate of Profit	Used Up c	Value of Commodities	Cost Price
I. 80c + 20v	100%	20	20%	50	90	70
II. 70c + 30v	100%	30	30%	51	111	81
III. 60c + 40v	100%	40	40%	51	131	91
IV. 85c + 15v	100%	15	15%	40	70	55
V. 95c + 5v	100%	5	5%	10	20	15
390c + 110v		110	100%			Total
78c + 22v		22	22%			Average

Now, if we consider capitals I to V once more as one single total capital, it will be seen that also in this case the composition of the sums of these five capitals amounts to 500, being $390c + 110v$, so that the average composition is once more

78c + 22v. The average surplus-value also remains 22%. If we allot this surplus-value uniformly to capitals I to V, we arrive at the following prices of the commodities:

Capitals	Surplus Value	Value	Cost Price of Commodities	Price of Commodities	Rate of Profit	Deviation of Price from Value
I. 80c + 20v	20	90	70	92	22%	+ 2
II. 70c + 30v	30	111	81	103	22%	− 8
III. 60c + 40v	40	131	91	113	22%	− 18
IV. 85c + 15v	15	70	55	77	22%	+ 7
V. 95c + 5v	5	20	15	37	22%	+ 17

Summing up, we find that the commodities are sold at $2 + 7 + 17 = 26$ above, and $8 + 18 + 26$ below their value, so that the deviations of prices from values mutually balance one another by the uniform distribution of the surplus-value, or by the addition of the average profit of 22 per 100 of advanced capital to the respective cost-prices of the commodities of I to V. One portion of the commodities is sold in the same proportion above in which the other is sold below their values. And it is only their sale at such prices which makes it possible that the rate of profit for all five capitals is uniformly 22%, without regard to the organic composition of these capitals. The prices which arise by drawing the average of the various rates of profit in the different spheres of production and adding this average to the cost-prices of the different spheres of production, are the *prices of production*. They are conditioned on the existence of an average rate of profit, and this, again, rests on the premise that the rates of profit in every sphere of production, considered by itself, have previously been reduced to so many average rates of profit. These special rates of profit are equal to s/C in every sphere of production, and they must be deduced out of the values of the commodities, as shown in volume I. Without such a deduction an average rate of profit (and consequently a price of production of commodities), remains a vague and senseless conception. The price of production of a commodity, then, is equal to its cost-price plus a percentage of profit apportioned according to the average rate of profit, or in other words, equal to its cost-price plus the average profit.

Since the capitals invested in the various lines of production are of a different organic composition, and since the different percentages of the variable portions of these total capitals set in motion very different quantities of labor, it follows that these capitals appropriate very different quantities of surplus-labor, or produce very different quantities of surplus-value. Consequently the rates of profit prevailing in the various lines of production are originally very different. These different rates of profit are equalised by means of competition into a general rate of profit, which is the average of all these special rates of profit. The profit allotted according to this average rate of profit to any capital, whatever may be its organic composition, is called the average profit. That price of any commodity which is equal to its cost-price plus that share of average profit on the total capital invested (not merely consumed) in its production which is allotted to it in proportion to its conditions of turn-over, is called its price of production. Take, for instance, a capital of 500, of which 100 are fixed capital, and let 10% of this wear out during one turn-over of the circulating capital of 400. Let the average profit for the time of this turn-over be 10%. In that case the cost-price of the product created during this turn-over will be 10c (wear) + 400 (c + v), circulating capital, or a total of 410, and its price of production will be 410 (cost-price) plus 10% of average profit on 500, or a total of 460.

While the capitalists in the various spheres of production recover the value of the capital consumed in the production of their commodities through the sale of these, they do not secure the surplus-value, and consequently the profit, created in their own sphere by the production of these commodities, but only as much surplus-value, and profit, as falls to the share of every aliquot part of the total social capital out of the total social surplus-value, or social profit produced by the total capital of society in all spheres of production. Every 100 of any invested capital, whatever may be its organic composition, draws as much profit during one year, or any other period of time, as falls to the share of every 100 of the total social capital during the same period. The various capitalists, so far as profits are concerned, are so many stockholders in a stock company in which the shares of profit are uniformly divided for every 100 shares of capital, so that profits differ in the case of the individual capitalists only according to the amount of capital invested by each one of them in the social enterprise, according to his investment in social production as a whole, according to his shares. That portion of the price of commodities which buys back the elements of capital consumed in the production of these commodities, in other words, their cost-price, depends on the investment of capital required in each particular sphere of production. But the other element of the price of commodities, the percentage of profit added to this cost-price, does not depend on the mass of profit produced by a certain capital during a definite time in its own sphere of production, but on the mass of profit allotted for any period to each individual capital in its capacity as an aliquot part of the total social capital invested in social production.

A capitalist selling his commodities at their price of production recovers money in proportion to the value of the capital consumed in their production and secures profits in proportion to the aliquot part which his capital represents in the total social capital. His cost-prices are specific. But the profit added to his cost-price is independent of his particular sphere of production, for it is a simple average per 100 of invested capital.

Let us assume that the five different investments of capital named I to V in the foregoing illustrations belong to one man. The quantity of variable and constant capital consumed for each 100 of the invested capitals in the production of commodities would be known, and these portions of the value of the commodities of I to V would make up a part of their price, since at least this price is required to recover the consumed portions of the invested capital. These cost-prices would be different for each class of the commodities I to V, and the owner would therefore mark them differently. But the different masses of surplus-value, or profit, produced by capitals I to V might easily be regarded by the capitalist as profits of his aggregate capital, so that each 100 would get its proportional quota. The cost-prices of the commodities produced in the various departments I to V would be different; but that portion of their selling price which comes from the addition of the profit for each 100 of capital would be the same for all these commodities. The aggregate price of the commodities of I to V would be equal to their aggregate value, that is to say, it would be equal to the sum of the cost-prices of I to V plus the sum of the surplus-values, or profits, produced in I to V. It would actually be the money-expression of the total quantity of past and present labor incorporated in the commodities of I to V. And in the same way the sum of all the prices of production of all commodities in society, comprising the totality of all lines of production, is equal to the sum of all their values.

This statement seems to be contradicted by the fact that

under capitalist production the elements of productive capital are, as a rule, bought on the market, so that their prices include profits which have already been realised. Accordingly, the price of production of one line of production passes, with the profit contained in it, over into the cost-price of another line of production. But if we place the sum of the cost-prices of the whole country on one side, and the sum of its surplus-values, or profits, on the other, it is evident that the calculation must come out right. For instance, take a certain commodity A. Its cost-price may contain the profits of B, C, D, etc., or the cost-prices of B, C, D, etc., may contain the profits of A. Now, if we make our calculation, the profits of A will not be included in its cost-price, nor will the profits of B, C, D, etc., be figured in with their own cost-prices. No one figures his own profit in his own cost-price. If there are n spheres of production, and every one of them makes a profit of p, then the aggregate cost-price of all of them is equal to k—np. Taking the calculation as a whole we see that the profits of one sphere which pass into the cost-prices of another have been placed on one side of the account showing the total price of the ultimate product, and so cannot be placed a second time on the profit side. If any do appear on this side, it can be only because this particular commodity was itself the ultimate product, so that its price of production did not pass into the cost-price of some other commodity.

If an amount equal to p, expressing the profits of the producers of means of production, passes into the cost-price of a commodity, and if a profit equal to p′ is added to this cost-price, then the aggregate profit P is equal to $p + p'$. The aggregate cost-price of a commodity, after deducting all amounts for profit, is in that case its own cost-price minus P. If this cost-price is called k, then it is evident that $k + P = k + p + p'$. We have seen in volume I, chapter IX, 2, that the product of every capital may be treated as though a part of it reproduced only capital, while the other part represented only surplus-value. Applying this mode of calculation to the aggregate product of society, it is necessary to make some rectifications. For, looking upon society as a whole, it would be a mistake to figure, say, the profit contained in the price of flax twice. It should not be counted as a portion of the price of linen and at the same time as the profit of the producers of flax.

To the extent that the surplus-value of A passes into the constant capital of B, there is no difference between surplus-value and profit. It is quite immaterial for the value of the commodities, whether the labor contained in them is paid or unpaid. We see merely that B pays for the surplus-value of A. But the surplus-value of A cannot be counted twice in the total calculation.

The essential difference is this: Aside from the fact that the price of a certain product, for instance the product of capital B, differs from its value, because the surplus-value realized in B may be greater or smaller than the profit of others contained in the product of B, the same fact applies also to those commodities which form the constant part of its capital, and which indirectly, as necessities of life for the laborers, form its variable part. So far as the constant part is concerned, it is itself equal to the cost-price plus surplus-value, which now means cost-price plus profit, and this profit may again be greater or smaller than the surplus-value in whose place it stands. And so far as the variable capital is concerned, it is true that the average daily wage is equal to the values produced by the laborers in the time which they must work in order to produce their necessities of life. But this time is in its turn modified by the deviation of the prices of production of the necessities of life from their values. However, this always amounts in the end to saying that one commodity receives too little of the surplus-value while another receives too much, so that the deviations from the value shown by the prices of production mutually compensate one another. In short, under capitalist production, the general law of value enforces itself merely as the prevailing tendency, in a very complicated and approximate manner, as a never ascertainable average of ceaseless fluctuations.

III, pp. 181-190

Now, if the commodities are sold at their values, then, as we have shown, considerably different rates of profit arise in the various spheres of production, according to the different organic composition of the masses of capital invested in them. But capital withdraws from spheres with low rates of profit and invades others which yield a higher rate. By means of this incessant emigration and immigration, in one word, by its distribution among the various spheres in accord with a rise of the rate of profit here, and its fall there, it brings about such a proportion of supply to demand that the average profit in the various spheres of production becomes the same, so that values are converted into prices of production.

III, p. 230

4. Market Prices and Market Values

Summary: Market prices and market values will continue to differ. The value of a commodity is determined by the labor time in it in only a "vague and meaningless form."

Nevertheless, the law of value (labor theory of value) dominates market prices. For commodities to exchange with one another at their values (of labor time contained in them), there must be (1) an established market ("The exchange of commodities must no longer be accidental or occasional"); (2) large quantities exchanged; and (3) no monopoly. Yet these values are only the "center of gravity" around which prices fluctuate—some commodities selling above and some selling below value. Daily market prices above or below value tend to balance out over definite periods. Despite the fact that day-to-day prices (due to demand and supply) continually differ from values, market prices cannot be understood without reference to the labor theory of value upon which demand-supply relationships rest.

---

*

. . . Only in this vague and meaningless form are we still reminded of the fact that the value of the commodities is determined by the labor contained in them.

III, p. 203

Whatever may be the way in which the prices of the various commodities are first fixed or mutually regulated, the law of value always dominates their movements. If the labor time required for the production of these commodities is reduced, prices fall; if it is increased, prices rise, other circumstances remaining the same.

Aside from the fact that prices and their movements are dominated by the law of value, it is quite appropriate, under these circumstances, to regard the value of commodities not only theoretically, but also historically, as existing prior to the prices of production. . . .

In order that the prices at which commodities are exchanged with one another may correspond approximately to their values, no other conditions are required but the following: 1) The exchange of the various commodities must no longer be accidental or occasional, 2) So far as the direct exchange of commodities is concerned, these commodities must be produced on both sides in sufficient quantities to meet mutual requirements, a thing easily learned by experience in trading, and therefore a natural outgrowth of continued trading, 3) So far as selling is concerned, there must be no accidental or artificial monopoly which may enable either of the contracting sides to sell commodities above their value or compel others to sell below value. An accidental monopoly is one which a buyer or seller acquires by an accidental proportion of supply to demand.

The assumption that the commodities of the various spheres of production are sold at their value implies, of course, only that their value is the center of gravity around which prices fluctuate, and around which their rise and fall tends to an equilibrium. We shall also have to note a *market value,* which must be distinguished from the individual value of the commodities produced by the various producers. Of this more anon. The individual value of some of these commodities will be below the market-value, that is to say, they require less labor-time for their production than is expressed in the market-value, while that of others will be above the market-value. We shall have to regard the market-value on one side as the average value of the commodities produced in a certain sphere, and on the other side as the individual value of commodities produced under the average conditions of their respective sphere of production and constituting the bulk of the products of that sphere. It is only extraordinary combinations of circumstances under which commodities produced under the least or most favorable conditions regulate the market-value, which forms the center of fluctuation for the market-prices, which are the same, however, for the same kind of commodities. If the ordinary demand is satisfied by the supply of commodities of average value, that is to say, of a value midway between the two extremes, then those commodities, whose individual value stands below the market-value, realise an extra surplus-value, or surplus-profit, while those, whose individual value stands above the market-value cannot realise a portion of the surplus-value contained in them.

It does not do any good to say that the sale of the commodities produced under the most unfavorable conditions proves that they are required for keeping up the supply. If the price in the assumed case were higher than the average market-value, the demand would be greater. At a certain price, any kind of commodities may occupy so much room on the market. This room does not remain the same in the case of a change of prices, unless a higher price is accompanied by a smaller quantity of commodities, and a lower price by a larger quantity of commodities. But if the demand is so strong that it does not let up when the price is regulated by the value of the commodities produced under the most unfavorable conditions, then these commodities determine the market-value. This is not possible unless the demand exceeds the ordinary, or the supply falls below it. Finally, if the mass of the produced commodities exceeds the quantity which is ordinarily disposed of at average market-values, then the commodities produced under the most favorable conditions regulate the market-value. These commodities may be sold exactly or approximately at their individual values, and in that case it may happen that the commodities produced under the least favorable conditions do not realise even their cost-prices, while those produced under average conditions realise only a portion of the surplus-value contained in them. The statements referring to market-value apply also to the price of production, if it takes the place of market-value. The price of production is regulated in each sphere, and this regulation depends on special circumstances. And this price of production is in its turn the center of gravity around which the daily market-prices fluctuate and tend to balance one another within definite periods. (See Ricardo on the determination of the price of production by those who produce under the least favorable conditions.)

No matter what may be the way in which prices are regulated, the result always is the following:

1) The law of value dominates the movements of prices, since a reduction or increase of the labor-time required for production causes the prices of production to fall or to rise. It is in this sense that Ricardo (who doubtless realised that his prices of production differed from the value of commodities) says that "the inquiry to which he wishes to draw the reader's attention relates to the effect of the variations in the relative value of commodities, and not in their absolute value."

2) The average profit which determines the prices of production must always be approximately equal to that quantity of surplus-value, which falls to the share of a certain individual capital in its capacity as an aliquot part of the total social capital. Take it that the average rate of profit, and therefore the average profit, are expressed by an amount of money of a higher value than the money-value of the actual average surplus-value. So far as the capitalists are concerned in that case, it is immaterial whether they charge one another a profit of 10 or of 15%. The one of these percentages does not cover any more actual commodity-value than the other, since the overcharge in money is mutual. But so far as the laborer is concerned (the assumption being that he receives the normal wages, so that the raising of the average profit does not imply

an actual deduction from his wages, in other words, does not express something entirely different from the normal surplus-value of the capitalist), the rise in the price of commodities due to a raising of the average profit must be accompanied by a corresponding rise of the money-expression for the variable capital. As a matter of fact, such a general nominal raising of the rate of profit and the average profit above the limit provided by the proportion of the actual surplus-value to the total invested capital is not possible without carrying in its wake an increase of wages, and also an increase in the prices of the commodities which constitute the constant capital. The same is true of the opposite case, that of a reduction of the rate of profit in this way. Now, since the total value of the commodities regulates the total surplus-value, and this the level of the average profit and the average rate of profit—always understanding this as a general law, as a principle regulating the fluctuations—it follows that the law of value regulates the prices of production.

Competition first brings about, in a certain individual sphere, the establishment of an equal market-value and market-price by averaging the various individual values of the commodities. The competition of the capitals in the different spheres then results in the price of production which equalises the rates of profit between the different spheres. This last process requires a higher development of capitalist production than the previous process.

In order that commodities of the same sphere of production, the same kind, and approximately the same quality, may be sold at their value, the following two requirements must be fulfilled:

1) The different individual values must have been averaged into *one* social value, the above-named market-value, and this implies a competition between the producers of the same kind

of commodities, and also the existence of a common market, on which they offer their articles for sale. In order that the market-price of identical commodities, which however are produced under different individual circumstances, may correspond to the market-value, may not differ from it by exceeding it or falling below it, it is necessary that the different sellers should exert sufficient pressure upon one another to bring that quantity of commodities on the market which social requirements demand, in other words, that quantity of commodities whose market-value society can pay. If the quantity of products exceeds this demand, then the commodities must be sold below their market-value; vice versa, if the quantity of products is not large enough to meet this demand, or, what amounts to the same, if the pressure of competition among the sellers is not strong enough to bring this quantity of products to market, then the commodities are sold above their market-value. If the market-value is changed, then there will also be a change in the conditions under which the total quantity of commodities can be sold. If the market-value falls, then the average social demand increases (always referring to the solvent demand) and can absorb a larger quantity of commodities within certain limits. If the market-value rises, then the solvent social demand for commodities is reduced and smaller quantities of them are absorbed. Hence if supply and demand regulate the market-price, or rather the deviations of market-prices from market-values, it is true, on the other hand, that the market-value regulates the proportions of supply and demand, or the center around which supply and demand cause the market-prices to fluctuate.

If we look closer at the matter, we find that the conditions determining the value of some individual commodity become effective, in this instance, as conditions determining the value of the total quantities of a certain kind. For, generally speaking, capitalist production is from the outset a mass-production. And even other, less developed, modes of production carry small quantities of products, the result of the work of many small producers, to market as co-operative products, at least in the main lines of production, concentrating and accumulating them for sale in the hands of relatively few merchants. Such commodities are regarded as co-operative products of an entire line of production, or of a greater or smaller part of this line.

We remark by the way that the "social demand," in other words, that which regulates the principle of demand, is essentially conditioned on the mutual relations of the different economic classes and their relative economic positions, that is to say, first, on the proportion of the total surplus-value to the wages, and secondly, on the proportion of the various parts into which surplus-value is divided (profit, interest, ground-rent, taxes, etc.). And this shows once more that absolutely nothing can be explained by the relation of supply and demand, unless the basis has first been ascertained, on which this relation rests.

III, pp. 208-214

D.

THE BREAKDOWN OF CAPITALISM

1. The Capitalist and Accumulation

Summary: The capitalist performs the social function (albeit a transitory one) of accumulating capital. It is in the nature of capitalist production that the capitalist constantly extends his capital. He is coerced by forces external to himself, to accumulate, "conquer the world of social wealth," and, by increasing the exploitation of the mass of human beings, extend his control of society.

The capitalist is motivated by avarice. As he gets rich, he spends more for luxury consumption. He does not need to restrict his consumption to amass wealth since he sucks it from others. Nevertheless, the capitalist is in conflict (psychologically) over his "passion for accumulation and the desire for enjoyment."

---

*

And so far only is the necessity for his own transitory existence implied in the transitory necessity for the capitalist mode of production. But, so far as he is personified capital, it is not values in use and the enjoyment of them, but exchange-value and its augmentation, that spur him into action. Fanatically bent on making value expand itself, he ruthlessly forces the human race to produce for production's sake; he thus forces the development of the productive powers of society, and creates those material conditions, which alone can form the real basis of a higher form of society, a society in which the full and free development of every individual forms the ruling principle. Only as personified capital is the capitalist respectable. As such, he shares with the miser the passion for wealth

194

as wealth. But that which in the miser is a mere idiosyncrasy, is, in the capitalist, the effect of the social mechanism, of which he is but one of the wheels. Moreover, the development of capitalist production makes it constantly necessary to keep increasing the amount of the capital laid out in a given industrial undertaking, and competition makes the immanent laws of capitalist production to be felt by each individual capitalist, as external coercive laws. It compels him to keep constantly extending his capital, in order to preserve it, but extend it he cannot, except by means of progressive accumulation.

So far, therefore, as his actions are a mere function of capital—endowed as capital is, in his person, with consciousness and a will—his own private consumption is a robbery perpetrated on accumulation, just as in book-keeping by double entry, the private expenditure of the capitalist is placed on the debtor side of his account against his capital. To accumulate, is to conquer the world of social wealth, to increase the mass of human beings exploited by him, and thus to extend both the direct and the indirect sway of the capitalist. . . .

At the historical dawn of capitalist production,—and every capitalist upstart has personally to go through this historical stage—avarice, and desire to get rich, are the ruling passions. But the progress of capitalist production not only creates a world of delights; it lays open, in speculation and the credit system, a thousand sources of sudden enrichment. When a certain stage of development has been reached, a conventional degree of prodigality, which is also an exhibition of wealth, and consequently a source of credit, becomes a business necessity to the "unfortunate" capitalist. Luxury enters into capital's expenses of representation. Moreover, the capitalist gets rich,

168 MARX ON ECONOMICS

not like the miser, in proportion to his personal labour and restricted consumption, but at the same rate as he squeezes out the labour-power of others, and enforces on the labourer abstinence from all life's enjoyments. Although, therefore, the prodigality of the capitalist never possesses the bonâ-fide character of the open-handed feudal lord's prodigality, but, on the contrary, has always lurking behind it the most sordid avarice and the most anxious calculation, yet his expenditure grows with his accumulation, without the one necessarily restricting the other. But along with this growth, there is at the same time developed in his breast, a Faustian conflict between the passion for accumulation, and the desire for enjoyment.

I, pp. 649-651

2. The Reserve Army of Unemployed, Crises, and Wages

Summary: In the process of capital accumulation, a shortage of labor may develop. Wages increase, improving the condition of the working class and thereby bringing about an increase in the numbers of the working class.

The demand for labor falls as the proportion of constant capital increases. The decline is relative. The absolute numbers of employed laborers may increase, but their numbers will decline relative to total capital. In the process of accumulation, there are violent fluctuations in employment. Surplus population (unemployment) is created as the proportion of variable to constant capital increases. As accumulation proceeds, the absolute supply of labor is increased to meet the requirements of economic growth—only to be dismissed as the organic composition of capital increases. As a consequence, an ever-growing industrial reserve army of unemployed develops. which is available for the self-expansion of industry.

The function of overpopulation is to provide labor for the periodic sudden expansion of industry.

The course of the business cycle (a decennial cycle), which is characteristic of modern society, depends upon the constant formation, the greater or less absorption, and the reformation of the industrial reserve army. The expansion by fits and starts of the scale of production would be impossible without a reserve army. Bourgeois economists look upon the business cycle as being due to the expansion and contraction of credit. This is a mere symptom of the business cycle.

Even Malthus recognizes the need of capitalist production for surplus labor. But his theory of population states that it may take sixteen to eighteen years for a rise in wages to bring laborers into the market to supply this need. Capitalist production cannot wait. In actuality, the number of laborers may remain the same or fall, so that in general the capitalist attempts to replace living labor with constant capital. This increases the effective supply of labor. The supply of labor can also be increased by more intensive exploitation—using unskilled labor to replace skilled, using women and children. Overwork of the employed part of the population swells the ranks of the reserve army. In turn, the competition of the idle forces the employed to submit to overwork.

Wages are exclusively determined by the expansion and contraction of the industrial reserve army, which are due to changes in the business cycle. Bourgeois economists explain wage increases as being due to accumulation, but decreases as due to long-run population increases—driving wages back to subsistence. The difficulty with this explanation is that it is not compatible with the fact of the duration of the business cycle, which encompasses a much shorter time than that allowed for by the long-run changes in the size of the population.

The despotism of capital is completed by the law of supply and demand. As soon as laborers see that as they produce more wealth, they endanger their livelihoods, as soon as they see that the reserve army keeps their wages down, they try to organize into trade unions. But when they do, capitalists invoke the "sacred law of supply and demand" and employ the state to interfere forcibly with trade unions. Low wages are a consequence only of the capitalist mode of production, and not of Lasalle's "iron law of wages" or the

Malthusian population theory. If these are both natural laws, changing the social relation of production cannot change them.

---

*

Growth of capital involves growth of its variable constituent or of the part invested in labour-power. A part of the surplus-value turned into additional capital must always be re-transformed into variable capital, or additional labour-fund. If we suppose that, all other circumstances remaining the same, the composition of capital also remains constant (*i.e.*, that a definite mass of means of production constantly needs the same mass of labour-power to set in motion,) then the demand for labour and the subsistence-fund of the labourers clearly increase in the same proportion as the capital, and the more rapidly, the more rapidly the capital increases. Since the capital produces yearly a surplus-value, of which one part is yearly added to the original capital; since this increment itself grows yearly along with the augmentation of the capital already functioning; since lastly, under special stimulus to enrichment, such as the opening of new markets, or of new spheres for the outlay of capital in consequence of newly developed social wants, &c., the scale of accumulation may be suddenly extended, merely by a change in the division of the surplus-value or surplus-product into capital and revenue, the requirements of accumulating capital may exceed the increase of labour-power or of the number of labourers; the demand for labourers may exceed the supply, and, therefore, wages may rise. This must, indeed, ultimately be the case if the conditions supposed above continue. For since in each year more labourers are employed than in its predecessor, sooner or later a point must be reached, at which the requirements of accumulation begin to surpass the customary supply of labour, and, therefore, a rise of wages takes place. A lamentation on this score was heard in England during the whole of the fifteenth, and the first half of the eighteenth centuries. The more or less favourable circumstances in which the wage-working class supports and multiplies itself, in no way alter the fundamental character of capitalist production. As simple reproduction constantly reproduces the capital-relation itself, *i.e.,* the relation of capitalists on the one hand, and wage-workers on the other, so reproduction on a progressive scale, *i.e.,* accumulation, reproduces the capital-relation on a progressive scale, more capitalists or larger capitalists at this pole, more wage-workers at that. The reproduction of a mass of labour-power, which must incessantly re-incorporate itself with capital for that capital's self-expansion; which cannot get free from capital, and whose enslavement to capital is only concealed by the variety of individual capitalists to whom it sells itself, this reproduction of labour-power forms, in fact, an essential of the reproduction of capital itself. Accumulation of capital is, therefore, increase of the proletariat.

I, pp. 672-673

. . . Since the demand for labour is determined not by the amount of capital as a whole, but by its variable constituent alone, that demand falls progressively with the increase of the total capital, instead of, as previously assumed, rising in proportion to it. It falls relatively to the magnitude of the total capital, and at an accelerated rate, as this magnitude increases. With the growth of the total capital, its variable constituent or the labour incorporated in it, also does increase, but in a constantly diminishing proportion. The intermediate pauses are shortened, in which accumulation works as simple extension of production, on a given technical basis. It is not merely that an accelerated accumulation of total capital, accelerated in a constantly growing progression, is needed to absorb an additional number of labourers, or even, on account of the constant metamorphosis of old capital, to keep employed those already functioning. In its turn, this increasing accumulation and centralisation becomes a source of new changes in the composition of capital, of a more accelerated diminution of its variable, as compared with its constant constituent. This accelerated relative diminution of the variable constituent, that goes along with the accelerated increase of the total capital, and moves more rapidly than this increase, takes the inverse form, at the other pole, of an apparently absolute increase of the labouring population, an increase always moving more rapidly than that of the variable capital or the means of employment. But in fact, it is capitalistic accumulation itself that constantly produces, and produces in the direct ratio of its own energy and extent; a relatively redundant population of labourers, *i.e.,* a population of greater extent than suffices for the average needs of the self-expansion of capital, and therefore a surplus-population.

Considering the social capital in its totality, the movement of its accumulation now causes periodical changes, affecting it more or less as a whole, now distributes its various phases simultaneously over the different spheres of production. In some spheres a change in the composition of capital occurs without increase of its absolute magnitude, as a consequence of simple centralisation; in others the absolute growth of capital is connected with absolute diminution of its variable constituent, or of the labour-power absorbed by it; in others again, capital continues growing for a time on its given technical basis, and attracts additional labour-power in proportion to its increase, while at other times it undergoes organic change, and lessens its variable constituent; in all spheres, the increase of the variable part of capital, and therefore of the number of labourers employed by it, is always connected with violent fluctuations and transitory production of surplus-population, whether this takes the more striking form of the repulsion of labourers already employed, or the less evident but not less real form of the more difficult absorption of the additional labouring population through the usual channels. With the magnitude of social capital already functioning, and the degree of its increase, with the extension of the scale of production, and the mass of the labourers set in motion, with the development of the productiveness of their labour, with the greater breadth and fulness of all sources of wealth, there is also an extension of the scale on which greater attraction of labourers by capital is accompanied by their greater repulsion; the rapidity of the change in the organic composition of capital, and in its technical form increases, and an increasing number of spheres of production becomes involved in this change, now simultaneously, now alternately. The labouring population therefore produces, along with the accumulation of capital produced by it, the means by which itself is made relatively superfluous, is turned into a relative surplus population; and it does this to an always increasing extent. This is a law of population peculiar to the capitalist mode of production; and in fact every special historic mode of production has its own special laws of population, historically valid within its limits alone. An abstract law of population exists for plants and animals only, and only in so far as man has not interfered with them.

But if a surplus labouring population is a necessary product of accumulation or of the development of wealth on a capitalist basis, this surplus population becomes, conversely, the lever of capitalistic accumulation, nay, a condition of existence of the capitalist mode of production. It forms a disposable industrial reserve army, that belongs to capital quite as absolutely as if the latter had bred it at its own cost. Independently of the limits of the actual increase of population, it creates, for the changing needs of the self-expansion of capital, a mass of human material always ready for exploitation. With accumulation, and the development of the productiveness of labour that accompanies it, the power of sudden expansion of capital grows also; it grows, not merely because the elasticity of the capital already functioning increases, not merely because the absolute wealth of society expands, of which capital only forms an elastic part, not merely because credit, under every special stimulus, at once places an unusual part of this wealth at the disposal of production in the form of additional capital; it grows, also, because the technical conditions of the process of production themselves—machinery, means of transport, &c. —now admit of the rapidest transformation of masses of surplus product into additional means of production. The mass of social wealth, overflowing with the advance of accumulation, and transformable into additional capital, thrusts itself frantically into old branches of production, whose market suddenly expands, or into newly formed branches, such as railways, &c., the need for which grows out of the development of the old ones. In all such cases, there must be the possibility of throwing great masses of men suddenly on the decisive points without injury to the scale of production in other spheres. Overpopulation supplies these masses. The course characteristic of modern industry, viz., a decennial cycle (interrupted by smaller oscillations), of periods of average activity, production at high pressure, crisis and stagnation, depends on the constant formation, the greater or less absorption, and the re-formation of the industrial reserve army of surplus population. In their turn, the varying phases of the industrial cycle recruit the surplus population, and become one of the most energetic agents of its reproduction. This peculiar course of modern industry, which occurs in no earlier period of human history, was also impossible in the childhood of capitalist production. The composition of capital changed but very slowly. With its accumulation, therefore, there kept pace, on the whole, a corresponding growth in the demand for labour. Slow as was the advance of accumulation compared with that of more modern times, it found a check in the natural limits of the exploitable labouring population, limits which could only be got rid of by forcible means to be mentioned later. The expansion by fits and starts of the scale of production is the preliminary to its equally sudden contraction; the latter again evokes the former, but the former is impossible without disposable human material, without an increase in the number of labourers independently of the absolute growth of the population. This increase is effected by the simple process that constantly "sets free" a part of the labourers; by methods which lessen the number of labourers employed in proportion to the increased production. The whole form of the movement of modern industry depends, therefore, upon the constant transformation of a part of the labouring population into unemployed or half-employed hands. The superficiality of Political Economy shows itself in the fact that it looks upon the expansion and contraction of credit, which is a mere symptom of the periodic changes of the industrial cycle, as their cause. As the heavenly bodies, once thrown into a certain definite motion, always repeat this, so is it with social production as soon as it is once thrown into this movement of alternate expansion and contraction. Effects, in their turn, become causes, and the varying accidents of the whole process, which always reproduces its own conditions, take on the form of periodicity. When this periodicity is once consolidated, even Political Economy then sees that the production of a relative surplus population—*i.e.,* surplus with regard to the average needs of the self-expansion of capital—is a necessary condition of modern industry.

"Suppose," says H. Marivale, formerly Professor of Political Economy at Oxford, subsequently employed in the English Colonial Office, "suppose that, on the occasion of some of these crises, the nation were to rouse itself to the effort of getting rid by emigration of some hundreds of thousands of superfluous arms, what would be the consequence? That, at the first returning demand for labour, there would be a deficiency. However rapid reproduction may be, it takes, at all events, the space of a generation to replace the loss of adult labour. Now, the profits of our manufacturers depend mainly on the power of making use of the prosperous moment when demand is brisk, and thus compensating themselves for the interval during which it is slack. This power is secured to them only by the command of machinery and of manual labour. They must have hands ready by them, they must be able to increase the activity of their operations when required, and to slacken it again, according to the state of the market, or they cannot possibly maintain the pre-eminence in the race of competition on which the wealth of the country is founded." Even Malthus recognises over-population as a necessity of modern industry, though, after his narrow fashion, he explains it by the absolute over-growth of the labouring population, not by their becoming relatively supernumerary. He says: "Prudential habits with regard to marriage, carried to a considerable extent among the labouring class of a country mainly depending upon manufactures and commerce, might injure it. . . . From the nature of a population, an increase of labourers cannot be brought into market in consequence of a particular demand till after the lapse of 16 or 18 years, and the conversion of revenue into capital, by saving, may take place much more rapidly; a country is always liable to an increase in the quantity of the funds for the maintenance of labour faster than the increase of population." After Political Economy has thus demonstrated the constant production of a relative surplus-population of labourers to be a necessity of capitalistic accumulation, she very aptly, in the guise of an old maid, puts in the mouth of her "beau ideal" of a capitalist the following words addressed to those supernumeraries thrown on the streets by their own creation of additional capital:—"We manufacturers do what we can for you, whilst we are increasing that capital on which you must subsist, and you must do the rest by accommodating your numbers to the means of subsistence."

Capitalist production can by no means content itself with the quantity of disposable labour-power which the natural increase of population yields. It requires for its free play an industrial reserve army independent of these natural limits.

Up to this point it has been assumed that the increase or diminution of the variable capital corresponds rigidly with the increase or diminution of the number of labourers employed.

The number of labourers commanded by capital may remain the same, or even fall, while the variable capital increases. This is the case if the individual labourer yields more labour, and therefore his wages increase and this although the price of labour remains the same or even falls, only more slowly than the mass of labour rises. Increase of variable capital, in this case, becomes an index of more labour, but not of more labourers employed. It is the absolute interest of every capitalist to press a given quantity of labour out of a smaller, rather than a greater number of labourers, if the cost is about the same. In the latter case, the outlay of constant capital increases in proportion to the mass of labour set in action; in the former that increase is much smaller. The more extended the scale of production, the stronger this motive. Its force increases with the accumulation of capital.

We have seen that the development of the capitalist mode of production and of the productive power of labour—at once the cause and effect of accumulation—enables the capitalist, with the same outlay of variable capital, to set in action more labour by greater exploitation (extensive or intensive) of each individual labour-power. We have further seen that the capitalist buys with the same capital a greater mass of labour-power, as he progressively replaces skilled labourers by less skilled, mature labour-power by immature, male by female, that of adults by that of young persons or children.

On the one hand, therefore, with the progress of accumulation, a larger variable capital sets more labour in action without enlisting more labourers; on the other, a variable capital of the same magnitude sets in action more labour with the same mass of labour-power; and, finally, a greater number of inferior labour-power by displacement of higher.

The production of a relative surplus-population, or the setting free of labourers, goes on therefore yet more rapidly than the technical revolution of the process of production that accompanies, and is accelerated by, the advances of accumulation; and more rapidly than the corresponding diminution of the variable part of capital as compared with the constant. If the means of production, as they increase in extent and effective power, become to a less extent means of employment of labourers, this state of things is again modified by the fact that in proportion as the productiveness of labour increases, capital increases its supply of labour more quickly than its demand for labourers. The over-work of the employed part of the working class swells the ranks of the reserve, whilst conversely the greater pressure that the latter by its competition exerts on the former, forces these to submit to over-work and to subjugation under the dictates of capital. The condemnation of one part of the working-class to enforced idleness by the over-work of the other part, and the converse, becomes a means of enriching the individual capitalists, and accelerates at the same time the production of the industrial reserve army on a scale corresponding with the advance of social accumulation. How important is this element in the formation of the relative surplus-population, is shown by the example of England. Her technical means for saving labour are colossal. Nevertheless, if to-morrow morning labour generally were reduced to a rational amount, and proportioned to the different sections of the working-class according to age and sex, the working population to hand would be absolutely insufficient for the carrying on of national production on its present scale. The great majority of the labourers now "unproductive" would have to be turned into "productive" ones.

Taking them as a whole, the general movements of wages are exclusively regulated by the expansion and contraction of the industrial reserve army, and these again correspond to the periodic changes of the industrial cycle. They are, therefore, not determined by the variations of the absolute number of the working population, but by the varying proportions in which the working class is divided into active and reserve army, by the increase of diminution in the relative amount of the surplus-population, by the extent to which it is now absorbed, now set free. For Modern Industry with its decennial cycles and periodic phases, which, moreover, as accumulation advances, are complicated by irregular oscillations following each other more and more quickly, that would indeed be a beautiful law, which pretends to make the action of capital dependent on the absolute variation of the population, instead of regulating the demand and supply of labour by the alternate expansion and contraction of capital, the labour-market now appearing relatively under-full, because capital is expanding, now again over-full, because it is contracting. Yet this is the dogma of the economists. According to them, wages rise in consequence of accumulation of capital. The higher wages stimulate the working population to more rapid multiplication, and this goes on until the labour-market becomes too full, and therefore capital, relatively to the supply of labour, becomes insufficient. Wages fall, and now we have the reverse of the medal. The working population is little by little decimated as the result of the fall in wages, so that capital is again in excess relatively to them, or, as others explain it, falling wages and the corresponding increase in the exploitation of the labourer again accelerates accumulation, whilst, at the same time, the lower wages hold the increase of the working-class in check. Then comes again the time, when the supply of labour is less than the demand, wages rise, and so on. A beautiful mode of motion this for developed capitalist production! Before, in consequence of the rise of wages, any positive increase of the population really fit for work could occur, the time would have been passed again and again, during which the industrial campaign must have been carried through, the battle fought and won. . . .

The above economic fiction confuses the laws that regulate the general movement of wages, or the ratio between the working-class—*i.e.,* the total labour-power—and the total social capital, with the laws that distribute the working population over the different spheres of production. If, *e.g.,* in consequence of favourable circumstances, accumulation in a particular sphere of production becomes especially active, and profits in it, being greater than the average profits, attract additional capital, of course the demand for labour rises and wages also rise. The higher wages draw a larger part of the working population into the more favoured sphere, until it is glutted with labour-power, and wages at length fall again to their average level or below it, if the pressure is too great. Then, not only does the immigration of labourers into the branch of industry in question cease; it gives place to their emigration. Here the political economist thinks he sees the why and wherefore of an absolute increase of workers accompanying an increase of wages, and of a diminution of wages accompanying an absolute increase of labourers. But he sees really only the local oscillation of the labour-market in a particular sphere of production—he sees only the phenomena accompanying the distribution of the working population into the different spheres of outlay of capital, according to its varying needs.

The industrial reserve army, during the periods of stagnation and average prosperity, weighs down the active labour-army; during the periods of over-production and paroxysm, it holds its pretensions in check. Relative surplus-population is therefore the pivot upon which the law of demand and supply of labour works. It confines the field of action of this law within the limits absolutely convenient to the activity of exploitation and to the domination of capital.

This is the place to return to one of the grand exploits of economic apologetics. It will be remembered that if through the introduction of new, or the extension of old, machinery, a portion of variable capital is transformed into constant, the economic apologist interprets this operation which "fixes" capital and by that very act set labourers "free," in exactly the opposite way, pretending that it sets free capital for the labourers. Only now can one fully understand the effrontery of these apologists. What are set free are not only the labourers immediately turned out by the machines, but also their future substitutes in the rising generation, and the additional con-

tingent, that with the usual extension of trade on the old basis
would be regularly absorbed. They are now all "set free," and
every new bit of capital looking out for employment can dispose
of them. Whether it attracts them or others, the effect on the
general labour demand will be nil, if this capital is just sufficient to take out of the market as many labourers as the
machines threw upon it. If it employs a smaller number, that
of the supernumeraries increases; if it employs a greater, the
general demand for labour only increases to the extent of the
excess of the employed over those "set free." The impulse that
additional capital, seeking an outlet, would otherwise have given
to the general demand for labour, is therefore in every case
neutralised to the extent of the labourers thrown out of employment by the machine. That is to say, the mechanism of capitalistic production so manages matters that the absolute increase of
capital is accompanied by no corresponding rise in the general
demand for labour. And this the apologist calls a compensation
for the misery, the sufferings, the possible death of the displaced
labourers during the transition period that banishes them into
the industrial reserve army! The demand for labour is not
identical with increase of capital, nor supply of labour with increase of the working class. It is not a case of two independent
forces working on one another. Les dés sont pipés. Capital
works on both sides at the same time. If its accumulation, on the
one hand, increases the demand for labour, it increases on the
other the supply of labourers by the "setting free" of them,
whilst at the same time the pressure of the unemployed compels
those that are employed to furnish more labour, and therefore
makes the supply of labour, to a certain extent, independent of
the supply of labourers. The action of the law of supply and
demand of labour on this basis completes the despotism of
capital. As soon, therefore, as the labourers learn the secret,
how it comes to pass that in the same measure as they work

more, as they produce more wealth for others, and as the productive power of their labour increases, so in the same measure
even their function as a means of the self-expansion of capital
becomes more and more precarious for them; as soon as they
discover that the degree of intensity of the competition among
themselves depends wholly on the pressure of the relative surplus-population; as soon as, by Trades' Unions, &c., they try
to organise a regular cooperation between employed and unemployed in order to destroy or to weaken the ruinous effects of
this natural law of capitalistic production on their class, so soon
capital and its sycophant, political economy, cry out at the
infringement of the "eternal" and so to say "sacred" law of
supply and demand. Every combination of employed and unemployed disturbs the "harmonious" action of this law. But,
on the other hand, as soon as (in the colonies, *e.g.,*) adverse
circumstances prevent the creation of an industrial reserve army
and, with it, the absolute dependence of the working class upon
the capitalist class, capital, along with its commonplace Sancho
Panza, rebels against the "sacred" law of supply and demand,
and tries to check its inconvenient action by forcible means and
State interference.

I, pp. 690-703

. . . Thus, in future, the German Workers' Party has got
to believe in Lassalle's "iron law of wages!" [1] That this shall not
be lost, the nonsense is perpetrated of speaking of the "abolition

[1] Lassalle formulated this "law" as follows: "The iron economic law
which, under present-day conditions, under the rule of the supply and
demand of labour, determines wages is this: that the average wage
always remains reduced to the necessary basis of subsistence that . . . is
requisite for existence and propagation." (*An Open Answer to the
Central Committee for Convening a General Congress of German
Workers at Leipzig,* Zurich, 1863.)

of the wage system" (it should read: system of wage labour) *together with* the "iron law of wages." If I abolish wage labour, then naturally I abolish its laws also, whether they are of "iron" or sponge. But Lassalle's attack on wage labour turns almost solely on this so-called law. In order, therefore, to prove that Lassalle's sect has conquered, the "wage system" must be abolished "*together* with the iron law of wages" and not without it.

It is well known that nothing of the "iron law of wages" belongs to Lassalle except the word "iron" borrowed from Goethe's "great, eternal, iron laws." The word *iron* is a label by which the true believers recognise one another. But if I take the law with Lassalle's stamp on it and consequently in his sense then I must also take it with his basis for it. And what is that? As Lange[2] already showed, shortly after Lassalle's death, it is the Malthusian theory of population (preached by Lange himself). But if this theory is correct, then again I can *not* abolish the law even if I abolish wage labour a hundred times over, because the law then governs not only the system of wage labour but *every* social system. Basing themselves directly on this, the economists have proved for fifty years and more that socialism cannot abolish poverty, *which has its basis in nature,* but can only *generalise* it, distribute it simultaneously over the whole surface of society!

A Critique of the Gotha Programme, pp. 22-23

[2] F. A. Lange (1828-75). A German Neo-Kantian philosopher, petty-bourgeois democratic writer, author of a work on social reform, *The Labour Question: Its Significance for the Present and the Future* (first published in 1865).

3. Monopoly, Capitalism, and Crises

Summary: The process of capital accumulation, once begun, becomes the means of further accumulation. Increasing wealth tends to increase the concentration of wealth in the hands of individual capitalists. The number of capitalists tends to increase due, for one thing, to the division of capital among members of a family. The concentration of capital in the hands of individual capitalists is characterized in two ways: (1) the amount of social wealth limits the degree of concentration in the hands of the capitalist; (2) capitalists are constantly competing with one another. Accumulation, then, involves two consequences—the growth of wealth in the hands of capitalists and competition among them.

Concentration increases as a consequence of competition. Under competitive conditions, commodities are cheapened and large concentrations of capital drive out smaller ones. The credit system also aids in the accumulation of huge aggregates of capital.

The centralization of capital (its accumulation in the hands of fewer and fewer capitalists) continues along with accumulation due, in part, to the economic advantages of size as the volume of social capital grows. However, centralization may occur simply through the process of the amalgamation of existing capital (through merger) into a single hand.

A consequence of centralization is that as the mass of capital in a single hand grows, fewer and fewer laborers are employed by it. The growth of monopoly capitalism therefore reduces the demand for labor.

And as monopoly capitalism develops, misery, oppression, degradation, and slavery grow; laborers revolt. "The knell of capitalist private property sounds. The expropriators are expropriated."

---

*

Every individual capital is a larger or smaller concentration of means of production, with a corresponding command over a larger or smaller labour-army. Every accumulation becomes the means of new accumulation. With the increasing mass of wealth which functions as capital, accumulation increases the concentration of that wealth in the hands of individual capitalists, and thereby widens the basis of production on a large scale and of the specific methods of capitalist production. The growth of social capital is effected by the growth of many individual capitals. All other circumstances remaining the same, individual capitals, and with them the concentration of the means of production, increase in such proportion as they form aliquot parts of the total social capital. At the same time portions of the original capitals disengage themselves and function as new independent capitals. Besides other causes, the division of property, within capitalist families, plays a great part in this. With the accumulation of capital, therefore, the number of capitalists grows to a greater or less extent. Two points characterise this kind of concentration which grows directly out of, or rather is identical with, accumulation. First: The increasing concentration of the social means of production in the hands of individual capitalists is, other things remaining equal, limited by the degree of increase of social wealth. Second: The part of social capital domiciled in each particular sphere of production is divided among many capitalists who face one another as independent commodity-producers competing with each other. Accumulation and the concentration accompanying it are, therefore, not only scattered over many points, but the increase of each functioning capital is thwarted by the formation of new and the subdivision of old capitals. Accumulation, therefore, presents itself on the one hand as increasing concentration of the means of production, and of the command over labour; on the other, as repulsion of many individual capitals one from another.

This splitting-up of the total social capital into many individual capitals or the repulsion of its fractions one from another, is counteracted by their attraction. This last does not mean that simple concentration of the means of production and of the command over labour, which is identical with accumulation. It is concentration of capitals already formed, destruction of their individual independence, expropriation of capitalist by capitalist, transformation of many small into few large capitals. This process differs from the former in this, that it only pre-supposes a change in the distribution of capital already to hand, and functioning; its field of action is therefore not limited by the absolute growth of social wealth, by the absolute limits of accumulation. Capital grows in one place to a huge mass in a single hand, because it has in another place been lost by many. This is centralisation proper, as distinct from accumulation and concentration.

The laws of this centralisation of capitals, or of the attraction of capital by capital, cannot be developed here. A brief hint at a few facts must suffice. The battle of competition is fought by cheapening of commodities. The cheapness of commodities depends, *caeteris paribus,* on the productiveness of labour, and this again on the scale of production. Therefore, the larger capitals beat the smaller. It will further be remembered that, with the development of the capitalist mode of production, there is an increase in the minimum amount of individual capital necessary to carry on a business under its normal conditions. The smaller capitals, therefore, crowd into spheres of production which Modern Industry has only sporadically or incompletely got hold of. Here competition rages in direct proportion to the number, and in inverse proportion to the magnitudes, of the antagonistic capitals. It always ends in the ruin of many small capitalists, whose capitals partly pass into the hand of their conquerors, partly vanish. Apart from this, with capitalist production an altogether new force comes into play—the credit system.

In its beginnings, the credit system sneaks in as a modest helper of accumulation and draws by invisible threads the money resources scattered all over the surface of society into the hands of individual or associated capitalists. But soon it becomes a new and formidable weapon in the competitive struggle, and finally it transforms itself into an immense social mechanism for the centralisation of capitals.

Competition and credit, the two most powerful levers of capitalism, develop in proportion as capitalist production and accumulation do. At the same time the progress of accumulation increases the matter subject to centralisation, that is, the individual capitals, while the expansion of capitalist production creates the social demand here, the technical requirements there, for those gigantic industrial enterprises, which depend for their realisation on a previous centralisation of capitals. Nowadays, then, the mutual attraction of individual capitals and the tendency to centralisation are stronger than ever before. However, while the relative expansion and energy of the centralisation movement is determined to a certain degree by the superiority of the economic mechanism, yet the progress of centralisation is by no means dependent upon the positive growth of the volume of social capital. This is the particular distinction between centralisation and concentration, the latter being but another expression for reproduction on an enlarged scale. Centralisation may take place by a mere change in the distribution of already existing capitals, a simple change in the quantitative arrangement of the components of social capital. Capital may in that case accumulate in one hand in large masses by withdrawing it from many individual hands.

Centralisation in a certain line of industry would have reached its extreme limit, if all the individual capitals invested in it would have been amalgamated into one single capital.

This limit would not be reached in any particular society until the entire social capital would be united, either in the hands of one single capitalist, or in those of one single corporation.

Centralisation supplements the work of accumulation, by enabling the industrial capitalists to expand the scale of their operations. The economic result remains the same, whether this consummation is brought about by accumulation or centralisation, whether centralisation is accomplished by the violent means of annexation, by which some capitals become such overwhelming centers of gravitation for others as to break their individual cohesion and attracting the scattered fragments, or whether the amalgamation of a number of capitals, which already exist or are in process of formation, proceeds by the smoother road of forming stock companies. The increased volume of industrial establishments forms everywhere the point of departure for a more comprehensive organisation of the co-operative labor of many, for a wider development of their material powers, that is, for the progressive transformation of isolated processes of production carried on in accustomed ways into socially combined and scientifically managed processes of production.

It is evident, however, that accumulation, the gradual propagation of capital by a reproduction passing from a circular into a spiral form, is a very slow process as compared with centralisation, which needs but to alter the quantitative grouping of the integral parts of social capital. The world would still be without railroads, if it had been obliged to wait until accumulation should have enabled a few individual capitals to undertake the construction of a railroad. Centralisation, on the other hand, accomplished this by a turn of the hand through stock companies. Centralisation, by thus accelerating and intensifying the effects of accumulation, extends and hastens at the same time the revolutions in the technical composition of capital, which increase its constant part at the expense of its variable part and thereby reduce the relative demand for labor.

The masses of capital amalgamated over night by centralisation reproduce and augment themselves like the others, only faster, and thus become new and powerful levers of social accumulation. Hence, if the progress of social accumulation is mentioned nowadays, it comprizes as a matter of course the effects of centralisation. The additional capitals formed in the course of normal accumulation (see chapter XXIV, 1.) serve mainly as vehicles for the exploitation of new inventions and discoveries, or of industrial improvements in general. However, the old capital likewise arrives in due time at the moment when it must renew its head and limbs, when it casts off its old skin and is likewise born again in its perfected industrial form, in which a smaller quantity of labor suffices to set in motion a larger quantity of machinery and raw materials. The absolute decrease of the demand for labor necessarily following therefrom will naturally be so much greater, the more these capitals going through the process of rejuvenation have become accumulated in masses by means of the movement of centralisation.

On the one hand, therefore, the additional capital formed in the course of accumulation attracts fewer and fewer labourers in proportion to its magnitude. On the other hand, the old capital periodically reproduced with change of composition, repels more and more of the labourers formerly employed by it.

I, pp. 685-689

Under competition, the increase in the minimum of capital required for the successful operation of an independent industrial establishment in keeping with the increase in productivity assumes the following aspect: As soon as the new and more expensive equipment has become universally established, smaller capitals are henceforth excluded from these enterprises. Smaller capitals can carry on an independent activity in such lines only during the incipient stage of mechanical inventions. On the other hand, very large enterprises, such as railroads, with an extraordinarily high relative proportion of constant capital, do not yield any average rate of profit, but only a portion of it, interest. Otherwise the rate of profit would fall still lower. At the same time, this offers direct employment to large aggregations of capital in the form of stocks.

An increase of capital, or accumulation of capital, does not imply a fall in the rate of profit, unless this growth is accompanied by the aforementioned alterations in the proportions of the organic constituents of capital. Now it so happens that in spite of the continual and daily revolutions in the mode of production, now this, now that, greater or smaller portion of the total capital continues for certain periods to accumulate on the basis of a given average proportion of those constituents, so that its growth does not imply any organic change, and consequently no fall in the rate of profit. This continual expansion of capital, and consequently expansion of production on the basis of the old method of production, which proceeds quietly while the new methods are already developing by its side, is another reason, why the rate of profit does not decrease in the same degree in which the total capital of society grows.

The increase of the absolute number of laborers, in spite of the relative decrease of the variable as compared to the constant capital, does not take place in all lines of production, and not uniformly in those in which it does proceed. In agriculture, the decrease of the element of living labor may be absolute.

By the way, it is but a requirement of the capitalist mode of production that the number of wage workers should increase absolutely, in spite of its relative decrease. Under this mode, labor-powers become superfluous as soon as it is no longer compelled to employ them for 12 to 15 hours per day. A development of the productive forces which would diminish the absolute number of laborers, that is, which would enable the entire nation to accomplish its total production in a shorter time, would cause a revolution, because it would put the majority of the population upon the shelf. In this the specific barrier of capitalist production shows itself once more, proving that capitalist production is not an absolute form for the development of the productive powers and creation of wealth, but rather comes in collision with this development at a certain point. This collision expresses itself partly through periodical crises, which arise from the circumstance that now this, now that, portion of the laboring population is rendered superfluous in its old mode of employment. The barrier of capitalist production is the superfluous time of the laborers. The absolute spare time gained by society does not concern Capitalism. The development of the productive powers concerns it only to the extent that it increases the surplus labor time of the working class, not to the extent that it decreases the labor time for material production in general. Thus capitalist production moves in contradictions.

We have seen that the growing accumulation of capital implies its growing concentration. Thus the power of capital, the personification of the conditions of social production in the capitalist, grows over the heads of the real producers. Capital shows itself more and more as a social power, whose agent the capitalist is, and which stands no longer in any possible relation to the things which the labor of any single individual can create. Capital becomes a strange, independent, social power, which stands opposed to society as a thing, and as the power of capitalists by means of this thing. The contradiction between capital as a general social power and as a power of private capitalists over the social conditions of production develops into an ever more irreconcilable clash, which implies the dissolution of these relations and the elaboration of the conditions of production into universal, common, social conditions. This elaboration is performed by the development of the productive powers under capitalist production, and by the course which this development pursues.

III, pp. 308-310

As soon as this process of transformation has sufficiently decomposed the old society from top to bottom, as soon as the labourers are turned into proletarians, their means of labour into capital, as soon as the capitalist mode of production stands on its own feet, then the further socialisation of labour and further transformation of the land and other means of production into socially exploited and, therefore, common means of production, as well as the further expropriation of private proprietors, takes a new form. That which is now to be expropriated is no longer the labourer working for himself, but the capitalist exploiting many labourers. This expropriation is accomplished by the action of the immanent laws of capitalistic production itself, by the centralisation of capital. One capitalist always kills many. Hand in hand with this centralisation, or this expropriation of many capitalists by few, develop, on an ever extending scale, the co-operative form of the labour-process, the conscious technical application of science, the methodical cultivation of the soil, the transformation of the instruments of labour into instruments of labour only usable in common, the economising of all means of production by their use as the means of production of combined, socialised labour, the entanglement of all peoples in the net of the world-market, and this, the international character of the capitalistic régime. Along with the constantly diminishing number of the magnates of capital, who usurp and monopolise all advantages of this process of transformation, grows the mass of misery, oppression, slavery, degradation, exploitation; but with this too grows the revolt of the working-class, a class always increasing in numbers, and disciplined, united, organised by the very mechanism of the process of capitalist production itself. The monopoly of capital becomes a fetter upon the mode of production, which has sprung up and flourished along with, and under it. Centralisation of the means of production and socialisation of labour at last reach a point where they become incompatible with their capitalist integument. This integument is burst asunder. The knell of capitalist private property sounds. The expropriators are expropriated.

I, pp. 836-837

4. Deficiency in Demand and Crises

Summary: The creation of surplus value, the object of production, is only the first action in the process of making profit. The second act, which may be separated from the first in time and place, is the sale of the commodities on the market. This last is limited by the consuming power of society. But the process of exploitation, the competitive struggle, and accumulation result in a reduction of the consuming power of society to a minimum. This is an internal contradiction of capitalism.

Periodically, overproduction (underconsumption) of necessaries of life reduces the realization of surplus value under conditions of distribution and consumption peculiar to capitalist production. This process of continuous overproduction and hence the failure of the capitalist to reap profit cannot continue without recurring explosions. It is not true overproduction, but overproduction (underconsumption) due to its capitalist form.

The last cause of all real crises is the inability of society to consume what it produces.

---

*

The creation of this surplus-value, is the object of the direct process of production, and this process has no other limits but those mentioned above. As soon as the available quantity of surplus-value has been materialised in commodities, surplus-value has been produced. But this production of surplus-value is but the first act of the capitalist process of production, it merely terminates the act of direct production. Capital has absorbed so much unpaid labor. With the development of the process, which expresses itself through a falling tendency of the rate of profit, the mass of surplus-value thus produced is swelled to immense dimensions. Now comes the second act of the process. The entire mass of commodities, the total product, which contains a portion which is to reproduce the constant and variable capital as well as a portion representing surplus-value, must be sold. If this is not done, or only partly accomplished, or only at prices which are below the prices of production, the laborer has been none the less exploited, but his exploitation does not realise as much for the capitalist. It may yield no surplus-value at all for him, or only realise a portion of the produced surplus-value, or it may even mean a partial or complete loss of his capital. The conditions of direct exploitation and those of the realisation of surplus-value are not identical. They are separated logically as well as by time and space. The first are only limited by the productive power of society, the last by the proportional relations of the various lines of production and by the consuming power of society. This last-named power is not determined either by the absolute productive power nor by the absolute consuming power, but by the consuming power based on antagonistic conditions of distribution, which reduces the consumption of the great mass of the population to a variable minimum within more or less narrow limits. The consuming power is furthermore restricted by the tendency to accumulate, the greed for an expansion of capital and a production of surplus-value on an enlarged scale. This is a law of capitalist production imposed by incessant revolutions in the methods of production themselves, the resulting depreciation of existing capital, the general competitive struggle and the necessity of improving the product and expanding the scale of production, for the sake of self-preservation and on penalty of failure. The market must, therefore, be continually extended, so that its interrelations and the conditions regulating them assume more and more the form of a natural law independent of the producers and become ever more uncontrollable. This internal contradiction seeks to balance itself by an expansion of the outlying fields of production. But to the extent that the productive power develops, it finds itself at variance with the narrow basis on which the condition of consumption rest. On this self contradictory basis it is no contradiction at all that there should be an excess of capital simultaneously with an excess of population. For while a combination of these two would indeed increase the mass of the produced surplus-value, it would at the same time intensify the contradiction between the con-

ditions under which this surplus-value is produced and those
under which it is realised.

III, pp. 286-287

On the other hand, there is periodically a production of too
many means of production and necessities of life to permit of
their serving as means for the exploitation of the laborers at a
certain rate of profit. Too many commodities are produced to
permit of a realisation of the value and surplus-value contained in them under the conditions of distribution and consumption peculiar to capitalist production, that is, too many
to permit of the continuation of this process without ever
recurring explosions.

It is not a fact that too much wealth is produced. But it is
true that there is periodical overproduction of wealth in its
capitalistic and self-contradictory form.

The barrier of the capitalist mode of production becomes
apparent:

1) In the fact that the development of the productive power
of labor creates in the falling rate of profit a law which turns
into an antagonism of this mode of production at a certain
point and requires for its defeat periodical crises.

2) In the fact that the expansion or contraction of production is determined by the appropriation of unpaid labor,
and by the proportion of this unpaid labor to materialised
labor in general, or, to speak the language of the capitalists,
is determined by profit and by the proportion of this profit
to the employed capital, by a definite rate of profit, instead of
being determined by the relations of production to social wants
to the wants of socially developed human beings. The capitalist
mode of production, for this reason, meets with barriers at a
certain scale of production which would be inadequate under

different conditions. It comes to a standstill at a point determined by the production and realisation of profit, not by the
satisfaction of social needs.

III, p. 303

Let us suppose that the whole society is composed only of
industrial capitalists and wage workers. Let us furthermore
make exceptions of fluctuations of prices, which prevent large
portions of the total capital from reproducing themselves under
average conditions and which, owing to the general interrelations of the entire process of reproduction, such as are developed particularly by credit, must always call forth general
stoppages of a transient nature. Let us also make abstraction of
the bogus transactions and speculations, which the credit
system favors. In that case, a crisis could be explained only
by a disproportion of production in various branches, and by
a disproportion of the consumption of the capitalists and the
accumulation of their capitals. But as matters stand, the reproduction of the capitals invested in production depends
largely upon the consuming power of the non-producing
classes; while the consuming power of the laborers is handi-
capped partly by the laws of wages, partly by the fact that it
can be exerted only so long as the laborers can be employed at
a profit for the capitalist class. The last cause of all real crises
always remains the poverty and restricted consumption of the
masses as compared to the tendency of capitalist production
to develop the productive forces in such a way, that only the
absolute power of consumption of the entire society would
be their limit.

III, p. 568

Summary: The above does not suggest that crises may be avoided by increasing wages, because it is observed that crises are always preceded by a period of increasing wages (which cut into profits by reducing surplus value).

*

It is purely a tautology to say that crises are caused by the scarcity of solvent consumers, or of a paying consumption. The capitalist system does not know any other modes of consumption but a paying one, except that of the pauper or of the "thief." If any commodities are unsaleable, it means that no solvent purchasers have been found for them, in other words, consumers (whether commodities are bought in the last instance for productive or individual consumption). But if one were to attempt to clothe this tautology with a semblance of a profounder justification by saying that the working class receive too small a portion of their own product, and the evil would be remedied by giving them a larger share of it, or raising their wages, we should reply that crises are precisely always preceded by a period in which wages rise generally and the working class actually get a larger share of the annual product intended for consumption. From the point of view of the advocates of "simple" (!) common sense, such a period should rather remove a crisis. It seems, then, that capitalist production comprises certain conditions which are independent of good or bad will and permit the working class to enjoy that relative prosperity only momentarily, and at that always as a harbinger of a coming crisis.

II, pp. 475-476

5. *Crises Due to Internal Contradictions*

Summary: A fall in the rate of profit speeds the process of accumulation and accumulation hastens the fall in the rate of profit. Also, a fall in the rate of profit hastens both the concentration of wealth and its centralization in the hands of a few capitalists. New accumulation is checked by the fall in the rate of profit and threatens the process of capitalist development by bringing about speculation, crises, and surplus capital and population. To Ricardo and other economists of his stamp, it is nature (in their theory of rent) which brings a halt to capitalist accumulation. Whatever the cause, the acceptance of the fact of the falling rate of profit on Ricardo's part testifies to the transitory, rather than the absolute, nature of capitalist production and explains the "horror" with which this fact is greeted.

Another contradiction is this: The process of accumulation goes on regardless of the value of surplus value contained in the newly created wealth and regardless of the social conditions under which capitalist production takes place. On the other hand, capitalist production has two aims: (1) to preserve existing capital values; and (2) to expand these values as far as possible. However, the two goals are in conflict. Increasing values is accomplished through a decline in the rate of profit which depreciates existing values. Periodical depreciation of existing values is the method by which the fall in the rate of profit is stopped. Sudden stagnation and crises accompany this process.

Capitalist production is continually engaged in the attempt to overcome these problems, but it overcomes them only by means which again create problems of a more formidable size.

Continuous capital growth is accomplished by the expropriation and pauperization of the great mass of producers. This means that there is continual conflict between the historical task of capitalism—to create productive capacity—and the conditions of social production corresponding to it—the tendency to bring about a decline in the rate of profit.

The concentration of capital into a few hands brings about new crises. Large capital concentrations with small rates of profit can accumulate faster than small capitals with high rates of profit. The usurping of profitable investment outlets by capital forces small capital into "adventurous channels—speculation, fraudulent credit, fraudulent stocks, crises." The result is a "so-called plethora of capital," which simply means that this is a mass of capital which cannot survive the decline in the rate of profit because it is not sufficiently large. (Large capitals can survive the decline in their values because they are large.) The net consequence is both unemployed capital and unemployed labor.

This condition is to be distinguished from an absolute overproduction of capital in that in the latter case overproduction would only be absolute when accumulation could no longer produce any absolute or relative surplus labor time. Then there would be a sudden drop in the average rate of profit. This would be due to rising wages (an increase in the money value of variable capital) and the consequent reduction in surplus value.

When there is an overproduction of capital, some portion of capital has to lie fallow. So that even if the productive capital were still producing surplus value, the rate of profit would have to be calculated on both capitals—the fallow and the productive. Thus the mass of profits (absolute amount) would remain the same, being produced by the same amount of old capital, while the rate of profit would decline due to the increase in total capital implied in this process (the new capital remaining idle).

It is to the advantage of capitalists to keep the new capital (which is continuously being produced by old capital) fallow to protect the value of the old capital and to exclude competitors. If competitors come upon the scene, their presence would force some old capital to become fallow. There is a continuous competitive struggle between old and new capitals to decide which part would go into a fallow state. That is, there is a continuous competitive struggle to minimize losses within the capitalist class. But the class, taken as a whole, must lose.

In the end, however, equilibrium is restored (under conditions of absolute overproduction) by the "slaughtering of the *values* of capital." Violent and acute crises force sudden depreciations, stagnation, and collapse of the process of reproduction.

Wages fall, due to unemployment, and surplus value is restored. There is a renewed impulse to accumulate, to produce goods more cheaply because their prices have fallen (to cut costs). The rate of profit will again rise because, although the mass of capital has increased, depreciation has reduced its *value* relative to variable capital. "And in this way the cycle would be run once more."

The absolute overproduction, it must be remembered, is not absolute in that society has too many means of production, but only in the sense that these means of production serve as capital in the capitalist mode of production.

---

*

A fall in the rate of profit and a hastening of accumulation are in so far only different expressions of the same process as both of them indicate the development of the productive power. Accumulation in its turn hastens the fall of the rate of profit, inasmuch as it implies the concentration of labor on a large scale and thereby a higher composition of capital. On the other hand, a fall in the rate of profit hastens the concentration of capital and its centralisation through the expropriation of the smaller capitalists, the expropriation of the last survivors of the direct producers who still have anything to give up. This accelerates on one hand the accumulation, so far as mass is concerned, although the rate of accumulation falls with the rate of profit.

On the other hand, so far as the rate of self-expansion of the total capital, the rate of profit, is the incentive of capitalist production just as this self-expansion of capital is its only purpose, its fall checks the formation of new independent capitals and thus seems to threaten the development of the process of capitalist production. It promotes overproduction, speculation, crises, surplus-capital along with surplus-population. Those economists who, like Ricardo, regard the capitalist mode of production as absolute, feel nevertheless, that this mode of production creates its own limits, and therefore they attribute this limit, not to production, but to nature (in their theory of rent). But the main point in their horror over the falling rate of profit is the feeling, that capitalist production meets in the development of productive forces a barrier, which has nothing to do with the production of wealth as such; and this peculiar barrier testifies to the finiteness and the historical, merely transitory character of capitalist production. It demonstrates that this is not an absolute mode for the production of wealth, but rather comes in conflict with the further development of wealth at a certain stage.

III, p. 283

Together with the development of the productive power grows the higher composition of capital, the relative decrease of the variable as compared to the constant capital.

These different influences make themselves felt, now more side by side in space, now more successively in time. Periodically the conflict of antagonistic agencies seeks vent in crises. The crises are always but momentary and forcible solutions of the existing contradictions, violent eruptions, which restore the disturbed equilibrium for a while.

The contradiction, generally speaking, consists in this that the capitalist mode of production has a tendency to develop the productive forces absolutely, regardless of value and of the surplus-value contained in it and regardless of the social conditions under which capitalist production takes place; while it has on the other hand for its aim the preservation of the value of the existing capital and its self-expansion to the highest limit (that is, an ever accelerated growth of this value).

Its specific character is directed at the existing value of capital as a means of increasing this value to the utmost. The methods by which it aims to accomplish this comprise a fall of the rate of profit, a depreciation of the existing capital, and a development of the productive forces of labor at the expense of the already created productive forces.

The periodical depreciation of the existing capital, which is one of the immanent means of capitalist production by which the fall in the rate of profit is checked and the accumulation of capital-value through the formation of new capital promoted, disturbs the existing conditions, within which the process of circulation and reproduction of capital takes place, and is therefore accompanied by sudden stagnations and crises in the process of production.

The relative decrease of variable capital as compared to the constant, which goes hand in hand with the development of the productive forces, gives an impulse to the growth of the laboring population, while it continually creates an artificial over-population. The accumulation of capital, so far as its value is concerned, is checked by the falling rate of profit, in order to hasten still more the accumulation of its use-value, and this, in its turn, adds new speed to the accumulation of its value.

Capitalist production is continually engaged in the attempt to overcome these immanent barriers, but it overcomes them only by means which again place the same barriers in its way in a more formidable size.

The real barrier of capitalist production is capital itself. It is the fact that capital and its self-expansion appear as the starting and closing point, as the motive and aim of production; that production is merely production for *capital,* and not vice versa, the means of production mere means for an ever expanding system of the life process for the benefit of the *society* of producers. The barriers, within which the preservation and self-expansion of the value of capital resting on the expropriation and pauperisation of the great mass of producers can alone move, these barriers come continually in collision with the methods of production, which capital must employ for its purposes, and which steer straight toward an unrestricted extension of production, toward production for its own self, toward an unconditional development of the productive forces of society. The means, this unconditional development of the productive forces of society, comes continually into conflict with the limited end, the self-expansion of the existing capital. Thus, while the capitalist mode of production is one of the historical means by which the material forces of production are developed and the world-market required for them created, it is at the same time in continual conflict with this historical task and the conditions of social production corresponding to it.

With the fall of the rate of profit grows the lowest limit of capital required in the hands of the individual capitalist for the productive employment of labor, required both for the exploitation of labor and for bringing the consumed labor time within the limits of the labor time necessary for the production of the commodities, the limits of the average social labor time required for the production of the commodities. Simultaneously with it grows the concentration, because there comes a certain limit where large capital with a small rate of profit accumulates faster than small capital with a large rate of profit. This increasing concentration in its turn brings about a new fall in the rate of profit at a certain climax. The mass of the small divided capitals is thereby pushed into adventurous channels, speculation, fraudulent credit, fraudulent stocks, crises. The so-called plethora of capital refers always essentially to a plethora of that class of capital which finds no compensation in its mass for the fall in the rate of profit—and this applies always to the newly formed sprouts of capital—or to a plethora of capitals incapable of self-dependent action and placed at the disposal of the managers of large lines of industry in the form of credit. This plethora of capital proceeds from the same causes which call forth a relative over-population. It is therefore a phenomenon supplementing this last one, although they are found at opposite poles, unemployed capital on the one hand, and unemployed laboring population on the other.

An overproduction of capital, not of individual commodities, signifies therefore simply an over-accumulation of capital—although the overproduction of capital always includes the overproduction of commodities. In order to understand what this over-accumulation is (its detailed analysis follows later), it is but necessary to assume it to be absolute. When would an overproduction of capital be absolute? When would it be an overproduction which would not affect merely a few important lines of production, but which would be so absolute as to extend to every field of production?

There would be an absolute overproduction of capital as soon as the additional capital for purposes of capitalist production would be equal to zero. The purpose of capitalist production is the self-expansion of capital, that is, the appropriation of surplus-labor, the production of surplus-value, of profit. As soon as capital would have grown to such a proportion compared with the laboring population, that neither the absolute labor time nor the relative surplus-labor time could be extended any further (this last named extension would be out of the question even in the mere case that the demand for labor would be very strong, so that there would be a tendency for wages to rise); as soon as a point is reached where the increased capital produces no larger, or even smaller, quantities of surplus-value than it did before its increase, there would be an absolute overproduction of capital. That is to say, the increased capital C + ΔC would not produce any more profit, or even less profit, than capital C before its expansion by ΔC. In both cases there would be a strong and sudden fall in the average rate of profit, but it would be due to a change in the composition of capital which would not be caused by the development of the productive forces, but by a rise in the money-value of the variable capital (on account of the increased wages) and the corresponding reduction in the proportion of surplus-labor to necessary labor.

In reality the matter would amount to this, that a portion of the capital would lie fallow completely or partially (because it would first have to crowd some of the active capital out before it could take part in the process of self-expansion), while the active portion would produce values at a lower rate of profit, owing to the pressure of the unemployed or but partly employed capital. Matters would not be altered in this respect, if a part of the additional capital were to take the place of some old capital crowding this into the position of additional capital. We should always have on one side the sum of old capitals, on the other that of the additional capitals. The fall in the rate of profit would then be accompanied by an absolute decrease in the mass of profits, since under the conditions assumed by us the mass of the employed labor-power could not be increased and the rate of surplus-value not raised, so that there could be no raising of the mass of surplus-value. And the reduced mass of profits would have to be calculated on an increased total capital.—But even assuming that the employed capital were to continue producing value at the old rate, the mass of profits remaining the same, this mass would still be calculated on an increased total capital, and this would likewise imply a fall in the rate of profits. If a total capital of 1,000 yielded a profit of 100, and after its increase to 1,500 still yielded 100, then 1,000 in the second case would yield only 66⅔. The self-expansion of the old capital would have been reduced absolutely. A capital of 1,000 would not yield any more under the new circumstances than formerly a capital of 666⅔.

It is evident that this actual depreciation of the old capital could not take place without a struggle, that the additional capital ΔC could not assume the functions of capital without an effort. The rate of profit would not fall on account of competition due to the overproduction of capital. The competitive struggle would rather begin, because the fall of the rate of profit and the overproduction of capital are caused by the same conditions. The capitalists who are actively engaged with their old capitals would keep as much of the new additional capitals as would be in their hands in a fallow state, in order to prevent a depreciation of their original capital and a crowding of its space within the field of production. Or they would employ it for the purpose of loading, even at a momentary loss, the necessity of keeping additional capital fallow upon the shoulders of new intruders and other competitors in general.

That portion of ΔC which would be in new hands would seek to make room for itself at the expense of the old capital, and would accomplish this in part by forcing a portion of the old capital into a fallow state. The old capital would have to give up its place to the new and retire to the place of the completely or partially unemployed additional capital.

Under all circumstances, a portion of the old capital would be compelled to lie fallow, to give up its capacity of capital and stop acting and producing value as such. The competitive struggle would decide what part would have to go into this fallow state. So long as everything goes well, competition effects a practical brotherhood of the capitalist class, as we have seen in the case of the average rate of profit, so that each shares in the common loot in proportion to the magnitude of his share of investment. But as soon as it is no longer a question of sharing profits, but of sharing losses, every one tries to reduce his own share to a minimum and load as much as possible upon the shoulders of some other competitor. However, the class must inevitably lose. How much the individual capitalist must bear of the loss, to what extent he must share in it at all, is decided by power and craftiness, and competition then transforms itself into a fight of hostile brothers. The antagonism of the interests of the individual capitalists and those of the capitalist class as a whole then makes itself felt just as previously the identity of these interests impressed itself practically on competition.

How would this conflict be settled and the "healthy" movement of capitalist production resumed under normal conditions? The mode of settlement is already indicated by the mere statement of the conflict whose settlement is under discussion. It implies the necessity of making unproductive, or even partially destroying, some capital, amounting either to the complete value of the additional capital ΔC, or to a part of it. But a graphic presentation of this conflict shows that the loss is not equally distributed over all the individual capitals, but according to the fortunes of the competitive struggle, which assigns the loss in very different proportions and in various shapes by grace of previously captured advantages or positions, so that one capital is rendered unproductive, another destroyed, a third but relatively injured or but momentarily depreciated, etc.

But under all circumstances the equilibrium is restored by making more or less capital unproductive or destroying it. This would affect to some extent the material substance of capital, that is, a part of the means of production, fixed and circulating capital, would not perform any service as capital;

a portion of the running establishments would then close down.
Of course, time would corrode and depreciate all means of
production (except land), but this particular stagnation would
cause a far more serious destruction of means of production.
However, the main effect in this case would be to suspend the
functions of some means of production and prevent them for
a shorter or longer time from serving as means of production.

The principal work of destruction would show its most dire
effects in a slaughtering of the *values* of capitals. That portion
of the value of capital which exists only in the form of claims
on future shares of surplus-value of profit, which consists in
fact of creditor's notes on production in its various forms, would
be immediately depreciated by the reduction of the receipts on
which it is calculated. One portion of the gold and silver money
is rendered unproductive, cannot serve as capital. One portion
of the commodities on the market can complete its process of
circulation and reproduction only by means of an immense
contraction of its prices, which means a depreciation of the
capital represented by it. In the same way the elements of
fixed capital are more or less depreciated. Then there is the
added complication that the process of reproduction is based
on definite assumptions as to prices, so that a general fall in
prices checks and disturbs the process of reproduction. This
interference and stagnation paralyses the function of money as
a medium of payment, which is conditioned on the development of capital and the resulting price relations. The chain of
payments due at certain times is broken in a hundred places,
and the disaster is intensified by the collapse of the credit-
system. Thus violent and acute crises are brought about,
sudden and forcible depreciations, an actual stagnation and
collapse of the process of reproduction, and finally a real
falling off in reproduction.

At the same time still other agencies would have been at

work. The stagnation of production would have laid off a part of the laboring class and thereby placed the employed part in a condition, in which they would have to submit to a reduction of wages, even below the average. This operation has the same effect on capital as though the relative or absolute surplus-value had been increased at average wages. The time of prosperity would have promoted marriages among the laborers and reduced the decimation of the offspring. These circumstances, while implying a real increase in population, do not signify an increase in the actual working population, but they nevertheless affect the relations of the laborers to capital in the same way as though the number of the actually working laborers had increased. On the other hand, the fall in prices and the competitive struggle would have given to every capitalist an impulse to raise the individual value of his total product above its average value by means of new machines, new and improved working methods, new combinations, which means, to increase the productive power of a certain quantity of labor, to lower the proportion of the variable to the constant capital, and thereby to release some laborers, in short, to create an artificial over-population. The depreciation of the elements of constant capital itself would be another factor tending to raise the rate of profit. The mass of the employed constant capital, compared to the variable, would have increased, but the value of this mass might have fallen. The present stagnation of production would have prepared an expansion of production later on, within capitalistic limits.

And in this way the cycle would be run once more. One portion of the capital which had been depreciated by the stagnation of its function would recover its old value. For the rest, the same vicious circle would be described once more under expanded conditions of production, in an expanded market, and with increased productive forces.

However, even under the extreme conditions assumed by us this absolute overproduction of capital would not be an absolute overproduction in the sense that it would be an absolute overproduction of means of production. It would be an overproduction of means of production *only to the extent that they serve as capital,* so that the increased value of its increased mass would also imply a utilisation for the production of more value. . . .

. . . the fall in the rate of profit calls forth the competitive struggle among capitalists, not vice versa. This competitive struggle is indeed accompanied by a transient rise in wages and a resulting further fall of the rate of profit for a short time. The same thing is seen in the overproduction of commodities, the overstocking of markets. Since the aim of capital is not to minister to certain wants, but to produce profits, and since it accomplishes this purpose by methods which adapt the mass of production to the scale of production, not vice versa, conflict must continually ensue between the limited conditions of consumption on a capitalist basis and a production which forever tends to exceed its immanent barriers.

III, pp. 292-301

6. *Crises—Say's Law, Monetary Crises, Disproportions in Production*

A. CAUSES OF CRISES IN GENERAL

Summary: Say's Law, which states that there can be no general overproduction, is based on the principle that products exchange against products. As Ricardo puts it, "No man produces but with

a view to consume or sell, and he never sells but with an intention
to purchase some other commodity, which may be immediately useful to him, or which may contribute to future production. . . ."

Here we note only that the problem is not the continuous use of
existing capital but the accumulation of new capital. Thus, if for
any reason the market price of commodities should fall below their
price of production, reproduction and accumulation will be held
back. Money lies as idle hoards in banks.

Stagnation could occur also (purchase and sale could come into
conflict) as a result of a failure to realize the "real preconditions"
for reproduction as, for example, if grain became dear, or not
enough constant capital *in natura* accumulated. Stagnation could
also result from this situation: If, due to a sharp increase in the
demand for the factors of production which are used for reproduction, their prices rise, interest rates will fall, leading to risky and
speculative ventures. The decline in reproduction leads to a decline
in the demand for labor, which in turn leads to falling wages and
unemployment. This has cumulative consequences resulting in renewed downward pressure on prices. Also, it must be remembered
that in the relatively long time between which capital is advanced
for production and its return, great changes in market conditions
and great changes in the productivity of labor must occur. Great
catastrophes and crises develop "—and these cannot in any way be
got rid of by the pitiful claptrap that products exchange against
products."

---

*

The view adopted by Ricardo from the inane Say, but which
was really Mill's (which we shall come back to when we
deal with that miserable fellow Say), that no *over-production,*
or at any rate *no general glut of the market* is possible, rests
on the principle that exchange is of *products against products.*
Or, as [James] Mill put it, on the "metaphysical equilibrium of
sellers and buyers," [which was] further developed [to the
principle of] demand being determined only by production

itself, or even of the identity of demand and supply. The same
principle is expressed also in the form of which Ricardo was
particularly fond, that any quantity of capital can be productively employed in any country. In Chapter XXI, on the
Effects of Accumulation on Profits and Interest, Ricardo says:

> M. Say has, however, most satisfactorily shown that there is no
> amount of capital which may not be employed in a country, because
> a demand is only limited by production. No man produces but with
> a view to consume or sell, and he never sells but with an intention
> to purchase some other commodity, which may be immediately
> useful to him, or which may contribute to future production. By
> producing, then, he necessarily becomes either the consumer of his
> own goods, or the purchaser and consumer of the goods of some
> other person. It is not to be supposed that he should, for any length
> of time, be ill-informed of the commodities which he can most
> advantageously produce, to attain the object which he has in view,
> namely, the possession of other goods; and, therefore, it is not
> probable that he will continually produce a commodity for which
> there is no demand (pp. 192-3).

Ricardo, who always tries to be consistent, discovers that his
authority Say has put something across him here. In a footnote
to this passage he says:

> Is the following quite consistent with M. Say's principle? "The
> more disposable capitals are abundant in proportion to the extent of
> employment for them, the more will the rate of interest on loans of
> capital fall" (Vol. II, p. 108). If capital to any extent can be em-
> ployed by a country, how can it be said to be abundant, compared
> with the extent of employment for it?

As Ricardo cites Say, we shall criticise Say's theories later,
when we deal with this humbug himself.

Meanwhile we note here only the following: In reproduction, just as in the accumulation of capital, the point is not
only the replacement of *the same* mass of use value as the
capital consists of, on the old scale or (in accumulation) on

an enlarged scale, but the replacement of the *value* of the capital advanced along with the usual rate of profit. If therefore through any circumstance whatever or a combination of circumstances the market price of the commodities (of all or of the majority—it makes no difference) falls far below their price of production, then, in the first place, the reproduction of the capital will be considerably curtailed. Even more, however, will accumulation be held back. The transformation into capital of surplus value piled up in the form of money (gold or notes) would only bring loss. It therefore lies idle as a hoard in the banks, or even in the form of credit money, which in essence makes no difference. This stagnation could occur as a result of the opposite causes, when the *real preconditions* for reproduction were lacking (as for example if grain became dear, or because not enough constant capital *in natura* had been accumulated). There is a check in reproduction, and therefore in the flow of circulation. Purchase and sale come into sharp conflict, and unemployed capital appears in the form of money lying idle. The same phenomenon (and this as a rule precedes crises) can occur if the production of surplus capital takes place at a very rapid rate, and its re-transformation into productive capital so increases the demand for all the elements of the latter that real production cannot keep pace, and consequently there is a rise in the prices of all commodities which enter into the formation of capital. In this case the rate of interest falls sharply, however much profits may rise, and this reduction in the rate of interest leads then to the most risky speculative ventures. The check in reproduction leads to the decrease of the variable capital, to a fall in wages and a fall in the amount of labour employed. This in turn reacts anew on prices and brings about a new fall in prices.

It must never be lost sight of that in capitalist production what matters is not direct use value, but exchange value, and in particular the expansion of surplus value. This is the driving motive of capitalist production, and it is a pretty conception that—in order to reason away the contradictions of capitalist production—abstracts from the basis of the latter and presents it as production whose aim is to meet the direct consumption of the producers.

Further: as the circulation process of capital is not a one-day affair, but extends over fairly long periods before the return of the capital to its original form; as these periods however coincide with the periods within which market prices equalise with prices of production; as in the course of these periods great upheavals and changes in markets take place, since great changes in the productivity of labour and therefore in the *real value* of commodities take place—it is therefore very evident that from the starting point—the advance of the capital—until its return at the end of one of these periods, great catastrophes must occur and elements of crises must accumulate and develop—and these cannot in any way be got rid of by the pitiful claptrap that products exchange against products. The equalisation of value in period with the value of the same commodity in a later period, which Mr. Bailey considers a scholastic fantasy, forms on the contrary the basic principle of the process of circulation of capital.

Theories of Surplus Value, pp. 369-372

B. OVERPRODUCTION OF COMMODITIES AND OVERABUNDANCE OF CAPITAL

Summary: Some economists have tried to deny the possibility of an overabundance of commodities while affirming the possibility of an overproduction of capital. For the most part, this is a "prevaricating expression" or thoughtlessness, or, more important, an attempt to deny a phenomenon against which people have prejudices. All this is nonsense, since the two expressions are identical. However, using the term "overproduction of capital" is a step forward, since it recognizes that "producers confront one another not as mere owners of commodities, but as capitalists."

---

*

Ricardo is always, to the best of his knowledge, consistent. Therefore for him the statement that no *overproduction* (of commodities) is possible is identical with the statement that no plethora or overabundance of capital is possible.

There cannot, then, be accumulated in a country any amount of capital which cannot be employed productively until wages rise so high in consequence of the rise of necessaries, and so little consequently remains for the profits of stock, that the motive for accumulation ceases (Chapter XXI, p. 193).

It follows, then, from these admissions, that there is no limit to demand—no limit to the employment of capital while it yields any profit, and that, however abundant capital may become, there is no other adequate reason for a fall of profit but a rise of wages, and further, it may be added that the only adequate and permanent cause for the rise of wages is the increasing difficulty of providing food and necessaries for the increasing number of workmen (Chapter XXI, p. 197).

What then would Ricardo have said to the stupidity of his successors, who deny overproduction in one form (general overabundance of commodities on the market), and in another form, as overproduction of capital, plethora of capital, overabundance of capital, not only admit it, but even make of it a cardinal point in their doctrine?

Not a single responsible economist of the post-Ricardo

period denies the [possibility of] overabundance of capital. On the contrary, they all explain crises by it (in so far as they do not trace their causes to phenomena arising from credit). Therefore they all admit overproduction in one form, but deny it in the other. So the only question that remains is: what are the relations between these two forms of overproduction— the form in which it is denied and the form in which it is asserted?

Ricardo himself actually had no knowledge of crises, of general crises on the world market arising out of the process of production itself. He could explain the crises of 1800 to 1815 by the increase in the price of wheat resulting from harvest failures, by the devaluation of paper currency, the depreciation of colonial commodities, and so forth, because as a result of the continental blockade the market was forcibly contracted, from political, not economic, reasons. He could similarly explain the crises after 1815, partly by a bad year and shortage of grain, partly by the fall in the price of corn due to the causes which, by his own theory, necessarily drove up grain prices during the war and the blockade of England from the Continent, having ceased to operate; partly by the transition from war to peace and the consequent "sudden changes in the channels of trade" (see Chapter XIX of his *Principles,* which deals with this). Later historical phenomena, especially the almost regular periodicity of crises on the world market, made it no longer possible for Ricardo's successors to deny the facts or to interpret them as accidental. Instead, they invented—apart from those who explain everything by credit, but then [admit] that they themselves have to presuppose in turn the overabundance of capital—the pretty distinction between *overabundance of capital* and *overproduction.* They keep to the phrases and good reasons used by Ricardo and Adam Smith in arguing against the latter, while from the former they seek to deduce phenomena otherwise inexplicable to them. Wilson for example explains certain crises by the overabundance of fixed capital, others by the overabundance of circulating capital. The overabundance of capital itself is affirmed by the best economists (like Fullarton) and has already become such a fixed prejudice that the phrase even occurs in the learned Roscher's *Compendium* as something that is self-evident.

The question therefore arises: what is overabundance of capital, and what distinguishes this thing from overproduction? According to the same economists capital is equivalent to money or commodities. Overproduction of capital is therefore overproduction of money or of commodities. And yet these two phenomena are supposed to have nothing in common with each other. Nor does even overproduction of money help, since for them money is a commodity, so that the whole phenomenon resolves itself into overproduction of commodities, which they admit under one name and deny under another. If moreover it is said that the overproduction is of fixed capital or of circulating capital, the basis of this statement is that commodities are here no longer considered simply as commodities, but in their designation as capital. However, this statement on the other hand is an admission that in capitalist production and its phenomena—for example, overproduction— we are dealing not only with the simple relation in which the product appears as *commodity,* but with its social determinants, through which it is *more than* and even something different from a commodity.

In general, the phrase *overabundance of capital* as against *overproduction of commodities* is often merely a prevaricating expression, or [that kind of] thoughtlessness that admits the same phenomenon as present and necessary when it is called A, but denies it when it is called B; that therefore in fact has scruples and doubts only about the *name to be given* to the phenomenon, but not about the phenomenon itself. Or [the phrase springs from the striving] to overcome the difficulty in explaining the phenomenon by denying it in a form in which it comes up against prejudices, and admitting it only in a form in which no one bothers about it. But apart from these aspects of it, the transition from the phrase *"overproduction of commodities"* to the phrase *"overabundance of capital"* represents in fact a *step forward*. In what does this consist? [In the recognition] that the producers confront one another not as mere owners of commodities, but as capitalists.

> *Theories of Surplus Value,* pp. 373-376

C. UNITY OF PURCHASE AND SALE, OF THE PROCESS OF PRODUCTION AND THE PROCESS OF CIRCULATION

Summary: Say's Law is refuted by the fact of crises. The unity of purchase and sale is brought about forcibly by crises. The unity of purchase and sale is not given in advance as the adherents to Say's Law claim. To deny the existence of crises is to deny capitalist production itself, its antagonisms, contradictions, and explosions.

For Ricardo, following Say, to assert that productions are always bought by productions and that money is only a medium of exchange is to fail to recognize that money is an essential and independent form of commodity. Economists, in this way, reason crises out of existence, because they deny the existence of separate phases in the exchange of commodities.

To say that the relationship between money and commodities opens up the *possibility* of there being crises does not explain *why* there are crises. Monetary phenomena make crises possible; they do not cause them. In pre-market societies crises are unheard of.

Ricardo claims that men produce only to sell. In a capitalist society one must sell, but may not be able to do so, except at a loss. Also, Ricardo claims that he only sells to purchase something else which may be useful to him (consumption) or useful in production. But during disturbances, the capitalist will not produce if there is no market. His aim is not the production of wealth but the accumulation of profit.

In the metamorphosis of commodities, the possibility of crises arises in two ways. First, a commodity in its form as a use-value is transformed into money (C-M), that is, sold for money. Once done, then a purchase may be made (M-C), which presents no difficulties since money is freely exchangeable for anything. In this simple form of metamorphosis, the possibility of crises comes in the separation of sales and purchases. In a barter society, the possibility of a crisis, under our assumptions, would disappear.

The possibility of crises, in its second form, arises out of money as a means of payment, because money figures in two phases separated in time and different in function. First let us examine money in the *process of reproduction* of capital. Commodity capital must pass through the process C-M-C, the metamorphosis of the commodity. Crises may arise here due to the separation of purchase and sale. The first metamorphosis consists of turning capital into money; the second, turning money into capital. Some capitals are in the process of turning themselves into money while others are turning themselves from money into capitals. This "mutual confluence and intertwining" of the production process is necessitated by the division of labor and is also to some extent accidental. Thus the exchange economy, by providing the means of exchange and permitting a complex division of labor, provides the possibility under which crises may develop.

Let us turn now to money as a *means of payment*. For example, a merchant buys cloth on credit, paying by means of a bill of exchange, and, in turn, flax growers sell to spinners, spinners to weavers, and so on, through a long chain, all based on the bill of exchange originally issued by the merchant. Should the merchant be unable to sell his product on the market, no one else along the chain is paid (no one else realizes the value of his commodities). In this way the *possibility* of general crises arises.

Economists who are unable to reason crises out of existence believe that crises which emerge in the forms described above are *caused* by monetary phenomena and are therefore simply accidents.

What they fail to perceive is that these are only the forms in which crises appear and are not "a determinate cause" which must be based upon "the real movement of capitalist production, competition, and credit. . . ."

---

*

In relation to crises, all authors who portray the actual movement of prices, or all practical people writing at particular stages of a crisis, have correctly ignored the allegedly theoretical twaddle and have been content to take it for granted that the doctrine of the impossibility of a market plethora, though it might be true in abstract theory, is in practice false. The regular repetition of crises has in fact reduced the rigmaroles of Say and others to a phraseology which is only used in times of prosperity, but in times of crisis is discarded.

In world market crises the contradictions and antagonisms of bourgeois production break through to the surface. But instead of investigating the nature of the conflicting elements which force their way through in the catastrophe, the apologists content themselves with denying the catastrophe itself; and, faced with its regular recurrence, with insisting that production would never lead to crises if it were carried on according to the textbooks. The apologetics consist, then, in falsifying the simplest economic relations, and especially in stubbornly maintaining the unity in face of the contradiction.

If for example purchase and sale, or the movement of metamorphosis of commodities, represent the unity of two processes—or rather the course of a single process through two opposite phases, and thus in essence the unity of the two phases—this movement is nevertheless, equally in essence, the separation of the two phases, making them independent of each other. Since in fact they belong together, the independence of the two linked phases can only show itself forcibly, as a destructive process. It is precisely the *crisis* in which their unity asserts itself—the unity of different things. The independence in relation to each other, which is assumed by these mutually dependent and complementary phases, is forcibly destroyed. The crisis therefore makes manifest the unity of the phases which have become independent of each other. No crisis would take place, were it not for this inner unity of what on the surface are phases unrelated to each other. But No!—says the apologist economist. Because there is unity, there can be *no* crisis. Which in turn is nothing but to say that the unity of opposite [factors] excludes their antagonism.

In order to prove that capitalist production cannot lead to general crises, all its conditions and definite forms, all its principles and *differentiae specificae* (specific differences) are denied; in short, capitalist production itself is denied. And in fact what is demonstrated is that if the capitalist mode of production—instead of being a specifically developed, unique form of social production—were a mode of production dating back to the crudest beginnings of social production, the antagonisms and contradictions peculiar to it, and therefore also their explosion in crises, would not exist.

"Productions," Ricardo, following Say, observes, "are always bought by productions, or by services; money is only the medium by which the exchange is effected."

Here therefore, in the first place, the *commodity,* in which the antagonism between exchange value and use value exists, is transformed into a simple product (use value), and consequently the exchange of commodities is transformed into a mere bartering of products, of simple use values. This is to go back not only to before capitalist production, but to before simple commodity production; and the most developed phenomenon of capitalist production—world market crisis—is flatly denied by the flat denial of the first condition of capitalist production, namely, that the product is a commodity and must therefore take the form of money and pass through the process of metamorphosis. Instead of speaking of wage labour, the term used is "services", a word in which the specific characteristic of wage labour and of its use—namely, that it increases the value of the commodities for which it is exchanged, that it produces surplus value—is again disregarded, and with it also the specific relation whereby money and commodities are transformed into capital. "Service" is labour considered only as *use value* (a secondary matter in capitalist production), just in the same way as in the word *"productions"* the essence of the *commodity* and of the contradiction contained in it is suppressed. Then, quite consistently, *money* is conceived as merely the intermediary in the exchange of products, not as an essential and necessary form of existence of the commodity, which must present itself as exchange value—general social labour. Inasmuch as, through the transformation of the commodity into mere use value (product), the essence of exchange value is expunged, it is then easy to deny—or rather it is then necessary to deny—*money* as an essential and independent form of the commodity in the process of the metamorphosis from its original form. In this way, therefore, crises are reasoned out of existence through losing sight of or denying the first preconditions of capitalist production: the nature of the product as a commodity, the duplication of the commodity in commodity and money, the consequent separate phases in the exchange of commodities, and finally the relation of money or commodities to wage labour.

These economists, however, are no better, who (like John Stuart Mill, for example) seek to explain crises by these simple *possibilities* of crisis contained in the metamorphosis of commodities—such as the separation between purchase and sale.

These characteristics, which explain the possibility of crisis, are very far from explaining their actuality, and still less, *why* the phases of the process come into such conflict that their inner unity can only assert itself through a crisis, through a violent process. This *separation* appears in the crisis; it is the elementary form of crisis. To *explain* the crisis by its elementary form is to explain the existence of the crisis by expressing its presence in its abstract form, that is, to explain the crisis by the crisis.

Ricardo says:

> No man produces but with a view to consume or sell, and he never sells but with an intention to purchase some other commodity, which may be immediately useful to him, or which may contribute to future production. By producing, then, he necessarily becomes either the consumer of his own goods, or the purchaser and consumer of the goods of some other person. It is not to be supposed that he should, for any length of time, be ill-informed of the commodities which he can most advantageously produce, to attain the object which he has in view, namely, the possession of other goods; and, therefore, it is not probable that he will continually produce a commodity for which there is no demand (Chapter XXI, pp. 192-3).

This is the childish babble of a Say, but it is not worthy of Ricardo. In the first place no capitalist produces in order to consume his product. And when we are speaking of capitalist production, then it is correct to say "No man produces with a view to consume his own product", even if he uses portions of his product for industrial consumption. But here it is private consumption that is in question. In the earlier passage, it was forgotten that the product is a commodity. Now even the social division of labour is forgotten. In conditions in which men produce for themselves, there are in fact no crises, but also no capitalist production. Nor have we ever heard that the ancients, with their slave production, at any time experienced crises, although among the ancients too individual producers went bankrupt. The first part of the alternative is nonsense. So is the second. A man who has produced has not the choice whether he will sell or not. He *must* sell. And in crises appears precisely the circumstance that he cannot sell, or only below the price of production, or even that he must sell at a positive loss. What does it avail him or us, therefore, that he has produced in order to sell? What concerns us is precisely to discover what has cut across this good intention of his.

Further: "No man sells but with a view to purchase some other commodity, which may be immediately useful to him, or which may contribute to future production". What a pleasant portrayal of bourgeois relations! Ricardo even forgets that a man may sell in order to pay, and that these compulsory sales play a very significant role in crises. The immediate purpose of the capitalist when he sells is to transform his commodities or rather his commodity capital back again into money capital, and thereby to realise his profit. Consumption—revenue—is consequently not the determining motive of this process, which it is, however, for the man who only sells commodities in order to transform them into means of subsistence. But this is not capitalist production, in which revenue appears as a result but not as the determining purpose. Everyone sells with the immediate aim of selling; that is, in order to transform commodities into money.

During the crisis the man may be very pleased when he has made a sale, without any immediate thought of a purchase. However, if the value that has been realised is now again to function as capital it must pass through the process of reproduction, that is, be exchanged once more for labour and commodities. But crisis is precisely the moment of disturbance and interruption in the process of reproduction. And this disturbance cannot be explained by the fact that it does not take place in periods when there is no crisis. There can be no doubt that nobody "will continually produce a commodity for which there is no demand", but no one is talking about such an absurd hypothesis. Also, it has nothing whatever to do with the matter. "The possession of other goods" is not the immediate aim of capitalist production, but the appropriation of value, of money, of abstract wealth.

The basis of Ricardo's approach is here also James Mill's principle of the "metaphysical equation of purchases and sales", which I have already examined—an equation that sees *only* the unity but not the separation in the process of purchase and sale. This is also the basis of Ricardo's statement (following James Mill).

Money is not only "the medium by which the exchange is effected", but equally it is the medium through which the exchange of product for product falls into two acts which are independent of each other and separate in space and time. With Ricardo this false conception of money comes however from the fact that he is always looking at the *quantitative determination* of exchange value, that is, that it is equal to a definite quantity of labour time, but on the other hand forgets the *qualitative* characteristic that the individual labour, through its alienation, must present itself as *abstract, general, social labour*.

Before we advance one further step, this must be said:

Through the disjunction between the direct production process and the circulation process, the *possibility* of crisis, which became apparent in the simple metamorphosis of the commodity, is once more and further developed. When these two processes do not pass from one to the other in a continuous stream, but become independent of each other, the crisis is there.

In the metamorphosis of commodities the possibility of crisis shows itself in this way:

First, the commodity, which exists in its real form as a use value, and in its notional form, in its price, as an exchange value, must be transformed into money: C-M. Once this difficulty, the sale, is solved, then the purchase, M-C, presents no difficulty, as money is immediately exchangeable for everything else. The use value of the commodity, the usefulness of the labour contained in it, must be assumed from the start— otherwise it is not in any sense a commodity. It is further assumed that the individual value of the commodity is equal to its social value, that is that the labour time materialised in it is equal to the labour time socially necessary for the production of this commodity. The possibility of crisis, in so far as it shows itself in the simple form of the metamorphosis, therefore comes from the mere fact that the differences in form—the phases—which in its movement it passes through, in the first place, are necessary complementary forms and phases; and secondly, in spite of this inner necessary connection with each other, are independent parts and forms of the process, existing independently of each other, separate in time and space, cut off and divided from each other. It lies therefore in the very separation between sale and purchase. It is only in the form of commodity that the commodity has this difficulty to overcome. As soon as it has the form of money it has got over the difficulty. But moreover, this too is due to the separation between purchase and sale. If the commodity could not be withdrawn from circulation in the form of money, or its retransformation into a commodity could not be deferred; if—as in direct barter—purchase and sale were one, the *possibility* of crisis, on the assumptions made, would disappear. . . .

Crisis in its second form [arises from the] function of money as means of payment, in which money figures in two different phases divided from each other in time, in two different functions. Both of these two forms are still quite abstract, although the second is more concrete than the first.

First, therefore, in considering the *process of reproduction* of capital, which coincides with its circulation, it is necessary to show that these above-mentioned forms are simply repeated over and over again, or rather here first receive a content, a foundation on which they can manifest themselves.

Let us examine the movement which capital passes through from the moment when it leaves the production process as commodity in order once again to come out of it as commodity. If we here abstract from everything else that determines its content, then the total commodity capital, and each individual commodity of which it consists, has to pass through the process C-M-C, the metamorphosis of the commodity. The general possibility of crisis which is contained in this form—the separation of purchase and sale—is therefore implicit in the movement of the capital, in so far as this capital is *also* commodity and nothing but commodity. The connection between the metamorphoses of commodities with each other results moreover in one commodity transforming itself into money, because the other is re-transforming itself from the form of money into commodity. Consequently, the separation of purchase from sale appears here also in such a way that the transformation of the one capital from the form commodity into the form money must correspond to the re-transformation of the other capital from the form money into the form commodity, the first metamorphosis of the one capital to the second of the other, the one capital leaving the production process and the other returning into the production process. This mutual confluence and intertwining of the reproduction or circulation processes of different capitals is on the one hand necessitated by the division of labour, and on the other is accidental; and thus the determination of the content of crisis is already a stage further.

Secondly, however, as concerns the possibility of crisis arising from the form of money as *means of payment,* there are already in capital a number of more concrete causes for this possibility being realised. For example, the weaver has to pay for his whole constant capital, the elements of which are supplied by spinner, flax grower, machinery manufacturer, iron manufacturer, timber merchant, coal producer, and so on. In so far as these latter produce constant capital which only enters into [the process of production] without entering into the final commodity, the cloth, they replace each other's means of production by means of an exchange of capital. Let us suppose that the weaver then sells his cloth to the *merchant* for £1,000, but in return for a bill of exchange, so that money figures as *means of payment*. Similarly, the flax grower has sold to the spinner in return for a bill of exchange, and the spinner to the weaver, ditto the machinery manufacturer to the weaver, ditto the iron manufacturer and timber merchant to the machinery manufacturer, ditto the coal producer to the spinner, weaver, machinery manufacturer, and iron and timber suppliers. In addition, the iron, coal, timber and flax producers have paid each other with bills of exchange. Then if the merchant does not receive money for his commodity, he cannot pay his bill of exchange to the weaver. The flax grower has drawn on the spinner, the machinery manufacturer on the weaver and the spinner. The spinner cannot pay, because the weaver cannot pay; neither of them pays the machinery manufacturer, and the latter does not pay the suppliers of iron, timber, and coal. And all of them in turn, because they do not realise the value of their commodities, cannot replace the portion of the value which is to replace their constant capital. In this way a general crisis arises. This is nothing other than the developed *possibility of crisis* arising from money as means of payment; but we see here, in capitalist production, that very connection between mutual claims and obligations, between purchases and sales, through which the possibility can develop into actuality.

In any case: if purchase and sale do not get held up recipro-

cally, and therefore do not require forcible adjustment—or if
money so functions as means of payment that claims are settled,
and the contradiction inherent in money as means of payment
is not realised—if therefore these two abstract forms of crisis
do not in actuality make their appearance as such, no crisis
exists. No crisis can exist unless sale and purchase become
separated from each other and come into conflict, or the contradictions inherent in money as means of payment come to
the surface; unless therefore crisis at the same time emerges in
the simple form—as the contradiction between purchase and
sale, or the contradiction inherent in money as means of payment. But these also are mere *forms,* general possibilities of
crises; and consequently also forms, abstract forms, of actual
crisis. In them the nature of crisis appears in its simplest forms,
and, in so far as this form is itself its simplest content, in its
simplest content. But it is not as yet a content which has
a determinate cause. The simple circulation of money and even
the circulation of money as means of payment—and both make
their appearance long *before* capitalist production, without
crisis occurring—are possible and in fact take place without
crises. On the basis of these forms alone, therefore, it is not
possible to explain why they show their critical side, why the
contradiction contained in them as a possibility emerges as a
real contradiction.

From this we can see how great is the stupidity of economists
who, when they are no longer able to reason out of existence
the phenomenon of overproduction and crisis, soothe themselves by saying that only the possibility of crises is given in
those forms, and that therefore their emergence is *accidental,*
and so the advent of crisis is itself a mere *accident.*

The contradictions developed in the circulation of commodities, and further developed in the circulation of money—and
the consequent possibilities of crisis—reproduce themselves

spontaneously in capital, inasmuch as the developed circulation of commodities and circulation of money in fact arise only on the basis of capital.

What has to be done, however, is to follow through the further development of the potential crisis—the real crisis can only be presented on the basis of the real movement of capitalist production, competition and credit—in so far as crisis arises from the forms characteristic of capital, its *properties* as capital, and not from its mere existence as commodity and as money. The mere direct *process of production* of capital cannot by itself add anything new in this connection. In order to exist at all, the conditions for it are assumed. For that reason, in the first section dealing with capital—the immediate process of production—no new element of crisis has to be added. *By its nature* crisis is present in it. For the process of production is appropriation and therefore production of surplus value. But this cannot appear in the process of production itself, because the latter is not concerned with the realisation of both the re-produced value, and the surplus value. Crisis can only appear in the process of circulation, which in essence is at the same time the process of reproduction.

Here it must further be noted that we must examine the process of circulation or process of reproduction *before* examining already existing capital—capital and profit—as we have to show not only how capital produces, but how capital is produced. The actual movement, however, starts from the capital in hand—that is, the actual movement that is based on developed capitalist production, beginning out of itself and presupposing itself. The reproduction process and the occasions of crises which are further developed in it are therefore not fully handled under this heading, and require further elaboration in the chapter on "Capital and Profit".

The circulation process as a whole or the whole process of

reproduction of capital is the unity of its production phase with its circulation phase, a process which runs through both those processes as its phases. Therein lies a further developed possibility or abstract form of crisis. The economists who deny crises therefore insist only on the unity of these two phases. If they were only separate without being a unity, then no forcible restoration of their unity would be possible, no crisis. If they were only a unity without being separate, then no forcible separation would be possible, which again is crisis. It is the forcible restoration of unity between independent phases, and the forcible separation from each other of processes which in essence are one.

Theories of Surplus Value, pp.
376-388

D. GENERAL AND PARTIAL OVERPRODUCTION

Summary: Ricardo, while affirming the possibility that single commodities may be overproduced, denies that *all* goods may be in overproduction at the same time. With the exception of money, this is nonsense for these reasons: Preceding a crisis, the general level of prices usually rises. Consequently, all prices fall during the crash. Although at low prices the market will absorb all goods, it will do so only at ruinous prices. Also, all that is required for a crisis to develop is that the principal articles of trade be overproduced.

Ricardo asserts that the reason for partial overproduction is a satiety of demand for a particular product or products. Actually, human needs are unlimited. The satiety of the demand for one product simply leads to the demand for another. In that sense there can never be absolute overproduction. One cannot even explain partial overproduction on the ground of satiety—let alone general overproduction.

The real problem is this: Consumers and producers are different people, performing different economic functions in capitalist production. Consumers buy only finished goods. They do not buy means of production (raw materials, etc.). They do not buy the bulk of the products which they produce. As a matter of fact, workers produce surplus value. They can consume only their subsistence. Since they produce more than their needs, the alleged unity of consumption and production can be seen to be false.

Ricardo says that the limit to demand is production and the limit to production is capital. This is true in that no more can be consumed than is produced. But what is true about Ricardo's statement is not what he intended. What is true is that production takes place without regard to consumption, that is, the limits of the market. This follows from the fact that capitalists strive for the appropriation of the greatest amount of surplus labor. Thus the mass of commodities is increased by the operation of the process of capitalist accumulation.

In the example of the overproduction of cotton goods as a consequence of the inability of consumers to purchase the quantities available, not only are workers directly employed in that industry affected, but workers (and producers) in other industries connected with the cotton-goods industry are equally adversely affected.

It is easy to understand how the overproduction of a few leading articles of consumption can bring in its train a more or less general overproduction. But it in no way explains how overproduction of the original articles (that is, cotton goods) can arise in the first place.

---

*

In Chapter XXI Ricardo says:

Too much of a *particular* commodity may be produced, of which there may be such a glut in the market as not to repay the capital expended on it; but this cannot be the case with respect to *all* commodities (p. 194).

That only *particular* but not *all* kinds of commodities can constitute a glut in the market, and that consequently overproduction can always only be partial, is a paltry evasion. In the first place, if the mere nature of a commodity is considered, there is nothing in it which would prevent *all* commodities being in over supply on the market and therefore all falling below their price. What is involved here is precisely the moment of crisis. In fact, all commodities [may be in over supply] except *money*. The necessity for *the* commodity to transform itself into money means only that the necessity exists for *all* commodities. And inasmuch as there is a difficulty in a single commodity making this metamorphosis, the difficulty can exist for all commodities. The general nature of the metamorphosis of commodities—which includes the separation of purchase and sale as well as their unity—instead of excluding the *possibility* of a general glut, is rather *the* possibility of a general glut.

Moreover, in the background of Ricardo's arguments and similar arguments put forward by others there is in fact not only the relation of purchase and sale, but also that of demand and supply, which we have to consider only when we investigate the competition of capitals. Just as Mill says that purchase is sale, etc., so is demand supply and supply demand; but they are equally separate, and can assume independence of each other. At a given moment the supply of all commodities may be greater than the demand for all commodities, because the demand for the general commodity, money, exchange value, is greater than the demand for all particular commodities; in other words, because the compulsion for the commodity to take the form of money, to realise its exchange value, is greater than the compulsion for the commodity to be reconverted into use value. If the relation between demand and supply is conceived in a wider and more concrete way, there enters into it the relation between production and consumption. Here again there must be borne in mind the *unity* of these two phases, which exists in their nature and forcibly asserts itself precisely in crisis, against the equally existent, and for bourgeois production even characteristic, separation and opposition of the two.

As for the antithesis between partial and universal over-production—that is, in so far as the former is emphasised only as a means of getting rid of the latter—the following further points may be noted:

First: A general rise of prices in all articles of capitalist production usually precedes a crisis. Consequently they all have a share in the following crash, and all constitute an overloading of the market at the prices which they had before the crash. The market can absorb a mass of commodities at falling prices, prices that have fallen below their prices of production, which it could not absorb at their former market prices. The excess of commodities is always relative, that is, it is an excess àt certain prices. The prices at which the commodities are then absorbed are ruinous for the producer or merchant.

Secondly:

For a crisis (and therefore also overproduction) to be general, it is sufficient for it to grip the principal articles of trade.

Let us examine more closely how Ricardo tries to argue away the possibility of a general glut of the market:

Too much of a particular commodity may be produced, of which there may be such a glut in the market as not to repay the capital expended on it; but this cannot be the case with respect to all commodities; the demand for corn is limited by the mouths which are to eat it, for shoes and coats by the persons who are to wear them; but though a community, or a part of a community, may have as much corn, and as many hats and shoes as it is able, or may wish to consume, the same cannot be said of every commodity produced by nature or by art. Some would consume more wine if they had the ability to procure it. Others, having enough of wine, would wish to increase the quantity or improve the quality of their furniture. Others might wish to ornament their grounds, or to en-large their houses. The wish to do all or some of these is implanted in every man's breast; nothing is required but the means, and nothing can afford the means but an increase of production (p. 194).

Can there be a more childish line of reasoning? It runs like this. More may be produced of a particular commodity than can be consumed. But that cannot be true of *all* commodities at the same time. Because the needs which are satisfied through commodities have no limits and all these needs are not satisfied at the same time. On the contrary. The satisfaction of one need makes another so to speak latent. Therefore nothing is required but the means to satisfy these needs, and these means can only be provided through an increase of production. Therefore no general overproduction is possible.

What is the relevance of all this? In times of overproduction a great part of the nation (especially the working class) is less than ever supplied with grain, shoes, etc., to say nothing of wine and furniture. If overproduction could only occur after all members of the nation had satisfied even their most essential needs, in the history of bourgeois society up to the present not only no general overproduction, but even no partial overproduction, could have occurred. If for example the market is over-supplied with shoes or calico or wines or colonial products, does this mean that perhaps even only two-thirds of the nation have over-satisfied their need for shoes, calico, etc.? What in any case has overproduction to do with absolute needs? It is only needs with capacity to pay that count. What is in question is not absolute overproduction—overproduction in itself, in relation to the absolute need or the desire to possess commodities. In this sense neither partial nor general overproduction exists. And [in this sense] they are not in any kind of contradiction with each other.

But, Ricardo may say, when there are numbers of people who need shoes and calico, why do they not acquire the means to buy them by producing something with which they can buy shoes and calico? Would it not be even simpler to say: why do they not produce shoes and calico for themselves? And what is even more strange in overproduction is that the actual producers of the very commodities which overfill the market —the workers—suffer from lack of them. In this case it cannot be said that they should produce the things in order to get them, for they have produced them, and yet they have not got them. Nor can it be said that the particular commodities are in glut on the market because no need for them exists. If therefore even *partial* overproduction is not to be explained by the fact that the commodities in excess on the market exceed the need for them, in the same way *universal* overproduction cannot be explained away by the fact that needs, unsatisfied needs, exist for many of the commodities which are on the market.

Let us keep to the cotton weaver by way of example. So long as reproduction continued without a check—therefore also the phase of this reproduction in which the product, the cotton, existing as a commodity, a saleable commodity, is reconverted into money at its value—for so long also, shall we say, the workers who produce the cotton consumed a portion of it; and with extended reproduction—that is, accumulation— they absorbed progressively more of it, or more workers too were employed in the production of the cotton, who also were in part consumers of it.

So long as the weaver reproduces and accumulates, his workers also buy a part of his product; they expend a part of their wages on cotton. Because he produces, they have the means to buy a part of his product, and thus in part provide him with the means of selling it. The worker can only buy— represent demand for—commodities which enter into individual consumption, as he does not himself make a profit from his labour, and does not himself possess the conditions for setting it to work—the means of labour and material of labour.

Where production is developed in capitalist form, this therefore already excludes the greatest part of the producers, the workers themselves, from being consumers, buyers, of means of production. They buy no raw material and no means of labour; they buy only means of subsistence, commodities which enter directly into individual consumption. Consequently there is nothing more ridiculous than to speak of the identity of producers and consumers, since for an extraordinarily great number of branches of production—all those not producing articles for direct consumption—the mass of those engaged in production are absolutely excluded from the purchase of their own products. They are never directly consumers or buyers of this great part of their own products, although they pay a part of the value of these products in the consumption articles which they buy. This also shows the ambiguity of the word consumer and the error of identifying it with the word buyer. Industrially, it is precisely the workers who consume the machinery and raw material, who use it up in the labour process. But they do not use it up for themselves, and consequently they are not buyers of it. For them they are not use values, not commodities, but objective conditions of a process of which they themselves are the subjective conditions.

It may however be said that their employer represents them in the purchase of means of labour and materials of labour. But he represents them under different conditions from those in which they would represent themselves; that is, on the market. He has to sell a mass of commodities embodying surplus value, unpaid labour. They would have to sell only a mass of commodities which reproduced the value advanced in production—the value of the means of labour, the material of labour and the wages. He therefore has need of a wider market than they would require.

They are therefore producers, without being consumers—

even when there is no interruption in the process of reproduction—in respect of all the articles which have to be consumed not individually but industrially.

So nothing is more preposterous as a means of denying crises than the assertion that consumers (buyers) and producers (sellers) are identical in capitalist production. They are completely separate. In so far as the reproduction process takes place, this identity can be asserted for only one out of every three thousand producers, that is to say, for the capitalist. It is just as false the other way round—that the consumers are producers. The landowner does not produce rent, and yet he consumes. The position is the same with the whole of money capital.

The apologetic phrases used to deny crises are important from this aspect—that they always prove the opposite of what they set out to prove. In order to deny crises, they assert unity where there is opposition and contradiction. This is important in so far as it can be said: they prove that, if the contradictions which they day-dream out of existence in fact did not exist, then too no crises would exist. But in fact crisis exists, because those contradictions exist. Every reason which they advance against crisis is a contradiction day-dreamed away—therefore a real contradiction, therefore a cause of crisis. The desire to day-dream contradictions out of the way is at the same time the expression of contradictions that are really present, but which they vainly desire *should* not exist.

What the workers in fact produce is surplus value. So long as they produce it, they are able to consume. As soon as [its production] ceases, their consumption ceases, because their production ceases. But it is in no way true that they are able to consume because they produce an equivalent for their consumption. Rather is it the case that the very moment they have produced such an equivalent, their consumption ceases, they have no equivalent to consume. Either their labour is dispensed with or cut down, or in any case their wages lowered. In the latter case—when the level of production remains the same—they do not consume any equivalent for their production. But then they lack the means of subsistence, not because they do not produce enough, but because they get too little of their product for themselves.

If therefore the relations are reduced to that simply of consumer and producer, the fact is lost sight of that the producing wage-labour and the producing capitalist are two producers of a very different kind, even if we leave out of account the consumers who produce nothing at all. Once again the antagonism is denied by abstracting from an antagonism that is actually present in production. The mere relationship between wage-labourer and capitalist involves:

(1) That the greatest part of the producers (the workers) are non-consumers (non-buyers) of a very considerable part of their product, namely, of the means of labour and the material of labour.

(2) That the greatest part of the producers, the workers, can only consume an equivalent for their product so long as they produce more than this equivalent—surplus value or surplus product. They must always be *over-producers,* must always produce over and above their needs, in order to be able to be consumers or buyers within the limits of their needs.

With this class of producers, therefore, the unity between production and consumption is in any case *prima facie* false.

When Ricardo says that the only limit of demand is production itself, and this is limited by capital, this means in fact, when stripped of the false assumptions, nothing more than that capitalist production finds its measure only in capital—the concept of capital including here also the labour power incorporated in the capital (bought by it) as one of its conditions of production. Here the question arises whether capital as such is also the limit for consumption. In any case this is true negatively; that is to say, no more can be consumed than is produced. But the question is whether this is the positive limit, whether as much can and must be consumed—on the basis of capitalist production—as is produced. What Ricardo says, correctly analysed, means the direct opposite of what he is trying to say—namely, that production takes place without regard to the existing limits of consumption, but is limited only by capital itself. And this, to be sure, is characteristic of this mode of production. . . .

In the analysis of the production process we saw that the whole striving of capitalistic production is directed towards the appropriation of the greatest possible amount of surplus labour, that is, to materialise the greatest possible amount of immediate labour time with the given capital. This may be done through the prolongation of the labour time, or reduction of the necessary labour time, development of the productive power of labour, the use of cooperation, division of labour, machinery, etc., in short, production on a higher level, that is, mass production. Production without regard to the limits of the market is therefore in the nature of capitalist production. . . .

The stagnation in the market, which is over-supplied with cottons, disturbs reproduction for the weaver. This disturbance first affects his workers. The latter therefore are now to a smaller extent, or not at all, consumers of his commodity—cotton—and of other commodities which enter into their consumption. They have, it is true, a need for cottons, but they cannot buy them because they have not the means to do so, and they have not the means because they cannot continue to produce, and they cannot continue to produce because too much has been produced, too many cotton goods are in store on the market. Neither Ricardo's advice "to enlarge their production", nor his alternative, "to produce something else", can help them. They now constitute a part of the temporary over-production, overproduction of workers, in this case of cotton producers, because there is an overproduction of cotton goods on the market.

But apart from the workers employed directly by the capital invested in cotton weaving, numbers of other producers are affected by this check in the reproduction of cotton: spinners, cotton growers, producers of spindles and looms, of iron, coal, and so on. All these would be similarly checked in their repro-duction, as the reproduction of cotton goods is the condition for their own reproduction. This would take place, even if they had not overproduced in their own spheres, that is, had not produced beyond the limit set by and justified by the cotton industry when it was going swimmingly. All these industries have only this in common: that they consume their revenue (wages and profit, in so far as the latter is consumed as revenue and not accumulated) not in the form of their own product, but in the product of the spheres which produce articles of consumption, of which cotton is one. So the consumption and the demand for cotton falls, precisely because there is too much of it on the market. But so also does that of all other com-modities on which, as articles of consumption, the revenue of these indirect producers of cotton cloth is spent. The means with which they can buy cotton cloth and other articles of con-sumption become restricted and contract, because there is too much cotton on the market. This affects also other commodities (articles of consumption). They are now suddenly in *relative* overproduction, because the means to buy them, and therewith the demand for them, have contracted. Even if there has been no overproduction in these spheres, now they are overpro-ducing.

But if it is not only cotton, but also linen, silk and woollen goods in which overproduction has taken place, it can be understood how overproduction in these few but leading articles brings about a more or less general (*relative*) overproduction over the whole market. On the one hand a superfluity of all things needed for reproduction, and a superfluity of all kinds of unsold commodities on the market. On the other hand bankrupt capitalists and hungry workers, destitute of everything.

Nevertheless, this argument has two sides to it. If it is easy to understand how overproduction in a few leading articles of consumption must bring in its train a more or less general overproduction—the manifestation of the former—this in no way explains how overproduction of those articles can arise. For the phenomenon of general overproduction is brought about by the interdependence not only of the worker directly employed in these industries, but of all branches of industry which produce the earlier elements of their products, their constant capital in different phases. For the latter branches of industry, overproduction is an effect. But whence comes it in the former? For the latter go on producing so long as the former continue to produce, and along with this continued production a general growth of revenue, and therefore of their own consumption, seems assured.

Theories of Surplus Value, pp. 391-402

E. EXPANSION OF PRODUCTION AND EXPANSION OF THE MARKET

Summary: In answering the question of the expansion of production and the expansion of the market, it is useful to point to two reasons why the production of a good continuously expands. (1) Capital invested is expanding, and (2) it is constantly used more productively. Crises arise because the market expands more slowly than productive capacity.

Ricardo is consistent in denying the necessity for an expansion in the market to correspond to an expansion of production since all available capital can be productively used within a country. Adam Smith, who does not see crises of overproduction, does see the development of foreign markets as being caused by the relative overproduction of internal markets. Ricardo is consistent in chiding him for it.

Overproduction is a misleading word, if one means more products are produced than there is need for. It is only in capitalist modes of production that overproduction occurs. In reality there is constant underproduction in terms of the *needs of producers*. The limit of production is capitalist profit. It is impossible for Ricardo to admit that the bourgeois mode of production creates its own barrier, which barrier comes to the surface in the form of crises.

Smith saw, and Ricardo approves of the view, that production is mainly devoted to satisfying the needs (use values) of producers (labor) for the necessities of life, not for luxuries. The necessities of life provide a limitless demand for output. This was even more true of ancient societies, where the wealthy amassed fortunes, paid the working class or slaves on a subsistence basis, and used the rest unproductively (not for capital accumulation) in expenditures for works of art and in general overconsumption. The ancients did not know how to use their surplus for capitalist accumulation.

Ricardo could not see that bourgeois production is not production pure and simple. He does not realize that when everyone works for himself, and particular labor takes the form of abstract labor, that there is constant disharmony of the spheres of production which must be neutralized. To him, whatever disharmony there is, is neutralized by competition, and *general* overproduction is impossible.

Bourgeois economists argue as follows: There is no universal overproduction (an equal degree of overproduction everywhere) because universal overproduction would be the equivalent of proportional overproduction, which is simply a greater than usual rate of development of productive capacity in all spheres.

Let us examine this "miserable sophistry." If iron is overproduced, it cannot be said that coal is overproduced, because to overproduce iron involves a similar overproduction of coal. One cannot speak of overproduction of the raw materials which enter into the production of goods which have been overproduced.

Yet it is possible, even probable, that coal could be overproduced —beyond the needs of the iron industry—because the production schedule of the coal (or any other) industry is determined by the rate at which other (non-iron) coal-using industries are expanding, rather than by the immediate demand. The calculation of coal requirements may be overshot. It is therefore nonsense to say (as bourgeois economists do) that overproduction in the coal industry is due to underproduction elsewhere.

When the problem is given an international setting, as Say and others have done, it is said that England has not overproduced, but that Italy has underproduced. If Italy had had industries complementary to English industries, so that they could pay in commodities useful to English capital-goods industry requirements, a Utopian conception, there would be no overproduction. This simply says that if supply and demand are equal, there is no overproduction. Or, it means that if production were proportionate, there would be no overproduction. So also in international trade, if all countries possess equal capacities for production, and their economies are complementary, no overproduction exists. Put another way, overproduction occurs only because the preceding conditions are not fulfilled.

Or in even more abstract form: There would be no overproduction at one point if there were an equal degree of overproduction everywhere. "But capital is not large enough to overproduce in this universal way, and consequently overproduction occurs."

"Let us examine this fantasy still more closely":

Bourgeois economists admit the possibility of overproduction in each particular branch of production. What prevents a general glut is that commodities exchange against commodities. The whole subterfuge rests upon the abstraction from money. The separation of production from sale implied by the use of money comprises the *possibility* of interruptions. For example, as money is reconverted into goods used for production (use values), it is essential that these new values be purchased at the same price (or, better, cheaper). But raw-material prices may rise above their old values if (1) the demand for them increases very rapidly because constant capital has been produced at a disproportionate rate, making raw materials relatively scarce; (2) due to a poor harvest, the prices of subsistence goods rise rapidly (there are also other reasons why this could occur); (3) overproduction of capital is admitted while overproduction of commodities is denied. But capital includes those commodities which are not produced for consumption but for reproduction; *i.e.,* for making more money. Overproduction simply means too much has been produced for accumulation—not enough for consumption.

Some economists argue this way, although Ricardo does not. How do these economists then explain overproduction of commodities? They say that certain articles of consumption have been underproduced and that production has not been sufficiently diversified. Of course, this cannot refer to industrial consumption, since an overproduction in linen increases the demand for yarn, and so on. Therefore, the reference must be to personal consumption—too much linen, too few oranges. So the statement that there is too much capital simply means that too little is consumed or can be consumed as revenue.

Why does the linen producer exhort the corn producer to consume more linen and vice versa? Why does not each producer consume more (personally)? Each will admit that, apart from the limit of his own requirements, what prevents him from consuming more of his own production is the need to capitalize it—to accumulate. "But collectively they will not admit it."

Thus far we have not discussed crises which arise because, due to innovation, goods are continually being offered on the market at depreciated prices.

However, in general crises, all contradictions of bourgeois production break through collectively; in particular crises they appear in a scattered, isolated, and one-sided form.

Overproduction is a consequence of the law of the production of capital, which requires continuous accumulation of the means of production, without regard to the limit of the market or social needs, and backed by the ability to pay. Capitalists must accumulate while the mass of producers (workers) must be restricted in their consumption of subsistence ("the average level of needs") and as a consequence "the basis of capitalist production must remain restricted."

*

This question may perhaps be answered by pointing to the constantly expanding production, which expands each year for two reasons: first, because the capital invested in production is constantly growing, and secondly, because it is constantly used more productively; in the course of reproduction and accumulation there is a constant aggregation of small improvements which eventually alter the whole level of production. There is a piling up of improvements, an accumulating development of productive powers. If anyone likes to reply that the constantly expanding production requires a constantly expanding market, and that production expands more rapidly than the market, this is only putting in another way the phenomenon that has to be explained—in its real form, instead of an abstract form. The market expands more slowly than production; or in the cycle through which capital passes in its reproduction—a cycle in which there is not merely reproduction, but reproduction on an extended scale; it describes not a circle, but a spiral—a moment comes when the market manifests itself as too narrow for production. This is at the close of the cycle. This however merely means: the market is overfilled. Overproduction is manifest. Had the extension of the market kept pace with the extension of production, there would be no glut of the market, no overproduction.

However, the mere admission that the market must expand along with production is also from another aspect one more admission of the possibility of overproduction, since the market is limited externally in the geographical sense, the internal market is limited as compared with a market that is both internal and external, the latter again as compared with the world market—which however at each moment of time is in turn limited, [even though] in itself capable of extension. Consequently the admission that the market must expand if overproduction is not to occur, is also an admission that overproduction can occur. For since market and production are two independent factors, it is therefore possible that the expansion of one may not correspond with the expansion of the other, that the limits of the market may not be extended rapidly enough for production, or that new markets—new extensions of the market—may be rapidly overtaken by production, so that the expanded market now appears just as much a barrier as the narrower one did previously.

Ricardo is therefore consistent in denying the necessity for *an expansion of the market* to correspond with an expansion of production and growth of capital: all capital available in a country can also be advantageously employed in that country. He therefore polemises against Adam Smith, who on the one hand put forward *his* (Ricardo's) view and, with his usual rational instinct, also contradicted it. Adam Smith too does not recognise the phenomenon of overproduction, crises resulting from overproduction. What he sees are mere credit and money crises, which come to the surface of their own accord along with the credit and banking system. In fact he sees in the accumulation of capital an unqualified increase in the total wealth and well-being of the nation. On the other hand he conceives the development of the internal market into the foreign, colonial and world market, as in itself evidence of what can be called a relative overproduction in the internal market. . . .

The word *overproduction* in itself leads to error. So long as the most urgent needs of a great part of society are not satisfied, or *only* its most immediate needs, there can naturally be absolutely no talk of an *overproduction of products*—in the sense that the mass of products would be excessive in relation to the need for them. What must be said is the opposite: that in this sense, on the basis of capitalistic production, there is constant *underproduction.* The limit of production is the *capitalist's profit,* and not at all the *need of the producers.* But overproduction of *products* and overproduction of *commodities* are two completely different things. If Ricardo thinks that the form *commodity* makes no difference to the product, and further, that the *circulation of commodities* is only formally different from barter, that in this circulation exchange value is only a form, without significance, of the exchange of things, and that therefore money is a merely formal means of circulation, this is in fact the outcome of his presupposition that the bourgeois mode of production is the absolute mode of production, and consequently is a mode of production without any precise specific character, that what is specific in it is only formal. It is therefore not possible for him to admit that the bourgeois mode of production contains within itself a barrier to the free development of the productive forces, a barrier which comes to the surface in crises, and incidentally in *overproduction*—the basic phenomenon in crises.

Ricardo saw, from the passages of Adam Smith which he quotes, approves and therefore repeats, that the limitless "desire" for all kinds of use value is constantly satisfied, on the basis of a state of things in which the mass of producers remains more or less restricted to necessities, in which this very considerable mass of producers therefore remains more or less excluded from the consumption of wealth—in so far as wealth oversteps the circle of the necessary means of subsistence.

Incidentally, this is also the case, and to a still higher degree, in the ancient form of production based on slavery. But the ancients never even thought of transforming the surplus product into capital. At least, only to a small extent. The widespread occurrence among them of the amassing of treasure in the narrow sense shows how much surplus product lay completely idle. They converted a great part of the surplus product into unproductive expenditure on works of art, religious monuments and public works. Still less was their production directed to the unfettering and development of the material forces of production —division of labour, machinery, use of natural forces and science in private production. Broadly speaking they never got beyond handicraft labour. The wealth which they produced for private consumption was consequently relatively small, and only seems large because it was amassed in the hands of a few people, who, incidentally, did not know what to do with it. If consequently there was no *overproduction* among the ancients, there was nevertheless *overconsumption* on the part of the rich, which in the final periods of Rome and Greece broke out into insane extravagance. The few trading peoples among them lived partly at the expense of all these essentially poor nations. It is the absolute development of the productive forces, and hence mass production, with the mass of producers confined within the circle of the necessary means of subsistence on the one hand, and on the other hand the barrier set by the capitalists' profit, which forms the basis of modern overproduction.

All the difficulties which Ricardo and others raise against overproduction, etc., rest on the fact that they either look on bourgeois production as a mode of production in which no distinction exists between purchase and sale—direct barter— or they regard it as *social* production, of such a kind that society distributes its means of production and productive forces as if according to a plan, in the degree and measure in which they are necessary for the satisfaction of its various needs; so that to each sphere of production falls the quota of social capital required for the satisfaction of the need to which it corresponds. This fiction arises entirely from the inability to grasp the specific form of bourgeois production; and this inability in turn from the obsession that bourgeois production is production pure and simple. Just like a man who believes in a particular religion and sees in it religion pure and simple, with only *false* religions outside it.

On the contrary, it would be much more pertinent to ask: on the basis of capitalist production, in which everyone works for himself, and particular labour must at the same time appear as its opposite, abstract general labour, and in this form as social labour—how can the necessary balance and interdependence of the various spheres of production, their dimensions and the proportions between them, be possible except through the constant neutralisation of a constant disharmony? This moreover is admitted when adjustments through competition are spoken of; for these adjustments always presuppose that there is something to be adjusted, and harmony therefore is always only a result of the movement which neutralises the existing disharmony. For this reason, too, Ricardo admits the glut of the market for particular commodities; and then a general simultaneous glut in the market is said to be *impossible*. Consequently the impossibility of overproduction for any particular sphere of production is not denied. What is said to be [impossible] is the *simultaneity* of this phenomenon for all spheres of production, and hence general overproduction. This last phrase is always to be taken *cum grano salis*, for in times of general overproduction the overproduction in some spheres is always only the *result*, the *consequence*, of overproduction in the leading articles of commerce; [in these it is] always only *relative*, overproduction because overproduction exists in other spheres. Apologetics twists this precisely into its opposite. Overproduction in the leading articles of commerce, in which alone active overproduction manifests itself—these are in general articles which can only be produced in the mass and on a factory scale, also in agriculture—[is supposed only to exist] because overproduction exists in the articles in which relative or

passive overproduction appears. According to this idea overproduction only exists because overproduction is not universal.
The relativity of overproduction—that actual overproduction in
some spheres leads to it in others—is expressed in this way:
There is no universal overproduction, because if overproduction
were universal, all spheres of production would retain the same
relation to one another; therefore universal overproduction is
equivalent to proportional production, which excludes overproduction. And this is supposed to be an argument against overproduction. That is to say, on the ground that universal
overproduction in the absolute sense would not be overproduction, but only a greater than usual development of productive
power in all spheres of production, it is said that actual overproduction, which is precisely not this non-existent, self-abrogat-
ing overproduction, does not exist—although it only exists
because it is not this. If this miserable sophistry is more closely
examined, we get the following result. Overproduction takes
place, say, in iron, cotton goods, linen, silk, cloth, etc. It cannot
then be said, for example, that too little coal has been produced
and that therefore this overproduction has occurred; for the
overproduction of iron, etc., involves an exactly similar overproduction of coal, just as an overproduction of woven cloth
involves that of yarn. (Overproduction of yarn as compared
with cloth, iron as against machinery, etc., would be possible.
This would always be a relative overproduction of constant
capital.) There can therefore be no question of the overproduction of articles whose overproduction is implied because they
enter as elements, raw materials, auxiliary materials or means of
labour into the articles the positive overproduction of which is
precisely the fact to be explained (the "particular commodity
of which too much has been produced, of which there may be
such a glut in the market as not to repay the capital expended
on it"). The discussion concerns other articles which directly

belong to other spheres of production, and can neither be sub-
sumed under the leading articles of commerce which, according
to the assumption, have been overproduced; nor do they belong
to spheres in which, because they form the intermediate product
for the leading articles of commerce, production must have
advanced at least as much as in the final phases of the product
—although there is no reason why they themselves should not
have gone still further ahead, and thus have brought about an
overproduction within the other overproduction. For example,
although sufficient coal must have been produced in order to
keep going all the industries into which coal enters as a necessary condition of production, and therefore the overproduction
of coal is implied in the overproduction of iron, yarn, etc. (the
coal having been produced only in proportion to the production
of iron and yarn), it is *also* possible that more coal was produced than even the overproduction in iron, yarn, etc., required.
This is not only possible, but very probable. For the production
of coal and yarn and of those other spheres of production which
produce only the conditions and earlier phases of the product
to be completed in another sphere, is not governed by the immediate demand, by the immediate production or reproduction,
but by the *degree, measure, proportion* in which these are expanding. And it is self-evident that in this calculation the goal
may be overshot. Nevertheless [overproduction is said to origi-
nate from the fact that] there has not been enough produced,
there has been underproduction, of other articles, such as for
example pianofortes, precious stones, and so forth. The absurdity of this statement emerges all the more clearly when it is
given an international setting, as Say and others after him have
done. Thus, for example, England has not overproduced, but
Italy has underproduced. If Italy, firstly, had had capital enough
to replace the English capital that had been exported to Italy
in the form of commodities; and secondly had so invested this

capital that it produced the specific articles which English capital needed (partly to replace itself and partly to replace the revenue flowing from it) there would have been no overproduction. That is, there would not have existed the fact of actual—in relation to the *actual* production in Italy—existing overproduction in England, but only the fact of *imaginary underproduction in Italy*—imaginary, because it presupposes a capital in Italy and a development of the productive forces which did not exist there; and secondly because it makes the same utopian presupposition that this *non*-existing capital in Italy had been applied exactly as required in order that the English supplies and Italian demand, English and Italian production, should be complementary to each other. This means in other words nothing [but]: No overproduction would occur if demand and supply corresponded to each other; if capital were distributed in such proportions in all spheres of production that the production of one article involved the consumption of the other and thus its own consumption. There would be no overproduction, if there were no overproduction. But as capitalistic production is only able to let itself go without restraint in certain spheres, in definite conditions, no capitalistic production at all would be possible if it had to develop in all spheres *simultaneously* and *in equal degree*. Because in these spheres absolute overproduction takes place, relative overproduction takes place also in the spheres where there has not been overproduction. This explanation of overproduction in one direction by underproduction in another means nothing [but]: If production were proportionate, there would be no overproduction. Ditto, if demand and supply corresponded to each other. Ditto, if all spheres comprised equal opportunities of capitalistic production and its expansion—division of labour, machinery, export to distant markets, production on a mass scale, etc. Or in still more abstract form: if all countries which trade with one another possessed an equal capacity for production, and indeed for different and complementary production. That is to say: overproduction takes place, because all these pious wishes are not fulfilled. Or in even more abstract form: there would be no overproduction at one point if overproduction took place at all points in equal degree. But capital is not large enough to overproduce in this universal way, and consequently universal overproduction occurs.

Let us examine this fantasy still more closely:

It is admitted that there can be overproduction in each *particular branch of production.* The one circumstance that might prevent overproduction in *all* at the same time is, so it is alleged, that commodity exchanges against commodity, that is to say, they take refuge in the conditions of barter which they assume. But this way of escape is cut off by the very fact that trade in commodities is not barter, and therefore the seller of a commodity is not necessarily at the same time the purchaser of another. This whole subterfuge therefore rests on abstracting from *money,* and abstracting from the fact that what is in question is not the exchange of products but the circulation of commodities, for which the separation of purchase and sale is essential.

The circulation of capital in itself comprises *possibilities* of interruptions. For example, in the reconversion of money into its conditions of production the point is not only to transform money back again into the same use values (in kind), but it is essential for the repetition of the process of reproduction that these use values are to be had at their old value (lower is naturally still better). The very significant part of these elements of reproduction which consists of raw materials can however rise in price for two reasons: *first* if the instruments of production increase in quicker proportion than the raw materials can be provided within a definite period of time. *Secondly,* as a result of the variable character of harvests. That is why weather conditions, as Tooke rightly observes, play such an important role in modern industry. That is also true of the means of subsistence in relation to wages. The reconversion from money into commodity can therefore come up against difficulties and bring about possibilities of crisis, just as well as the conversion of commodity into money. In so far as simple circulation is considered—not the circulation of capital—this difficulty does not arise.

There are besides a number of other factors, conditions and possibilities of crisis which can only be considered when examining the concrete relations, in particular of the competition of capitals and of credit.

The overproduction of commodities is denied, though the overproduction of capital is admitted. But capital itself consists of commodities, or in so far as it consists of money it must be reconverted into commodities of one kind or another in order to be able to function as capital. What then does overproduction of capital mean? Overproduction of quantities of value destined to produce surplus value, or, if considered in their material content, overproduction of commodities destined for reproduction—that is, reproduction on too large a scale, which is the same thing as overproduction pure and simple. Defined more exactly, this in turn means nothing but that too much has been produced for the purpose of enrichment, or that too large a part of the product has been destined, not for consumption as revenue, but for making more money, for accumulation; not to satisfy the personal requirements of its possessor, but to secure for him abstract social riches, money and more power over the labour of others—capital—or to increase the power in his hands. This is what some say. Ricardo denies it. How then do the others explain the overproduction of commodities? That production is not sufficiently widely diversified, that certain

articles of consumption have not been produced in sufficiently
great quantities. It is clear that this cannot refer to industrial
consumption; for the manufacturer who overproduces in linen
thereby of necessity increases his demand for yarn, machinery,
labour, etc. Therefore the reference must be to personal consumption. Too much linen has been produced, but perhaps too
few oranges. Previously money was denied, for the purpose of
[denying] the separation between purchase and sale. Here,
capital is denied, in order to transform the capitalists into people
who carry out the simple operation C-M-C, and for individual
consumption, not as capitalists with the aim of getting richer,
with the aim of reconverting a part of the surplus value into
capital. But the statement that there is *too much capital* in fact
means nothing but that too little is consumed, and in the given
conditions can be consumed, as *revenue* (Sismondi). Why then
does the producer of linen demand of the producer of corn that
he consume more linen, or the latter demand of the former
that he consume more corn? Why does the man who deals in
linen not himself realise a larger part of his revenue, his surplus
value, in linen, and the farmer in corn? Each of them individually will admit that, apart from the limit to his requirements,
what prevents him from doing this is his need to capitalise it.
But collectively they will not admit it.

In this treatment we have completely abstracted from that
element of crises which arises from the fact that commodities
are reproduced more cheaply than they have been produced.
Hence depreciation of the commodities on the market.

In the general crises on the world market, all the contradictions of bourgeois production break through collectively; in
particular crises (particular as to content and in extent) they
appear only in a scattered, isolated and one-sided form.

Overproduction is specifically conditioned by the general law
of the production of capital: production is in accordance with

the productive forces, that is, with the possibility that the given quantity of capital has of exploiting the maximum quantity of labour, without regard to the actual limits of the market, the needs backed by the ability to pay; and this takes place through the constant expansion of reproduction and accumulation, and therefore the constant reconversion of revenue into capital; while on the other hand the mass of producers remain restricted to the average level of needs, and on the basis of capitalist production must remain so restricted.

Theories of Surplus Value, pp. 402-414

Part **III** *The Nature of a Communist Society*

A.

VALUE, RENT, AND MONEY IN A COMMUNIST SOCIETY

Summary: When production is under the control of a planned society, the market prices of goods will be equal to their value. Goods will be sold according to the social labor employed in their production.

*

. . . (Only when production will be under the conscious and prearranged control of society, will society establish a direct relation between the quantity of social labor time employed in the production of definite articles and the quantity of the demand of society for them.) The commodities must then be sold below their market-value, and a portion of them may even become unsaleable. The opposite takes place, if the quantity of social labor employed in the production of a certain kind of commodities is too small to meet the social demand for them. But if the quantity of social labor spent in the production of a certain article corresponds to the social demand for it, so that the quantity produced is that which is the ordinary on that scale of production and for that same demand, then the article is sold at its market-value. The exchange, or sale, of commodities at their value is the rational way, the natural law of their equilibrium.

III, p. 221

Summary: In a capitalist society, due to differential rent, the market prices of products of the soil are above their values (labor time embodied in their production). This surplus of price over value, which under capitalism goes to the landlord, would in a socialist society go to the state. While price would remain the same in both cases, "it is wrong to say that the value of the products would remain the same. . . ."

*

The general rule in differential rent is that the market-value always stands above the total price of production of the mass of products. For instance, take Table I. The ten quarters of the total product are sold at 600 shillings, because the market price is determined by the price of production of A, which amounts to 60 shillings per quarter. But the actual price of production is:

A 1 qr. = 60 sh.		1 qr. = 60 sh.
B 2 qrs. = 60 sh.		1 qr. = 30 sh.
C 3 qrs. = 60 sh.		1 qr. = 20 sh.
D 4 qrs. = 60 sh.		1 qr. = 15 sh.
10 qrs. = 240 sh.	Average	1 qr. = 24 sh.

The actual price of production of these 10 quarters is 240 shillings. But they are sold at 600 shillings, 250% too dear. The actual average price for 1 quarter is 24 shillings; the market price is 60 shillings, also 250% too dear.

This is a determination by the market-value, which is enforced on the basis of capitalist production by means of competition; it creates a false social value. This arises from the law of the market-value, to which the products of the soil are subject. The determination of the market-value of the products, including the products of the soil, is a social act, although performed by society unconsciously and unintentionally. It rests necessarily upon the exchange-value of the product, not upon the soil and its differences in fertility.

If we imagine that the capitalistic form of society is abolished and society is organized as a conscious and systematic association, then those 10 quarters represent a quantity of independent labor, which is equal to that contained in 240 shillings. In that case society would not buy this product of the soil at two and a half times the labor time contained in it. The basis of a class of land owners would thus be destroyed. This would have the same effect as a cheapening of the product to the same amount by foreign imports. While it is correct to say that, by retaining the present mode of production but paying the differential rent to the state, the prices of the products of the soil would remain the same, other circumstances remaining unchanged, it is wrong to say that the value of the products would remain the same, if capitalist production were superseded by association. The sameness of the market prices for commodities of the same kind is the way in which the social character of value asserts itself on the basis of capitalist production, as it does of any production resting on the exchange of commodities between individuals. What society in its capacity as a consumer pays too much for the products of the soil, what constitutes a minus for the realisation of its labor time in agricultural production, is now a plus for a portion of society, for the landlords.

III, pp. 773-774

Summary: In a socialist society, money would be abolished, to be replaced by non-circulating paper checks.

*

. . . In the case of socialized production, the money-capital is eliminated. Society distributes labor-power and means of production to the different lines of occupation. The producers may eventually receive paper checks, by means of which they withdraw from the social supply of means of consumption a share corresponding to their labor-time. These checks are not money. They do not circulate.

II, p. 412

B.

THE ALLOCATION OF OUTPUT AND LABOR IN A SOCIALIST AND COMMUNIST SOCIETY

Summary: Under Communism, we return to that characteristic of the primitive state exemplified by Robinson Crusoe in which production is for use (not profit), except that now it is for social, rather than for personal use. There still remains the problem of distribution. One portion of production will remain social for use in further production. The mode of distribution of the rest will vary with the historical development of the society, but as a first approximation, each will share according to his contribution of labor time. The social direction of labor time would perform two functions: (1) to allocate labor to perform the different kinds of work desired by a community; and (2) to serve as a measure of the value of each laborer's contribution to society, as well as to measure his share in that portion of output available for consumption.

*

Let us now picture to ourselves, by way of change, a community of free individuals, carrying on their work with the means of production in common, in which the labour-power of all the different individuals is consciously applied as the combined labour-power of the community. All the characteristics of Robinson's labour are here repeated, but with this difference, that they are social, instead of individual. Everything produced by him was exclusively the result of his own personal labour, and therefore simply an object of use for himself. The total product of our community is a social product. One portion serves as fresh means of production and remains social. But another portion is consumed by the members as means of subsistence. A distribution of this portion amongst them is consequently necessary. The mode of this distribution will vary with the productive organization of the community, and the degree of historical development attained by the producers. We will assume, but merely for the sake of a parallel with the production of commodities, that the share of each individual producer in the means of subsistence is determined by his labour-time. Labour-time would, in that case, play a double part. Its apportionment in accordance with a definite social plan maintains the proper proportion between the different kinds of work to be done and the various wants of the community. On the other hand, it also serves as a measure of the portion of the common labour borne by each individual and of his share in the part of the total product destined for individual consumption. The social relations of the individual producers, with regard both to their labour and to its products, are in this case perfectly simple and intelligible, and that with regard not only to production but also to distribution.

I, pp. 90-91

C.

THE RELATIONSHIP OF MAN TO WORK, MAN TO MAN, AND MAN TO THE STATE

Summary: So long as a split exists between the individual and the common interest, the division of labor, by circumscribing man's activities to certain narrow spheres, enslaves him. To attempt to escape is to lose one's livelihood. In a Communist society, where common production is regulated by society, an individual can choose his career freely, moving from occupation to occupation at will. Man will be freed from the slavery of the division of labor.

All history is the history of man's enslavement to an alien power, the world market. After the Communist revolution, with the abolition of private property, this power will be dissolved. Then genuine spiritual riches will be available to each individual. He will be free of national and local limitations, be enabled to enjoy the "all-sided production of the whole earth." The natural co-operation of men, hitherto forced by the rule of the market system, will arise spontaneously in the wake of the Communist revolution.

---

*

. . . the division of labour offers us the first example of how, as long as man remains in natural society, that is as long as a cleavage exists between the particular and the common interest, as long therefore as activity is not voluntarily, but naturally, divided, man's own deed becomes an alien power opposed to him, which enslaves him instead of being controlled by him. For as soon as labour is distributed, each man has a particular, exclusive sphere of activity, which is forced upon him and from which he cannot escape. He is a hunter, a fisherman, a shepherd, or a critical critic, and must remain so if he does not want to lose his means of livelihood; while in communist society, where nobody has one exclusive sphere of activity but each can become accomplished in any branch he wishes, society regulates the general production and thus makes it possible for me to do one thing to-day and another to-morrow, to hunt in the morning, fish in the afternoon, rear cattle in the evening, criticize after dinner, just as I have a mind, without ever becoming hunter, fisherman, shepherd or critic.

This crystallization of social activity, this consolidation of what we ourselves produce into an objective power above us, growing out of our control, thwarting our expectations, bringing to naught our calculations, is one of the chief factors in historical development up till now. . . .

In history up to the present it is certainly an empirical fact that separate individuals have, with the broadening of their activity into world-historical activity, become more and more enslaved under a power alien to them (a pressure which they have conceived of as a dirty trick on the part of the so-called universal spirit), a power which has become more and more enormous and, in the last instance, turns out to be the *world-market*. But it is just as empirically established that, by the overthrow of the existing state of society by the communist revolution (of which more below) and the abolition of private property which is identical with it, this power, which so baffles the German theoreticians, will be dissolved; and that then the liberation of each single individual will be accomplished in the measure in which history becomes transformed into world-history. From the above it is clear that the real intellectual wealth of the individual depends entirely on the wealth of his real connections. Only then will the separate individuals be liberated from the various national and local barriers, be brought into practical connection with the material and intellectual production of the whole world and be put in a position to acquire the capacity to enjoy this all-sided production of the whole earth (the creations of man). Universal dependence, this natural form of the world-historical co-operation of individuals, will be transformed by this communist revolution into the control and conscious mastery of these powers, which, born of the action of men on one another, have till now overawed and governed men as powers completely alien to them. . . .

The German Ideology, pp. 22-23, 27-28

Summary: In the future society, men will be free of class antagonisms. Political power, necessary only where class antagonisms exist, will disappear.

---

*

The essential condition of the emancipation of the working class is the abolition of all classes. . . .

The working class will substitute, in the course of its development, for the old order of civil society an association which will exclude classes and their antagonism, and there will no longer be political power, properly speaking, since political power is simply the official form of the antagonism in civil society.

The Poverty of Philosophy, p. 190

Editor's Note: The third point in the program of the German Workers' Party, presented to the congress of this party in Gotha in May

1875, called for the nationalization of the means of production, the "co-operative regulation of the total labour," and "equitable" distribution of the output of labor.

Summary: What is "equitable" distribution, and should all members of society, even those who do not work, share in it? This question devolves into the issue of whether all members of society are to receive the "undiminished proceeds of labour." Before there is anything to divide, funds must be deducted from total production for depreciation, for industrial expansion, insurance and reserves, for the costs of administration, for the requirements of communal consumption, such as schools, health services, etc., and for the unemployed.

Then to divide what remains according to productive input (labor time) is a bourgeois formula for equitable distribution. Some workers may have more children than others. Thus to right the defect of bourgeois society, namely, that mere physical or mental superiority makes one man richer than another, distribution should be "from each according to his ability, to each according to his needs!"

---

*

3. "The emancipation of labour demands the promotion of the instruments of labour to the common property of society, and the co-operative regulation of the total labour with equitable distribution of the proceeds of labour."

"Promotion of the·instruments of labour to the common property" ought obviously to read, their "conversion into the common property," but this only in passing.

What are the "proceeds of labour"? The product of labour or its value? And in the latter case, is it the total value of the product or only that part of the value which labour has newly added to the value of the means of production consumed?

The "proceeds of labour" is a loose notion which Lassalle has put in the place of definite economic conceptions.

What is "equitable distribution"?

Do not the bourgeois assert that the present-day distribution is "equitable"? And is it not, in fact, the only "equitable" distribution on the basis of the present-day mode of production? Are economic relations regulated by legal conceptions or do not, on the contrary, legal relations arise from economic ones? Have not also the socialist sectarians the most varied notions about "equitable" distribution?

To understand what idea is meant in this connection by the phrase "equitable distribution," we must take the first paragraph and this one together. The latter implies a society wherein "the instruments of labour are common property, and the total labour is co-operatively regulated;" and from the first paragraph we learn that "the proceeds of labour belong undiminished with equal right to all members of society."

"To all members of society"? To those who do not work as well? What remains then of the "undiminished proceeds of labour"? Only to those members of society who work? What remains then of the "equal right" of all members of society?

But "all members of society" and "equal right" are obviously mere phrases. The kernel consists in this, that in this communist society every worker must receive the "undiminished" Lassallean "proceeds of labour."

Let us take first of all the words "proceeds of labour" in the sense of the product of labour, then the co-operative proceeds of labour are the *total social product.*

From this is then to be deducted:

Firstly, cover for replacement of the means of production used up.

Secondly, additional portion for expansion of production.

Thirdly, reserve or insurance fund to provide against mis-adventures, disturbances through natural events, etc.

These deductions from the "undiminished proceeds of labour" are an economic necessity and their magnitude is to be determined by available means and forces, and partly by calculation of probabilities, but they are in no way calculable by equity.

There remains the other part of the total product, destined to serve as means of consumption.

Before this is divided among the individuals, there has to be deducted from it:

Firstly, the general costs of administration not belonging to production.

This part will, from the outset, be very considerably restricted in comparison with present-day society and it diminishes in proportion as the new society develops.

Secondly, that which is destined for the communal satisfaction of needs, such as schools, health services, etc.

From the outset this part is considerably increased in comparison with present-day society and it increases in proportion as the new society develops.

Thirdly, funds for those unable to work, etc., in short, what is included under so-called official poor relief today.

Only now do we come to the "distribution" which the programme, under Lassallean influence, alone has in view in its narrow fashion, namely that part of the means of consumption which is divided among the individual producers of the co-operative society.

The "undiminished proceeds of labour" have already quietly become converted into the "diminished" proceeds, although what the producer is deprived of in his capacity as a private individual benefits him directly or indirectly in his capacity as a member of society.

Just as the phrase "undiminished proceeds of labour" **has** disappeared, so now does the phrase "proceeds of labour" disappear altogether.

Within the co-operative society based on common ownership of the means of production, the producers do not exchange their products; just as little does the labour employed on the products appear here *as the value* of these products, as a material quality possessed by them, since now, in contrast to capitalist society, individual labour no longer exists in an indirect fashion but directly as a component part of the total labour. The phrase "proceeds of labour," objectionable even today on account of its ambiguity, thus loses all meaning.

What we have to deal with here is a communist society, not as it has *developed* on its own foundations, but, on the contrary, as it *emerges* from capitalist society; which is thus in every respect, economically, morally and intellectually still stamped with the birthmarks of the old society from whose womb it emerges. Accordingly the individual producer receives back from society—after the deductions have been made—exactly what he gives to it. What he has given to it is his individual amount of labour. For example, the social working day consists of the sum of the individual labour hours; the individual labour time of the individual producer is the part of the social labour day contributed by him, his share in it. He receives a certificate from society that he has furnished such and such an amount of labour (after deducting his labour for the common fund), and with this certificate he draws from the social stock of means of consumption as much as costs the same amount of labour. The same amount of labour which he has given to society in one form, he receives back in another.

Here obviously the same principle prevails as that which regulates the exchange of commodities, as far as this is exchange of equal values. Content and form are changed, because under the altered circumstances no one can give anything except his labour, and because, on the other hand, nothing can pass into the ownership of individuals except individual means of consumption. But, as far as the distribution of the latter among the individual producers is concerned, the same principle prevails as in the exchange of commodity-equivalents, so much labour in one form is exchanged for an equal amount of labour in another form.

Hence, *equal right* here is still in principle—*bourgeois right,* although principle and practice are no longer in conflict, while the exchange of equivalents in commodity exchange only exists on the *average* and not in the individual case.

In spite of this advance, this *equal right* is still stigmatised by a bourgeois limitation. The right of the producers is *proportional* to the labour they supply; the equality consists in the fact that measurement is made with an *equal standard,* labour.

But one man is superior to another physically or mentally and so supplies more labour in the same time, or can labour for a longer time; and labour, to serve as a measure, must be defined by its duration or intensity, otherwise it ceases to be a standard of measurement. This *equal* right is an unequal right for unequal labour. It recognises no class differences, because everyone is only a worker like everyone else; but it tacitly recognises unequal individual endowment and thus productive capacity as natural privileges. *It is therefore a right of inequality in its content, like every right.* Right by its very nature can only consist in the application of an equal standard; but unequal individuals (and they would not be different individuals if they were not unequal) are only measurable by an equal standard in so far as they are brought under an equal point of view, are taken from one *definite* side only, *e.g.,* in the present case are regarded *only as workers,* and nothing more seen in them, everything else being ignored. Further, one worker is married, another not; one has more children than another and so on and so forth. Thus with an equal output, and hence an equal share in the social consumption fund, one will in fact receive more than another, one will be richer than another, and so on. To avoid all these defects, right, instead of being equal, would have to be unequal.

But these defects are inevitable in the first phase of communist society as it is when it has just emerged after prolonged birth pangs from capitalist society. Right can never be higher than the economic structure of society and the cultural development thereby determined.

In a higher phase of communist society, after the enslaving subordination of individuals under division of labour, and therewith also the antithesis between mental and physical labour, has vanished; after labour, from a mere means of life, has itself become the prime necessity of life; after the productive forces have also increased with the all-round development of the individual, and all the springs of co-operative wealth flow more abundantly—only then can the narrow horizon of bourgeois right be fully left behind and society inscribe on its banners: from each according to his ability, to each according to his needs!

A Critique of the Gotha Programme, pp 8-14

Sources
Index

SOURCES

The extracts from Karl Marx's writings used in this book were taken from the following:

Capital: A Critique of Political Economy. Volume I: *The Process of Capitalist Production.* Chicago: Charles H. Kerr and Co., 1906. Copyright 1906 by Charles H. Kerr and Co. This work was originally published as *Das Kapital: Kritik der politischen Oekonomie,* Volume I: *Der Produktions prozess des Kapitals,* by Otto Meissner in Hamburg in 1867. It was first published in England by Swan Sonnenschein and Co. in 1886, translated from the third German edition (1883) by Samuel Moore and Edward Averling. The first American edition (1906) is the third edition as revised and amplified by Ernest Untermann from the fourth German edition (edited and enlarged by F. Engels and published by Meissner in 1890).

Capital: A Critique of Political Economy. Volume II: *The Process of Circulation of Capital.* Chicago: Charles H. Kerr and Co., 1907. Copyright 1907 by Charles H. Kerr and Co. A translation by Ernest Untermann of the second German edition (probably 1893) of *Das Kapital: Kritik der politischen Oekonomie,* Volume II: *Der Circulation prozess des Kapitals,* originally published by Otto Meissner in Hamburg in 1885.

Capital: A Critique of Political Economy. Volume III: *The Process of Capitalist Production as a Whole.* Chicago: Charles H. Kerr and Co., 1909. Copyright 1909 by Charles H. Kerr and Co. A translation by Ernest Untermann of the first German edition of *Das Kapital: Kritik der politischen Oekonomie,* Volume III: *Der Gesamptprozess der Kapitalistischen Produktion,* originally published by Otto Meissner in Hamburg in 1894.

A Contribution to the Critique of Political Economy. Bharati Library, Calcutta: Abinash Chandra Saha. Copyright 1904 by the International Library Publishing Co. This work was originally published as *Zur Kritik der politischen Oekonomie* by Franz Duncker in Berlin in 1859. The translation, by N. I. Stoke, "with an appendix containing Marx's Introduction to the *Critique,* recently published among his Posthumous Papers," was made from the second German edition (published by J.H.W. Dietz in Stuttgart in 1897).

A Critique of the Gotha Programme. With Appendices by Marx, Engels and Lenin. A Revised Translation, based on the Russian Edition of the Marx, Engels, Lenin Institute. Edited by C. P. Dutton. New York: International Publishers. Copyright 1938. This work is based on marginal notes written by Marx in 1875 on a copy of the program of the German Workers' Party at Gotha in 1875. These notes, a severe criticism, were sent in a letter to Wilhelm Bracke, and were published by Engels in 1891 in *Die Neue Zeit* under the title *Zur Kritik des Sozialdemokratischen Parteiprogramms aus dem nachlasz von Karl Marx.* The first English translation, *The Gotha Program by K. Marx and did Marx err?* by Daniel DeLeon, National Executive Committee Socialist Labor Party, was published in New York in 1922.

"Wage-Labor and Capital" in *The Essentials of Marx.* By Karl Marx and Frederick Engels. With Introduction and Notes by Algernon Lee. New York: Vanguard Press, Inc., 1926. Copyright 1926 by Vanguard Press, Inc. This work, based on lectures given by Marx in 1847 before the German Workingmen's Club in Brussels, originally appeared as columns in the *Neue Rheinische Zeitung* in April 1849. It was published as a pamphlet in Zurich in 1884.

The German Ideology. By Karl Marx and Frederick Engels. Edited with an Introduction by R. Pascal. New York: International Publishers, Inc., 1939. This work was written in 1845-46 as *Die Deutsche Ideologie: Kritik der neuesten deutschen Philosophie in Ihren Repräsentanten Feuerbach, B. Bauer und Steiner, und des deutschen Socialismus in Seinen verschiedenen Propheten.* A small part was apparently published as an article in 1847. Other parts were published in *Dokumente des Sozialismus* by Ed. Bernstein in 1902-03; and still another part was published by G. Mayer in *Archiv für Sozial Wissenschaft und Sozialpolitik* in 1921. Parts I and III, translated by W. Looch and C. P. Magill, were published as *German Ideology* by Lawrence and Wishart in London in 1938.

Manifesto of the Communist Party. By Karl Marx and Friedrich Engels. Authorized English Translation. Edited and Annotated by Friedrich Engels. Translated by Samuel Moore. New York: International Publishers, 1932. Three anonymous editions of the *Manifest des Kommunistischen Partei* appeared in 1848, two with J. E. Burghard as printer, and the third with R. Hirschfeld. An English translation, by Helen MacFarlane, was published in the *Red Republican* in London in 1850.

The Poverty of Philosophy. With a Preface by Frederick Engels. Translated by H. Quelch. Chicago: Charles H. Kerr and Co., 1920. This was originally published as *Misère de la Philosophie: Réponse à la Philosophie de la Misère de M. Proudhon* by A. Franck in Paris in 1847.

Theories of Surplus Value. Selections. Translated from the German by G. A. Bonner and Emile Burns. New York: International Publishers, 1952. Copyright 1952 by International Publishers Co., Inc. The original work, edited by Karl Kautsky, was published, in three volumes, as *Theorien über den Mehrwert* by J.H.W. Dietz in Stuttgart between 1905 and 1910.

INDEX